Louder
Than
Words

An Introduction to Nonverbal Communication

Lo

AN INTRODUCTION TO

MARJORIE

THE IOWA STATE UNIVERSITY PRESS / AMES

uder—

Than

Words

NONVERBAL COMMUNICATION

FINK VARGAS

©1986 The Iowa State University Press

All rights reserved

Composed and printed by The Iowa State University Press, Ames, Iowa

First edition, 1986

Library of Congress Cataloging-in-Publication Data

Vargas, Marjorie Fink, 1935–
   Louder than words.

   Includes index.
    1. Nonverbal communication (Psychology).   2. Interpersonal communication.   1. Title.
BF637.N66V37   1986   153.6   86–2882
ISBN 0-8138-1113-9

Contents

Preface, vii

Author's Note to the Teacher, viii

Louder Than Words — A Picture Essay, 1

1 *Nonverbal Communication — An Introduction, 9*

2 *Communication and the Human Body, 18*

3 *Kinesics, 32*

4 *Eye Behavior, 53*

5 *Paralanguage, 67*

6 *Silence, 76*

7 *Tacesics and Stroking, 83*

8 *Proxemics, 95*

9 *Chronemics, 121*

10 *Color, 138*

11 *And the Feat Goes On, 157*

Appendix, 177

Index, 183

Preface

Louder Than Words did not begin as a text but as a high school teacher's unit resource file. For ten years I taught nonverbal communication units at Malcolm Price Laboratory School in Cedar Falls, Iowa, all the while looking for a student textbook that would substitute for the background lectures I was forced to give. Nothing appropriate was available. To substitute, I developed dozens of activities through which the students could discover for themselves the power of nonverbal languages. My one file grew to be ten, each with an accompanying activity folder. These ultimately became the chapters in this book.

My resources ranged from dissertations and research reports in scholarly journals to current newspaper and magazine articles. But perhaps more significant than any of these were the discoveries made by my students as they pursued their original research. Time and time again, they were surprised and amazed by the consistency of fellow Iowans in nonverbal communicative behaviors. Without that student input, this book would not have been written.

I must not ignore, however, the significant contribution of my family. My own heritage as the daughter of a naturalized American from West Germany provided insights unavailable by any other means. Living with my Bolivian immigrant husband and visiting his family and friends in La Paz made me aware of cultural behaviors far different from my own. These experiences caused me to explore consciously the practices that exist in other cultures and subcultures.

As is true of all languages, variations exist everywhere. Dialects and idiolects are the rule not the exception, whether the language be verbal or nonverbal. The purpose of this book is not to provide definitive explanations but to make its readers, learners all, more sensitive to the nonverbal cues transmitted by others and to those messages others receive from them.

Author's Note to the Teacher

THE ACTIVITIES at the end of each chapter are considered an important aid to learning—perhaps more important than some of the examples given within the chapter itself. They are written as directions to the student reader, but each activity should be considered separately and seriously by the teacher assigning it.

Activities requiring the reading of selections in the appendix can be assigned to the entire class, but some other activities ask students to find and read full-length books, a far greater task that should be given only to pupils who show particular interest in the topic.

The films and other visual aids suggested for group viewing and analysis have been tested in my own high school classes and proven highly beneficial. A rental source has been given for each of them, but many may also be available in area and metro educational film libraries. For maximum instructional value, they should be ordered well in advance so that they may be viewed while the chapter is being discussed.

The majority of the activities require student experimentation. While such tests can be done casually, they are far more meaningful if more formally planned and carried out, and the results recorded. Many can be done by individual students, but others are more successful if conducted by pairs or small groups. The teacher should provide in-class planning time so that the students can devise and write out a controlled research design that specifies the time, place, number of subjects, and other variables. Careful investigative designs, techniques, and written reports have long been a part of high school science courses. While studying nonverbal communication, students may also be introduced to the exciting world of human behavioral and ethnographic research.

Regardless of which activities are done by the students, class discussion should follow their completion, preceding any written report that may be required. Clearly, time for such discussion should be built into the teacher's lesson plan so that the observations of even a few students can provide learning for all.

Louder
Than
Words

An Introduction to
Nonverbal Communication

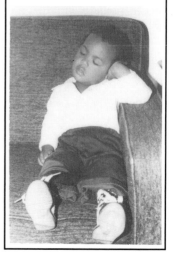

*Most kinesic behaviors are
learned. Young boys and girls
imitate the male and female
role models in their lives.
(Photos by Symone Ma)*

People who hold similar views often assume congruent or mirror postures in a meeting or discussion group.

Americans are members of a low tactile culture. Acceptable public embraces are limited to a few clearly defined situations.

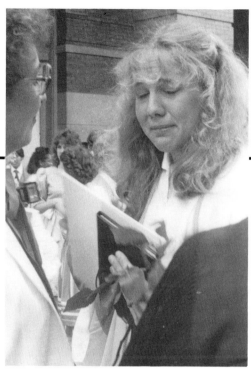

Affect displays sometimes belie the emotions we wish to convey to others. For graduating seniors joy and sadness are frequently separated by a fine line.

Other people receive thousands of messages simply by watching the movements of our eyes, brows, cheeks, jaw, mouth, and lips.

Posture, even when relaxed, is a good indicator of student interest in a class.

When interpreting nonverbal messages, the entire context must be considered. This senior's laid-back posture may indicate detachment—or simply limbs that are too long for the furniture.

At a dress-up banquet, few diners wish to be caught finding out if the chicken is "finger lickin' good." In the kitchen, eating meals we have prepared for ourselves, we use the informal behaviors we have learned.

These workers are clearly lending more than a hand to the project.

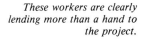

When we know that we look our best, self-confidence is also increased. If the task at hand is speaking to a group, as it is for this student, communication effectiveness may be greatly enhanced.

At times we don't care where the action is. We just want to be alone.

Faces clearly reflect emotions when excitement and anticipation are high, as on this bus traveling to a theater production in Minneapolis.

*When pictures are posed,
they seldom show us as
we really are.*

*A sweeping gesture shows this student's
intrepid attitude.*

*Good eye contact causes listeners to
judge a speaker to be more sincere,
honest, and informed.*

*Some things — the fish that got away, for
example — are difficult to describe
without gestures.*

Concern and receptiveness are conveyed nonverbally by this student's kinesic behaviors.

When conversing in cramped quarters, Americans introduce physical barriers to compensate for the lack of comfortable social distance.

Conveying age through stage makeup consists of accentuating existing facial lines, adding a full beard, greying the hair, and changing its style appropriately.

Those who work with children successfully know the benefits of addressing them at their own eye level.

Their faces, not the notes these students are making, give their true reactions to French cheeses.

Nonverbal Communication —
An Introduction

"DON'T WORRY," my friends told me, "most people there study English. You won't have any serious language problems." Their advice was familiar, but I had my doubts. It was too late to learn more Spanish than I'd been able to master in one semester of night school. As a crutch, I'd have to lean on Judy, my fellow traveler, who had previously spent time in Bolivia as a Peace Corps volunteer.

Although Judy didn't spend time practicing Spanish with me, we did spend hours talking about Bolivian culture, the Indian influence, and economic class contrasts. We discussed family life, foods and serving practices, and bartering in the markets. I was ready for the cold Andean nights and life devoid of technological comforts. Above all, I was determined not to be an ugly American.

Some of the things she told me struck a chord. Once, several years before, I had criticized my father for not teaching me German, his native language. "Ja," he had said, "it would have been easy to speak German. But to be Americans, we had to live like Americans. 'When in Rome...' " his voice had trailed off. "So now you teach English instead."

The week before our trip, while my mind was preoccupied with other things, Judy taught me the Bolivian embrace or *abrazo*. We had hardly passed through immigration when I encountered my first hearty handshake, followed by a right arm thrown around my shoulder to pat my back, followed by another squeeze of my right hand. During the half-dozen repeat performances in the next five minutes, I smiled broadly, remembering Judy's insistence that I get out of my beanbag and practice the *abrazo* back home.

9

My head was reeling from the cacophony of new faces, sounds, and smells — not to mention *soroche* caused by the thirteen thousand–foot altitude. Thus I appreciated the woman in the welcoming party who took me by the elbow and steered me toward the baggage claim area. A few minutes later, after our hosts had matched us each with our luggage and assigned us to vehicles and drivers, we shook hands all around once again before separating for the trip into the city.

Halfway there I found the proper words tucked away in my brain — *mucho gusto enconocerle* — but by then it was too late. The first encounter had passed.

That night I felt terrible. My head ached, I hadn't remembered a single word other than *gracias,* and I was sure I'd made an absolute fool of myself. Judy assured me that I'd performed admirably. I'd not only executed the *abrazo* smoothly but had smiled profusely, shaken hands with everyone, walked arm in arm with my hostess, responded to every toast as expected and danced with gusto if not grace. Relieved, I fell asleep, trying to decide if my headache was caused by the altitude or the pisco cocktails.

Sixty-five Percent of Human Communication Is Nonverbal

Ray L. Birdwhistell, a leader in the field of nonverbal communication, analyzes interpersonal communication this way: In a conversation between two people, only 35 percent of the social message is conveyed by the words. The remaining 65 percent is communicated nonverbally, by how they speak, move, gesture, and handle spatial relationships.[1]

This is not to suggest that American travelers should not learn languages spoken by other nations, but that on the global scale nonverbal languages are perhaps more important than verbal.

Dozens of nonspoken systems serve as symbols to communicate between human beings, as this book will explain. Research indicates that nine such nonverbal languages contribute significantly to all human communication, regardless of the spoken language they accompany:

1. THE HUMAN BODY, those genetically related physical characteristics of the sender or receiver that give a message, such as sex, age, physique, or skin color
2. KINESICS, the language of body position and movement
3. THE EYES, their contact and use
4. PARALANGUAGE, those voice qualities and characteristics that accompany spoken words
5. SILENCE

6. TACESICS AND STROKING, the language of touch and its substitutes

7. PROXEMICS, the way that humans use space to communicate

8. CHRONEMICS, time in both its cultural and physiological dimensions

9. COLOR

Forces Eliminate Universal Meanings

Contrary to popular thought, the meanings conveyed by nonverbal
languages vary as greatly as those in spoken languages. In other words, no
gesture or movement, no sign or symbol is used and interpreted the same
way by people everywhere in the world. Four powerful forces modify each
of the nonverbal languages: (1) personal variation, (2) sexual variation, (3)
cultural variation, and (4) situational variation.

For example, an individual's personality, chemistry, and genetic
makeup will affect his or her kinesic behavior under stress or the size of the
space bubble he strives to maintain around himself in a social group.

Sex differences determine timbers of voice as well as variations in
preening behavior, regardless of cultural background.

Culture, on the other hand, controls such concepts as being on time.
Sometimes even among subcultures in a single verbal language group, vari-
ations in nonverbal symbols exist. A gesture meaning "come here" to many
Greeks might be interpreted as "stay where you are" by Americans.

Every bit of language, verbal or nonverbal, is sent and received within
a situational context that might well change its meaning. When a man
winks at a woman in a cocktail lounge, it probably has a very different
meaning from the wink a man gives his wife over the head of their child
who has been bragging about how badly he beat Daddy.

Obviously these few examples do not show the range and depth of
influence exerted by the four modifying forces. Further discussion of them
will be included within chapters 2–10, which will each examine a nonverbal
language. At this point it is important to remember only that there is no
universal language, spoken or unspoken.

Verbal and Nonverbal Cues Are Related

Normally nonverbal communication accompanies and complements a
spoken language. Table pounding and increased vocal volume serve to underscore the verbal message. Pointing the way repeats the directions given

orally. A slow, soft voice caresses a loved one and reinforces spoken words.

We watch the intended recipient of our messages to see if our cues are being accepted and understood. Often the feedback is nonverbal — a head nod, eye movement, or slight change in facial expression. Such cues serve to regulate the future flow of communication.

Sometimes nonverbal communication takes the place of a verbal exchange. When a dejected high school student comes home after losing an athletic match, his posture and facial expression say all that his caring father wants to know.

Occasionally the nonverbal message contradicts the message being spoken. As a child, I never could understand how my mother knew everytime I told her a lie. As a teacher, I find myself watching for telltale clues such as changes in eye contact, facial expression, and posture to help me determine whether to accept a student's excuse. Sometimes the contradiction is hard to detect. At other times the discrepancy is obvious.

Consider the student speaker who states confidently, "I'm not nervous," while beads of perspiration appear on his face and his knees tremble; or the young woman who protests, "Of course you're the only one," as her eyes repeatedly scan the room full of other men. In cases of contradictory messages, we are inclined to believe and trust the nonverbal message over the spoken one.

Why? Perhaps because we believe that nonverbal behaviors are harder to fake. To some extent this is true. Nonverbal messages do not usually occur in isolation. When a person becomes angry, for example, his facial muscles tighten and a smile becomes difficult, his body tenses in preparation for conflict, and his voice reflects this emotional state. His personal space bubble expands; he requires more space.

Another reason that we trust nonverbal messages is that we did not consciously learn to decode them as we did verbal communications. Thus we ascribe our understanding of the nonverbal cues to intuition and assume it is accurate because it cannot be discounted logically.

Nonverbal Cues Communicate Self

While much nonverbal communication accompanies and modifies our spoken words, some unspoken language communicates primarily our attitudes, personalities, and emotions. A trained observer is able to decode these cues and separate them from the other subject matter being exchanged.

Who a person is cannot be eliminated from interpersonal communication. One's self-concept shows itself in the postures and movements of the body, the use of the eyes and of the space available, and the nature of the vocal qualities.

Consider this situation. You are ushered into an empty office by a nurse, who points to a chair and says the doctor will be with you shortly. Minutes later he bursts through the door. Crossing to you, he sits on the corner of the desk as he questions you regarding your symptoms. You begin your explanation, but before you've finished he has broken eye contact, turned his back, and walked to his chair behind the desk. There he sits down, opens the bottom drawer of his desk, and rests his feet on its edge. He leans back in his chair, places his hands behind his head, and spreads his elbows wide. Finally he speaks, shooting a question at you.

Your reaction is defensive, almost apologetic. Why? You're there for good reason, and you expect to pay for his services. He has conveyed nonverbal messages of power and dominance, which you were helpless to counter.

Naturally most people don't proclaim who they are as obviously or as intensely as this hypothetical doctor. But everyone has characteristic postures, facial expressions, voice qualities, eye contact, and space usage patterns that communicate to those around him or her.

Who a person wants others to think he or she is may not be the same as who a person is. But culture has given us ample opportunities to learn how to behave so as to impress others, temporarily at least.

Looking for an example? Tell a four-year-old child to stay clean and be good. Then watch for the next five minutes. Or, if you prefer, watch a televised beauty contest. All of the girls have been trained to use body language so as to appear poised and attractive. The result may be no less convincing than the behavior of the four-year-old, but their movements and gestures are accurate and proven successful.

Candidates for public office, especially on the national level, also become students of nonverbal communication. Either they develop behaviors that convince the public of their sincerity and capability, or they step quietly and quickly back into obscurity.

Finally, nonverbal communication will reveal *who others think a person is.*

A classic example of this is provided by a survey conducted at the University of Pittsburgh. Male Pittsburgh graduates six feet two inches to six feet four inches tall received starting salaries 12.4 percent higher than those men under six feet.[2] Further support for discrimination against the short man can be found in a study of 140 corporate recruiters who were asked to make a choice between two men just by reading their applications for employment. Applications were exactly the same except one listed a height of six feet one inch and the other five feet five inches. Only about 1 percent favored the shorter man.[3] Personnel managers and employing officials clearly *think* tall men are more capable employees.

Most Nonverbal Languages Are Learned

With only a few exceptions, nonverbal communication is learned. Seldom formally, and often unconsciously, children learn as they grow up by observing and imitating the adults around them. Little girls imitate their mothers and other women. Little boys mimic their fathers and older males. By this method they develop the gender cues appropriate for their sex. Appropriate behaviors for their ethnic group, region, and class are assimilated in the same way.

The most obvious exceptions to the generalization that nonverbal communication is learned are the physical characteristics of the sender or receiver that clearly communicate but are related to heredity. Certainly no one learns to communicate blonde or sixty pounds overweight or five feet three inches tall. Nevertheless, each cultural subgroup has a fashionable ideal against which individuals may compare themselves, sometimes painfully.

We cut and curl — or straighten — our hair. We grow beards or shave our faces and bodies. We diet and exercise, use deodorants, colognes, and makeup — all in the hope of better approximating what we have *learned* is the ideal of our sex, age, and ethnic group.

We don't learn to scratch when parts of our bodies itch — but we certainly do learn when and where it is unacceptable to scratch in public. No one learns to yawn or sneeze — but to stifle either or to cover it is carefully cultivated behavior. From examples such as these, we can conclude that unlearned nonverbal behaviors are frequently recognized and modified so as not to communicate in a manner contrary to our desires.

Culture Is a Powerful Teacher

Our social environment, our cultural corner of the world, is a powerful and effective teacher. It determines which languages children will learn and provides them with opportunities to observe, decode, and evaluate their success, coupled with opportunities to practice encoding and transmitting messages of their own.

Such learning affects even the way a boy learns to walk or to stand. In the United States, fashionable black males walk with catlike looseness and coordination, which to white males appears sexually provocative. Urban blacks move from the hips, unlike their white American counterparts, who seem almost mechanically stiff in their walk.[4] Some French middle-class males walk in yet another manner, with a bounce and seemingly double-jointed looseness that Americans consider almost comical. French mime Marcel Marceau has made this walk known the world over.[5]

A young child imitates those whom he admires to the point of losing the ability to be comfortable moving or standing differently. Consider, for example, the relaxed stance of the Shilluk of Africa's Nile basin, who stand on one foot resting the other foot against the inside of the knee. To anyone unaccustomed to this stance, it is not at all relaxing but awkward and tiring.

My Bolivian friends of all ages find a deep squat as comfortable as sitting on a chair and assume this position for long periods of time. I simply could not join them. They laughed and told me of course I could. At least a quarter of mankind uses that sitting posture regularly. I protested, "Can't I sit directly on the floor?" In reply they asked, "And if it's cold and wet?" I could see their point and tried my best to force my atrophied muscles to let me bend. I had almost reached the desired depth when I lost my balance. I had learned and practiced the postures of my own culture too well.

Benjamin Whorf, who spent many years studying the culture and language of the Shawnee and Hopi Indians, first proposed the hypothesis that language is more than just a medium for expressing thought. It is, in fact, a major element in the shaping of thought.[6] To illustrate, Whorf points to the language of the Eskimos, which has dozens of different words for snow in varied states. The Eskimo child learns to look at snow with an eye for differentiation. He actually perceives snow differently than does a child in the United States.[7]

Let's test the Whorfian hypothesis closer to home to see if having separate words for different aspects of a thing really makes a difference in our perception or awareness. Americans commonly identify a segment of the spectrum as orange, red, pink, and purple. People who have a special interest in art will have words in their vocabularies like copper, salmon, vermilion, cerise, magenta, crimson, scarlet, burgundy, maroon, and mahogany. Those in fashion and interior design might add tangerine, apricot, fuchsia, cherry, poppy, carnation, ruby, cardinal, and cranberry. Although about ten million colors are said to be distinguishable, the fine distinctions denoted by these words are not normally made by most Americans. These hues are identified regularly, however, by people working with color. The best color dictionary in use today includes approximately four thousand color names. Most male Americans would have difficulty naming twenty.[8]

In making finer color distinctions, women surpass men, as they do in their ability to decipher nonverbal messages generally. This is not to say that all women are better than some men. But in experiment after experiment, more female subjects were able to recognize and accurately decode unspoken cues than were male subjects.[9]

Why this should be true cannot be proven. One theory is that men more frequently refine abilities controlled by the right hemisphere of the brain. They tend to be more abstract, more adept at visual-spatial tasks, and less dependent on context. Women, on the other hand, use abilities governed by the brain's left hemisphere including verbal skills and sensitivity to people and context.[10]

A second, equally plausible theory surfaces repeatedly. In British and American culture, women have traditionally been subordinate to men in power and influence. In order to achieve their goals, women have had to resort to indirect means of working around and through men. To that end they have developed an awareness of the variables of language as a compensatory skill.

Everyone Can Improve Nonverbal Communication Skills

The purpose of this book is to help you become aware of the range and depth of nonverbal communication so that you might (1) respond more intelligently to the nonverbal cues sent by others and (2) understand the messages that you transmit nonverbally. The subtleties of nonverbal languages make this a difficult but interesting task.

The approach to this task will be systematic.

Step one will be to *sensitize* you, the reader, to the range and complexities of each nonverbal language. In addition to examples from American behavior, numerous illustrations from foreign cultures and subcultures will be cited. You may never encounter people who practice these behaviors, but the purpose of examining them extends beyond the practical. Through an understanding of ways very different from your own, abstractions and generalizations about nonverbal communication will become meaningful. This is not unlike a math student studying a base-two, base-five, or base-twelve number system in order to better understand the base-ten system. And who knows what the future may bring? Knowledge of the base-two (binary) number system opened the door to the world of computers. Knowledge of the principles of nonverbal communication may enable you to better communicate with people from other cultures when you encounter them.

Step two will ask you to *analyze* the examples of nonverbal communication you encounter. An extended list of suggested activities at the end of each chapter should aid in completion of this step.

Step three will occur back in the classroom. Through discussion, you

will *organize* your observations and reactions into meaningful concepts.
Step four will be to *utilize* the new learning in your own interpersonal
communication.

Notes

1. Ray L. Birdwhistell, *Kinesics and Context: Essays on Body Motion Communication* (Philadelphia: Univ. of Pennsylvania Press, 1970), p. 158.
2. Study cited in Mark L. Knapp, *Essentials of Nonverbal Communication* (New
   York: Holt, Rinehart and Winston, 1980), p. 107.
3. Ibid.
4. Kenneth R. Johnson, "Black Kinesics: Some Non-verbal Communication Patterns in the Black Culture," in *With Words Unspoken,* ed. Lawrence B. Rosenfeld and Jean M. Civikly (New York: Holt, Rinehart and Winston, 1976), pp.
   232–34.
5. Edward T. Hall and Mildred Reed Hall, "The Sounds of Silence," in *Language:
   Introductory Readings,* ed. Virginia P. Clark, Paul A. Eschholz and Alfred F.
   Rosa (New York: St. Martin's 1972), p. 468.
6. Benjamin L. Whorf, *Language, Thought and Reality* (Cambridge, Mass.: MIT
   Press, 1956).
7. Ibid., p. 216.
8. Clarence Rainwater, *Light and Color* (New York: Golden, 1971), p. 125.
9. R. Rosenthal, D. Archer, J. H. Koivumaki, M. R. Di Matteo, and D. L.
   Rogers, "Assessing Sensitivity to Nonverbal Communication: The PONS Test,"
   Division 8 Newsletter, Division of Personality and Social Psychology of the
   American Psychological Association, January 1974, pp. 1–3.
10. Camilla Persson Benbow, quoted in Jo Durden-Smith and Diane DeSimone "Is
    There a Superior Sex?" *Playboy,* May 1982, p. 159.

2

Communication and the Human Body

TWO PERSONS approach one another, a situation of potential interpersonal communication. They may not know one another and perhaps will never speak to each other, but unless they are in a crowded place or are preoccupied by other thoughts, they will probably communicate as they pass.

Personal communication is a process which involves at least two people: a sender bearing an encoded message and a receiver who perceives the stimuli via the senses and decodes them within his or her field of experience. At the same time, the receiver is consciously or unconsciously transmitting messages back to the sender who receives and processes those cues.

The message or transmitted signal serves as a cue or stimulus to the receiver. That message may be heard, felt, smelled, tasted, or seen. We can and do communicate by physical appearance, gestures, eye contact, touch, and smell as well as by sounds and words.

Nonverbal Communication Requires All Senses

Hearing is, of course, the most important sense in the reception of spoken communication. But all of the human senses receive messages when the communication has been sent nonverbally.

The auditory sense receives nonverbal as well as verbal messages. Paralanguage is heard; these vocal characteristics and qualifiers are, by definition, audible though nonverbal. The human ear is capable of amazing sensitivity to variations of tone. Consider for a moment the piano tuner

18

who hears not only half-tone but even quarter-tone differences in pitch over a wide range from treble to bass.

Silence as a communicator denotes the absence of sound and may or may not be accompanied by messages for other senses.

The human sense of touch is one of the first to develop in newborn infants. Within hours of birth a child responds to all the variations of touch — contact, pressure, cold and heat, and pain. (Dampness is not considered a separate variation but is a contributor to perceived cold and heat.) Soon after birth, children are held, caressed, and patted by their mothers and other adults in their world. Babies' favorite toys are tactile ones, soft rubber figures, stuffed animals, teething rings — anything they can feel and put into their mouth in an effort to touch more intensely.

They touch everything within reach and play with themselves, touching their fingers, toes, hair, nose, and genitals — until they learn that picking their nose and touching their genitals are "no-no's." Some children love to stroke a special blanket. More and more of the world comes within their grasp as they begin to crawl and then to walk, and more and more things are touched and tasted. With such a wide world for children to explore, is it any wonder that adults' first efforts at educating them are frequent repetitions of "No, no! Don't touch!"?

Being held and stroked by others continues to be a warm, soothing condition for children. Touching as nonverbal communication between adults will be examined further in chapter 7, "Tacesics and Stroking." Let it suffice here to say that being touched continues to tell the recipients that someone cares and feels a commitment to them, unless, of course, the touch is in combat.

Smell is a sense that is much more fully developed in animals than it is in humans. Odors can reach the membrane of the nasal passage via the nostrils or upward from the throat. In interpersonal communication situations, most olfactory stimulation enters through the nose. The odor of an individual conveys a message which modifies all other messages received from that person.

Long before infants can transmit verbal messages, they can communicate to their parents' senses of smell and taste. Doctors and parents of some mentally retarded children have noticed, for example, that those children carry with them an odor that has been described as musty or mousy. Research has proven that the chemical imbalance phenylketonuria (PKU), which causes some people to be retarded, also produces this unique odor. The enzyme that should metabolize the amino acid phenylalanine in these people is deficient or defective. Undigested phenylalanine accumulates in the tissues and gives their urine and perspiration a peculiar odor. If the condition is diagnosed early enough, the retarding effects of PKU can be greatly diminished and sometimes arrested completely. Observant parents have been thankful, therefore, to have responded to this nonverbal message.

A mother's kiss can also be a test for cystic fibrosis, according to information disseminated by the Cystic Fibrosis Foundation. Children suffering from this inherited respiratory and degenerative disease produce perspiration that contains three to five times the chloride or sodium levels found in normal children. Thus an excessively salty taste to the skin is a strong basis for suspecting cystic fibrosis.

The majority of nonverbal messages are received through sight. Kinesics is the study of body movements that communicate to us visually. Proxemics deals with space and distance, usually perceived by sight, occasionally by touch. Finally, there's color, another purely visual language.

If any of our senses are deficient, it follows that we are limited in our ability to receive and decode nonverbal communication. Defective color vision, or color blindness, is rarely thought to be a handicap, although it affects about 8 percent of the male population and almost 1 percent of females.[1]

Physical Characteristics Are Messages

Let us now examine the possible messages conveyed by our bodies, not by the ways we move or dress but by the qualities we've acquired primarily through heredity.

Two people see each other for the first time. As they approach one another bodily characteristics become evident one by one. The first four are height, physique, sex, and age. As the distance closes, they are able to recognize skin color and tone, hair length and style, body modifications, and eyes. Finally as they reach one another, body and breath odors are perceived and general attractiveness is assessed. All of these messages will be perceived before a word is said and, indeed, may determine whether anything will be said.

In the United States, the conclusions drawn from the messages will determine the level and variety of usage chosen for any verbal communication that may follow. Before we speak, we infer the relative status and degree of intimacy felt for the person being addressed. We then phrase our greetings and verbal exchanges accordingly. Consider the following possibilities:

"Hey, kid! D'ya know what time it is?"
"Good morning, Mr. Johnson. Will you tell me the time?"
"Excuse me, ma'am. May I bother you for the time?"
"Hi, stupid! What time y'got?"

Each of these indicates a distinct evaluation by the speaker of the person being addressed. It is possible, however, for an American to stop someone who looks only vaguely familiar and, without committing himself to further conclusions, to ask, "Excuse me, do you have the time?"

In some cultures interpreting the nonverbal body cues is essential in choosing the grammatical structures to be used verbally. In Java, for example, a speaker must choose one of three basic styles of the language — the plain, the fancy, or the elegant. Then he has to decide whether or not to use honorifics, which permit him to raise his style a half notch more. As a result, the Javanese cannot escape from telling a listener exactly what they think of him. Their choice of any one of the six styles reveals all.[2]

Many other languages used in Japan, China, and other countries of the Far East also oblige the speaker to choose whether or not to use honorifics. Most Indo-European languages reflect the degree of intimacy and respect felt toward a person by the speaker's selection of second person pronouns. Still other languages display whether the person being addressed is male or female.

But perhaps the greatest evaluation-before-speech task is required of the Nootka Indians of Vancouver Island. Their language requires choices to indicate the sex of the person speaking, the sex of the person being addressed, and whether the speaker is more or less important than the person spoken to. In addition they have a special way of talking to a person who is left-handed, and a special way of talking to a man who has been circumcised.[3]

One wonders how they could deal with a stranger on the telephone!

Decoding Resurrects Stereotypes

Examining the interpretations ascribed to various body characteristics takes us into the field of prejudice and discrimination, for many conclusions in our decoding are based on stereotypes. We have seen in chapter 1 how a man's height alone affected an employer's evaluation of his qualifications and overall worth to the company. The simple fact that a person is female and not male causes the observer of that person to infer a wide number of generalizations, some accurate, some not. Accounts of the injustices suffered by black men and women on the basis of their skin color alone could fill a library. People who appear to be Indian or Latin American or Oriental or Jewish also feel the effects of stereotypes associated with their features.

Stereotypes have also caused untold misery for men and women whose vocal characteristics or manner of walking or sitting has been judged as indicating homosexuality. And consider the plight of homosexuals whose

intellects, talents, and training have prepared them for meaningful participation in the straight world, but whose sexual preference becomes known
to their colleagues, clients, and social acquaintances. Otherwise well-
schooled people have turned against such men and women. Why? Because
they suddenly expect lesbian or gay behaviors, which exist only in their own
minds as a result of stereotypes and ignorance.

So discrimination goes on. Laws and logic notwithstanding, our minds
quickly jump to conclusions.

Study Associates Temperaments with Body Types

Back in the 1940s Dr. W. H. Sheldon developed a classification for
body physiques. The *endomorph* was identified as soft, round, and fat; the
mesomorph, hard, muscular, and athletic; the *ectomorph,* tall, thin, and
fragile. Naturally few humans matched one of these extremes. Most of us
are a combination of all three. So Sheldon developed a system to reflect
that assumption.

A person's characteristics in each body type are rated on a scale from
one to seven — seven representing the highest degree of an extreme body
type. A person's composite is thereby represented by three numbers. The
first refers to his or her degree of *endomorphy,* the second to *mesomorphy,*
and the third to *ectomorphy.* An extremely obese person would be 7/1/1, a
Mr. Universe type 1/7/1, and a very skinny person 1/1/7. To determine the
degree of each body type present in a given individual, Sheldon divided the
body into five regions and made a number of measurements in each zone. It
is estimated that Muhammed Ali is roughly a 2/7/1 and Abraham Lincoln
a 1/4/6.[4]

Dr. Sheldon followed this first study with a second, which categorized
the varieties of human temperament. At the end of these studies he found a
high correlation between his three classes of temperament and the three
body types he had identified earlier.

Endomorphy correlated very closely with *viscerotonia.* The viscerotonic person, according to Sheldon, displays a temperament that is relaxed,
dependent, affable, contented, sociable, affectionate, calm, tolerant,
leisurely, forgiving, complacent, and generous. Closely correlated with *mesomorphy* was *somatotonia,* a temperament Sheldon described as adventurous, dominant, confident, reckless, energetic, enthusiastic, determined, active, assertive, courageous, efficient, and optimistic. *Ectomorphy* correlated with *cerebrotonia,* which Sheldon characterized as a temperament that
is tense, self-conscious, precise, cautious, withdrawn, suspicious, reflective,
shy, tactful, detached, serious, and thoughtful.[5]

For these conclusions (which have been highly simplified for this book), Sheldon has been attacked repeatedly by the scientific community. He is accused of creating classifications to support his prejudices and measuring for them nonscientifically.

Be that as it may, popular opinion and stereotyping has long supported Sheldon's conclusions. We do associate certain personality and temperament types with certain body physiques. These expectations may or may not be accurate, but they do exist and affect our thinking. Like the tall man who is judged deserving of a higher beginning salary, the fat individual is considered lazy, sociable, and soft-hearted simply by virtue of his physique.

There isn't much any of us can do about the prejudices of others, but we can try to avoid making the same mistakes ourselves.

Fe, Fi, Fo, Fum, *Can You Smell the Blood of an Englishman?*

Limited scientific research has been done regarding human biological odors. How does one test subjects' reactions to variables that cannot be controlled, preserved, recorded, or duplicated precisely? Even our words to describe them are vague.

Furthermore, the human olfactory sense is not highly developed. Yet Americans are very concerned about how they smell to others. Even if our parents and best friends hadn't told us, we'd be brainwashed by the advertisers of soap, deodorant, perfume, mouthwash, toothpaste, and breath mints to believe that no self-respecting human would allow natural body scents to reach the nostrils of others. We've come to believe that almost any scent is better than our own biological odors. We buy approximately eight million dollars worth of products annually to make us smell like flowers, fruits, herbs, antiseptics, animal musk, or sick whales, anything but what we are.[6]

Other cultures spend much less money and effort to cover up their natural odors. In many areas of the world, groups of people acquire characteristic odors from the foods they eat, chemicals or other products they use in their work, clothing they wear, or tobacco they smoke. For example, people who use a lot of garlic in their cooking emit a resultant odor.

In Arabian life, olfaction plays an important role. Arabs enjoy natural odors. In conversation, they characteristically stand close enough to share each other's breath and consider it pleasant to do so. They use pleasant scents to help build relationships and are not hesitant to tell a good friend or relative that his stomach smells sour on a given day and to suggest that he not speak too close to others. It has even been reported that the scent of a prospective bride has been considered in assessing her temperament. Personality characteristics such as chronic anger and discontent, they believe, produce an odor that can be recognized.[7]

There may be some truth to that claim. It is common knowledge that individuals' body chemistries differ and as a result the same cologne does not produce the same odor on everyone. Animals can smell the odor of a human's skin oils and perspiration and react accordingly. Bloodhounds are renowned for their ability to trail someone they've never seen after simply smelling a piece of clothing worn by that person. Dogs and other animals are able to smell if a human is afraid of them and will attack when that scent is evident. Scientists have done some research regarding this "smell of fear" as produced by mice and other species and have isolated it in these animals.[8] If there is a fear scent in humans too, might there not be scents of satisfaction, anxiety, contempt, or sadness?

Although tests have shown that humans differ widely in their sensitivity to scents, most people are able to recognize at least four thousand distinct odors. Some can distinguish up to ten thousand.[9] By paying attention to scents from childhood on as the Arabian culture does, we can learn a great deal about ourselves and others.

"Beauty" Is a Changing Thing

Research has shown that physical beauty or attractiveness can be influential in establishing social contact, that is, in determining whether a person will be sought out. It may have a bearing on whether one is able to persuade or manipulate others and may also be an important factor in the selection of dating and marriage partners. But what is an attractive woman or a handsome man?

Three hundred years ago a northern European man would have described a pleasingly plump girl with wavy tresses and lily white skin. Recently the American ideal has been the "California girl," a slim, long-limbed nymphet with long blonde hair and a year-round suntan. The china doll–white skin, once valued as an indication that the woman was a lady and not a field hand, is now scorned as anemic. A tanned body communicates a carefree outdoor life-style and is greatly prized as a status symbol especially in parts of the country where ice and snow dominate the winter months.

During the first half of the twentieth century every American girl's dream man was "tall, dark, and handsome." Defined muscles were not as important as the way he looked in a dress suit. His eyes and hair had to be dark and shiny. He might possibly have a well-shaped moustache but not a full beard. The slick, well-groomed image was in vogue.

Then, during the sixties, college girls saw the nonconforming male as attractive. His hair had to be at least shoulder length; the longer the better. A full beard and clothes that bore no trace of style nearly covered his form.

Male clothes in the early eighties reveal a firm physique, muscular from exercise. A man's hair is casually styled with a fluffy windblown look. A beard or other facial hair is fully acceptable if shaped and styled for a casual appearance. A rugged and tanned skin communicates a healthy lifestyle.

Until recent years, many black Americans, male and female, did not think their racial characteristics attractive. The civil rights movement of the 1960s generated racial pride, however; and the slogan "black is beautiful" soon became more than a rallying cry. The ideal black image was reinforced by the increased appearance of black models in advertising. By 1983 the entire country was ready to recognize a black woman as Miss America.

Today Americans of both sexes have their hair styled, shave parts of their bodies, use lotions to retain soft skins, and exercise to develop parts of their bodies that nature created smaller than the perceived ideal.

But they don't stop there. They replace missing teeth with false ones, have their nose reshaped surgically, and get their ears pierced so that they can insert metal studs or rings. Men with bald heads may glue on an artificial hairpiece or try having hair plugs implanted.

Women may have face-lifts. Even more women spend time daily applying creams, eye shadow and liner, mascara, and perhaps false eyelashes. They use blush and lip colors that imitate the natural flush of female sexual excitement. Then, before polishing their nails with colored enamel, they file and shape them, occasionally covering imperfect ones with artificial.

In the traditional Fiji Island society men dyed their hair red and yellow with lime and mangrove sap. They allowed it to grow into long, frizzy mops, which were then clipped and teased into fantastic shapes up to four feet wide. The higher one's status, the longer he would spend with his hairdresser.[10] Modern punkers look like kittens beside these lions with their full manes.

When Bo Derek was rated a perfect "10" with her hair plaited into cornrows and tiny braids, thousands of white women spent hours trying to make their hair look the same. The style is far from new in Africa where similar styles have been traditional for people as widely separated as the Herero of Namibia and the Masai of Kenya and Tanzania. The style is much easier to achieve and maintain given the hair texture and dryness of most blacks, as "California girls" quickly discovered.

In the days of silent movies, a single dark beauty mark on the cheek of a woman was considered sexually attractive. Among the Eskimos, women formerly tattooed their cheeks and chins with fine dark lines achieved by drawing a thread covered with soot just below the top layer of skin.

Tattooing is widely practiced among women and men, particularly in Polynesia. Until the twentieth century, Maori men in New Zealand traditionally tattooed every part of their bodies. Men of high status received their first tattoos as small boys and the process did not end until their entire bodies were decorated with glowing patterns.

Dark-skinned people, on whom tattoos would not be clearly visible, frequently adorn their bodies by scarification. First the skin is hooked and snipped with a blade. Then an irritant such as ashes is rubbed into the wound so that a raised scar will form. This practice has been discovered in New Guinea on one side of the world and as far away as Africa on the other. It is particularly widespread in the African Sudan where each tribal group has its own lacelike scarification patterns. The result is considered not only attractive but an indication of high status.

Stylish young American women generally wear earrings through pierced earlobes. In recent years, men too have joined in the practice and both sexes sometimes have the lobe pierced twice and wear two earrings in the same ear. Many American men and women over fifty do not find earrings in pierced ears any more attractive than they do the polished bone through the pierced septum of the nose of some South American Indians, Australian Aborigines, and many Pacific islanders.

In East Africa, young Kikuyu girls insert ear plugs into the holes pierced in their lobes. They replace them regularly with larger and larger plugs until the earlobes touch the shoulders or can meet over the crown of the head.

Until recently, many western Eskimo men inserted bone labrets or short pegs into holes pierced at the lower corners of the mouth to enhance their appeal to the opposite sex. The Sara women of the Lake Chad region of Africa have their lips pierced by their future husbands when they are betrothed. They insert short pegs, which are steadily replaced with larger ones until huge lip discs are worn.

Flattened foreheads that sloped back to the hairline were considered beautiful by the Olmec peoples of Central America and people as far away from them as Borneo. To attain what nature did not regularly supply, they bound special wooden apparatuses to the skulls of infants, who wore them until the desired incline was reached.

Along the northwest coast of North America and in the New Hebrides in the Pacific, the back of the head was flattened or the entire skull bound to produce an elongated, cone-shaped head.

For over a thousand years, China had a tradition of foot-binding for women. Like the lily white skin of European ladies, tiny female feet were a sign of high class and seen by men as the ultimate of feminine beauty. From an early age, girls' feet were tightly bandaged and crushed until they became tiny triangular hooves that fit into three- and four-inch embroidered shoes. Chinese literature extolled the fashion by referring to them as "lily feet," "golden lotus," "jade bamboo shoots," and "twin wild ducks." Naturally a woman with such misshapen feet could not perform demanding physical labor. She could barely ambulate within the walls of her home. Lower class Chinese, who could not afford to thus limit their daughters' usefulness, looked upon those who could with envy. The practice was not discontinued until well into the twentieth century.

Another crippling practice is the tradition among the Padaung of Burma to elongate women's necks by coiled spirals of gold, copper, or brass. The practice begins when a girl is about five years old at which time the first coil, about four inches high, is wrapped around her neck. About two years later, it is replaced by a longer one. By this time the unused neck muscles can no longer support the head, and extreme caution must be taken while making the change. Before adulthood, changes are made several more times, until the women can no longer move easily or see their babies at their breasts. However, the consequences of removing the coils from a woman's neck are fatal, for the weakened vertebrae have collapsed.

How did such a terrible practice become a symbol of beauty and status? The explanation seems reasonable: Padaung villages are surrounded by the wilderness domain of the tiger. Little boys were taught to handle weapons to defend themselves; girls had to be defended by others. Survivors noted that whenever tigers attacked, they lunged at the throats of their victims. So caring parents encircled the necks of their little girls with metal rings, adding more as they grew. The atrophy of neck muscles and vertebrae was an unfortunate result, so the coils had to be retained for life. The tradition developed not as an attempt to destroy but in an effort to protect human life. Long necks surrounded by metal coils became symbols of beauty and status, indicating that these girls were valued and loved.

Uneducated people will ridicule these body modifications as "uncivilized," or "barbaric." But these labels display the speakers' ignorance, little more. *Uncivilized* means "lacking civilization." The practices cited here have been traditions in differing civilizations or cultures with different concepts of what makes a person attractive. *Differing* is not the same as *lacking*. Just because a practice is strange doesn't make it bad or inferior.

"But," some diehards will protest, "no American would support such painful practices in order to be considered beautiful. We don't do anything so drastic to our bodies."

Nothing painful? Ask anyone who has spent time in an orthodontist's office about what has to be endured for beautiful teeth. None of them will tell you having your teeth straightened doesn't hurt.

Nothing so drastic? Piercing the ear lobes or nose septum or snipping the skin for scarification is nothing compared to the surgical process to implant silicone or other foreign substances in the breast.

Thus when, as Americans, we see another person approaching, our senses record a wide array of body characteristics and our minds compare them to the standards and expectations our society has helped us formulate. Had we lived in another place or at another time, our standards and expections might have been quite different.

When I visited Bolivia for the first time, I was accompanied by two other young women who like me wore corrective lenses to improve their vision. Back in the States, the others wore contact lenses, but the dry, dusty atmosphere of La Paz made wearing contacts for long periods of time uncomfortable; and we all, therefore, wore our glasses. Every time we met a new group of Bolivians and got to know them slightly, they would inevitably ask us, "Why do you wear glasses?" At first I was puzzled by the question and said something like, "They help me see better." Unwittingly, I'd insulted the man, who said he knew that, but did I need them? My linguistic ability was taxed to the limit as I tried to explain that although I didn't need glasses for reading, I wore them all the time because I couldn't read signs or enjoy the beauty of La Paz without them. The next time the question was asked, it fortunately wasn't directed at me, so I listened sympathetically as my friend tried to explain her vision problems.

The Bolivian curiosity caused me to investigate the situation. I quickly realized that although many Bolivians owned glasses and wore them when careful visual examination was a necessity, the only people who wore them in public were those who, in the United States, would probably be considered legally blind.

I had no intention of abandoning my glasses, but neither did I want to go through that long explanation again. I looked up the Spanish equivalent of *myopia,* which was, with only a slight variation of pronunciation, *miopia.* After that my problem was solved. Whenever I was asked why I wore glasses, I'd simply reply, "Tengo miopia." I doubt if many of those who asked had heard of the condition, but it sounded impressive and serious enough to shut off further questions.

The issue did not surface again until our last weeks in the city when we were invited to a party by some of our new friends. By that time I'd learned to know Federico Vargas, who was to be my escort for the evening. He was dark and handsome, though rather short and skinny — but that's another story. As we dressed for the party, the girls decided to wear their contact lenses for the evening since it was a dressy occasion. Because I did not own contacts and probably wouldn't really need to see well, they convinced me to leave my glasses in our room. When we met our dates downstairs, their first question was, "Where are your glasses?" My friends quickly explained that they were wearing contact lenses. I smiled and said nothing.

Because contact lenses are so difficult to wear in La Paz, they are uncommon, even though the city is a large cosmopolitan capital. Each of the men, therefore, curiously examined the eyes of his date until he could see her impressive bits of American technology. Federico Vargas was just as curious as the others. "I don't see anything," he said quietly.

"No, because I don't have them," I replied. He stepped back and shook his head sadly. "Go upstairs and get your glasses," he said. "I like you better with them on."

Now there was a man who appreciated inner beauty! I put my glasses back on, and we were married three years later.

Activities

1. Self-description test

Try completing each of the following statements about yourself. Fill in each blank in items a–e with a word from the list following it. (Three words that fit you exactly may not be listed but select the words that seem to fit most closely.) Then answer question f.

a. I feel _____, _____, and _____ most of the time.

calm, anxious, cheerful, contented, relaxed, confident, tense, impetuous, complacent, reticent, energetic, self-conscious

b. When I study or work, I seem to be _____, _____, and _____.

efficient, enthusiastic, reflective, placid, sluggish, competitive, leisurely, meticulous, precise, determined, thoughtful, cooperative

c. Socially, I am _____, _____, and _____.

outgoing, affable, tolerant, gentle-tempered, considerate, awkward, affected, soft-tempered, argumentative, shy, talkative, hot-tempered

d. I am rather _____, _____, and _____.

active, warm, domineering, introspective, forgiving, courageous, suspicious, cool, sympathetic, serious, soft-hearted, enterprising

e. Other people consider me rather _____, _____, and _____.

generous, adventurous, withdrawn, dominant, optimistic, affectionate, reckless, detached, sensitive, kind, cautious, dependent

f. Underline one word out of the three in each of the following lines which most closely describes the way you are.

(1) assertive, relaxed, tense
(2) hot-tempered, cool, warm
(3) withdrawn, sociable, active
(4) confident, tactful, kind
(5) dependent, dominant, detached
(6) enterprising, affable, anxious

This test was designed to find out if by temperament you are viscerotonic, somatotonic, or cerebrotonic.[11] To score your test, count the number of adjectives that you selected from each of the following categories. The heading on the list from which the greatest number of your traits was selected should indicate your dominant temperament. The tendency toward the other temperaments should also be indicated by the number of terms selected from them. For example, if your totals are 11/6/4, you have predominantly viscerotonic traits.

Viscerotonia	Somatotonia	Cerebrotonia
affable	active	anxious
affected	adventurous	awkward
affectionate	argumentative	cautious
calm	assertive	considerate
complacent	cheerful	cool
contented	competitive	detached
cooperative	confident	gentle-tempered
dependent	courageous	introspective
forgiving	determined	meticulous
generous	dominant	precise
kind	domineering	reflective
leisurely	efficient	reticent
placid	energetic	self-conscious
relaxed	enterprising	sensitive
sluggish	enthusiastic	serious
sociable	hot-tempered	shy
soft-hearted	impetuous	suspicious
soft-tempered	optimistic	tactful
sympathetic	outgoing	tense
tolerant	reckless	thoughtful
warm	talkative	withdrawn

You will recall that Dr. Sheldon associated viscerotonia with the endomorph, who is soft, round, and fat; somatotonia with the mesomorph, who is hard and muscular; and cerebrotonia with the ectomorph, who is tall, thin, and fragile. Do you think a test based on a series of physical measurements would have suggested the same body types as did this questionnaire? Discuss your results and conclusions with your classmates.

2. Prepare and administer a test evaluating your classmates' sense of smell. Collect a dozen clean screwtop baby-food jars that will seal tight. In each jar, place a cotton ball saturated with a different scent. Be imaginative in collecting samples. Be sure, however, that each scent is familar to everyone being tested. Number the jars. Then let the subjects open the jars and try to identify the scents one by one. Discuss your findings with the subjects tested.

3. Read Helen Keller's autobiography *The Story of My Life* (available in most public and school libraries). Note passages in which she reports learning by smell, taste, or touch. Discuss to what extent sighted and hearing people respond to the same stimuli.

4. It has been said that after years of living together, husbands and wives begin to resemble one another. From newspapers, collect anniversary photos to illustrate this

theory. For each couple, identify verbally the details that strike you particularly (e.g., set of the jaw, smile wrinkles, lip line, or other features).

5. At a dog show, obedience class, or veterinarian's office, photograph dogs with their owners. When the film has been printed, compare the owners with their pets. To what extent are their appearances similar?

6. Examine the public image of a political candidate or popular entertainer. Describe the nonverbal "package" that his or her promoters try to sell the public. How is the person's physical appearance groomed to complement the package?

7. Formulate and administer a true-false questionnaire to probe the stereotypes held in your school and community regarding the expected behaviors and personal qualities of men as compared with women, of homosexuals, and of members of other nationalities and races. Discuss your findings and their implications.

Notes

1. Clarence Rainwater, *Light and Color* (New York: Golden, 1971), p. 113.
2. Peter Farb, *Word Play: What Happens When People Talk* (New York: Alfred A. Knopf, 1973), pp. 48–49.
3. Lister Sinclair, "A Word in Your Ear," from "The Ways of Mankind" (radio series), 1954. (LP recording of original radio program available from National Association of Educational Broadcasters, Univ. of Illinois, Urbana, Ill.)
4. William H. Sheldon, *The Varieties of Human Physique* (New York: Harper and Row, 1940).
5. William H. Sheldon and S. S. Stevens, *The Varieties of Temperament* (New York: Harper and Row, 1942).
6. ABC News, "Sex and Scents," on "20/20," 24 June 1982.
7. Edward T. Hall, *The Hidden Dimension* (Garden City, N.Y.: Doubleday and Co., 1966), p. 160.
8. Lowell Ponte, "Secret Scents That Affect Behavior," *Reader's Digest,* June 1982, p. 124.
9. Ibid., p. 122.
10. This and most of the other non-Caucasian ornamental body modifications reported in this chapter are described in Dale Idiens and Jennifer M. Scarce, "Man Attired," vol. 19 of *Peoples of the Earth,* ed. Edward Evans-Prichard (Danbury, Conn.: Danbury, 1973), pp. 58–71.
11. Juan B. Cortes and Florence M. Gatti, "Physique and Self-Description of Temperament," *Journal of Consulting Psychology* 29 (1965):pp. 432–39. Copyright 1965 by the American Psychological Association. Reprinted by permission of the publisher.

3

Kinesics

WITH HIS HAIR DISHEVELED, his shoulders drooping, and his eyes down-cast, a man in a white lab coat slowly enters the room. We see him from across the room, a waiting room judging by the persons on the far right of the screen, who look up from their magazines only briefly.

One woman, however, rises immediately and rushes toward him. We don't see her face, but her hand reaches out to touch his upper arm. The camera zooms in on their profiles. His face is gaunt with fatigue.

"How is she, Doctor?" she asks in a tense voice. "She'll be all right, won't she?"

The scene continues from a new camera angle. From a point just over the doctor's shoulder, we watch her face as he speaks, "I'm sorry. We did everything we could, but . . . "

Her expression changes. What we first saw as anxiety and tension drops to dismay and hopelessness. We aren't told how the women feels; we're expected to empathize with her and feel for ourselves as the music rises. The writer and actors feel they have made the context so clear that the viewers can't err in decoding what they see.

Novelists often do our interpreting for us. They frequently verbalize the thoughts and feelings of the major characters. But screen writers and film producers force the public to accept nonverbal cues and to infer the thoughts and emotions of their characters.

Given this current emphasis in mass communication, the popularity of body language study should come as no surprise. Any well-stocked book-store in the United States today will have two or three paperbacks on the subject. This is not bad, but the thrust of these books, judged by their covers, is that a person can easily learn to read the unconscious, unintentional messages conveyed by the bodies of others. The casual reader-turned-expert might zero in on individual behaviors, postures, or gestures and jump to conclusions. This is the danger. Human prejudice can cause untold misery and certainly should not be encouraged.

Context Is Essential

A knowledge of the way movements of our bodies can communicate is a useful tool in the hands of someone who has learned how to use it. When learning about kinesics, as the study of body movement is known in the world of scientific investigation, the key word is *context*. We must consider every little movement within the context of the situation, the context of place, the context of verbal communication, the context of time, and the context of culture.

Remembering then that kinesic behaviors do not communicate in isolation, let us examine the aspects of behavior included under that general heading. Derived from the Greek work *kinein* meaning "to move," *kinesics* denotes the study of (1) facial expressions, (2) gestures and movements of the torso, head, legs and feet, arms and hands, and (3) body postures, both sitting and standing, moving and static. Researchers often choose to include eye behavior as well, but that will be considered in chapter 4.

Two current researchers, Paul Ekman and Wallace V. Friesen, have classified body movement on the basis of origins, functions, and coded behavior. Their five categories are (1) emblems, (2) illustrators, (3) affect displays, (4) regulators, and (5) adapters.[1] Other classification systems have been proposed by other scientists, but the Ekman-Friesen categories are clear-cut enough for even the layman to understand.

Emblems Are Word Substitutes

Emblems, according to Ekman and Friesen, are those behaviors that are substituted for specific words or phrases. Frequently, emblems are used when verbal communication is impractical or impossible. For example, baseball catchers develop movements to signal to their pitchers; scuba divers communicate with each other and with those on the surface nonverbally; water skiers send messages by means of body movements to those in the speedboat pulling them; radio and television personnel use a standard set of gestures to communicate to one another while on the air; and sports referees signal infractions of the rules and penalties imposed. As these examples indicate, some emblems are devised by and limited to the individuals who use them; other movements are part of the shoptalk of a profession, standardized and used the world over.

Clearly, emblems must be learned, either consciously or subconsciously. The message they communicate is sent intentionally and deliberately. Furthermore, the use of emblems is not limited to special-interest groups. Every one of us sends and receives messages via emblems daily. The safe movement of traffic depends upon our recognition of police and drivers' hand signals to stop and turn right or left. A person standing beside the road with a thumb extended conveys a request for a ride.

Students raise their hands to gain their teachers' attention. We cross our fingers for good luck and shrug our shoulders when we don't know the answer. Babies are taught to come when someone stands before them with outstretched arms, to be quiet when adults put an index finger vertically to their lips, and to wave "hello" and "bye-bye."

Like words and phrases in any living language, emblems are constantly being added, modified, or dropped from use. During World War II, Winston Churchill raised his right hand and extended his index and middle fingers in an emblem the citizens of the allied nations readily recognized as "victory." During the years of the Vietnam conflict, the same gesture was used to symbolize "peace!" But when an Englishman turns his wrist so that the fingered V-sign is made with the palm facing the gesturer himself, the emblem becomes the worst obscenity his hand can make.[2]

The middle-finger jerk, which commonly conveys "up yours" to American viewers, has been in use for nearly two thousand years. The forearm jerk version of the same message is of much more recent origin. Arabs often reverse the middle-finger jerk, holding the palm downward and all fingers extended except the middle finger which is thrust downward.

Shaking a fist in another's face is a common threat emblem used worldwide. Its intimidating quality has made it a popular salute by Communists and black power advocates. Adults use a modified version of this threat emblem when they shake a raised forefinger at misbehaving children.

To insult their opponents, American children frequently stick out their tongues or thumb their noses. Adults more commonly use obscene insult emblems. In Elizabethan times the hand was made into a fist and the thumbnail snicked against the upper teeth in a gesture called biting the thumb. William Shakespeare records this gesture in act I, scene I of *Romeo and Juliet*. Sampson of the house of Capulet bites his thumb at Abram and Balthasar of the house of Montague, "which is disgrace to them if they bear it" (l. 45). The Montagues do not let the insult pass unnoticed but twice challenge Sampson, "Do you bite your thumb at us, sir?" (ll. 46, 48). Few words are exchanged before a sword fight erupts. One obscene, insulting emblem starts the world's best known feud between families.

Emblems, like words, often must be translated from country to country. A gesture with a clear meaning in one society may mean something else in another setting. The American circles his thumb and forefinger to mean "okay," but in Japan the same emblem indicates the shape of a coin and means "money." The French frequently combine that gesture with a disparaging facial expression to mean "zero" or "worthless." In some Mediterranean countries, the fingers are slightly flattened and the gesture becomes obscene. Thus a person must be careful when using kinesics as a substitute for learning a foreign language.

While in college, several of my friends worked as waitresses in elegant restaurants catering to wealthy, cosmopolitan customers. I recall a group of us sitting in my dorm room complaining about "those foreigners." Most of them had accents that were hard to understand, a forgivable flaw, but every so often there would be a table of them who wouldn't leave any tip whatsoever, or someone who treated the waitresses like dogs, snapping his fingers at them. We talked about the "proper" way of letting a waitress know that one is ready to order. A person should first close the menu; second, try to catch the eye of the waitress; and as a last resort, say, "Miss, Miss," as she passes nearby. Now, thinking back, I'm surprised that none of us could defend the foreign guest who assumed that a 10 to 15 percent service charge would be added to the check as it would have been in much of the rest of the world or the finger-snapping foreigner, who was simply following the custom of his own culture. Instead, we quickly judged everyone by our standards and found them lacking in etiquette.

The Greek people are friendly, it is said, but the manner in which they wave at Americans often puzzles us. No matter whether the Greeks are saying "hello" or "goodbye," they wave with their palms toward themselves, a movement which Americans interpret as "come here." In modern Greece, the rudest gesture possible is the *moutza,* a gestural relic from Byzantine times. It consists of an open hand thrust toward the insulted person's face and is commonly interpreted as "go to hell." Thus in the back window of an American automobile, a waving hand conveys a friendly hello. The same hand mounted on a car in Greece insults the driver behind should he approach too close.

The emblems of some societies cannot be translated, for they are a part of culture not practiced everywhere else. The elaborate greeting patterns practiced in France and South America, for example, have no equivalent in most of the United States. In Bolivia, for instance, men and women seem to be shaking hands wherever you look. Whenever two friends meet and pause to chat, their greeting includes a handshake. Even on the street and in stores and markets, encountering a friend means shaking his or her hand. If a particularly hearty greeting is desired, the handshake leads into an *abrazo.*

But that's not the end of it. When the conversation ends, whether it be two minutes or four hours later, another, parting handshake is exchanged. If your friend is accompanied by a girlfriend, a brother, and two cousins, none of whom you've met before, you will shake their hand as you are introduced and then once more when you and your friend say goodbye.

To fail to shake a person's hand is considered an insult. The handshaking rules for women are a bit more relaxed, particularly for older women, but I found it safest to offer my hand regularly.

When you are invited to enter a Bolivian home, it is imperative that you greet everyone there, particularly the older adults of the family. It doesn't matter that you plan to have an extended conversation with only one member of the family; the entire group must be recognized. After all, you are a guest in their home too. To fail to do so just because they are in another room or out in the patio is to treat them as less than human. Greeting them does not mean simply calling *"Hola"* through the open door or across the room either. You must shake hands or, in the case of a senior relative, embrace him or her in a full *abrazo*.

When large families get together, every man, woman, and child greets every other family member and guest as they arrive. When the visit has ended, the entire procedure is repeated, including hunting down Tia Maria in the kitchen.

Television has to some extent helped us learn the emblems of other cultures. Watching the Olympic Games, for example, has taught us that while Americans are apt to whistle in approval and boo or hiss when they're displeased, Europeans hiss for silence, whistle when they're displeased, and applaud in approval. The Soviet athlete who shakes his fist at the dissatisfied whistling audience is not expressing anger or violence toward the crowd but saying by this behavior, "I'll try harder. I have power I haven't used yet."

When operas, ballets, and concerts were first telecast live from Europe, American viewers were shocked to see the performers respond to a hearty ovation at the end of the concert by joining in the applause. Typically the troupe would appear for a curtain call and the audience would begin its applause. As the enthusiasm grew, a few patrons might rise for their ovation. Then the chorus members would begin applauding and finally the soloists too would begin clapping. Many Americans marveled, asking, "What kind of egotists are these people? Chorus members might be forgiven yet for applauding the principals, who are probably their idols, but how can a prima donna, a concertmaster, or a conductor applaud?" When these reactions reached the television producers, they added an English-speaking commentator to later telecasts to explain that in Europe this is a common practice. The performers are not applauding their own performance but thanking the audience for its support and approval.

Illustrators Reinforce Speech

Illustrators, Ekman and Friesen's second category of kinesic behaviors, accompany and illustrate spoken messages.

We are using illustrators to emphasize or accent spoken phrases when we pound the table or reach out toward the audience as we talk. We are using illustrators when we use our hands to draw an imaginary path while giving someone directions to reach a specific site. We are using illustrators when we point to objects we are talking about or indicate the dichotomy of our thoughts by using our bodies to show ideas "on one hand" and those "on the other hand." We are using illustrators when we nod approval or shake our heads "no."

Illustrators may not be as explicit or as deliberately used as emblems; nevertheless, we are aware of employing them whenever we do.

Liké our use of emblems, using illustrators is learned behavior. However, most illustrators were learned subconsciously by imitation as we learned speech from those around us. Illustrators accompany our speech so naturally and easily that we might well assume that they, of all forms of kinesic behavior, bear universal meanings. Ray Birdwhistell, one of the leaders in body motion research, insists this is not true. "We have found no gesture or body motion which has the same social meaning in all societies," he writes. All people everywhere open and close their eyes, turn their heads on their necks, and move their hands and arms, but the significance of these nonverbal cues varies from culture to culture, from society to society.[3]

Linguists have long noted that speakers of different languages vary in the number and types of gestures employed as they speak. Male Italian speakers will converse with both arms in motion almost constantly. They will make broad, sweeping symmetrical gestures with both arms while gesturing with their fingers and hands simultaneously. Native speakers of Yiddish, on the other hand, hold their upper arms close to their bodies while making choppy, staccato, one-handed gestures with their hands and forearms.

Fiorello La Guardia, the colorful mayor of New York City during the 1930s and 1940s, was the son of an Italian father and a Jewish mother, and he lived much of his life in New York. Thus he spoke Italian, Yiddish, and the New York English dialect with equal fluency and maintained the good will of those in each speech community by addressing them in their own language. Newsreel cameras followed him everywhere, sometimes catching his spoken words, sometimes not. Nevertheless, anyone who was familiar with the three languages could identify which language he was speaking simply by watching his kinesic behavior. Even his body language was trilingual.

By comparison to the speakers of Italian and Yiddish, speakers of English use their hands and arms very little. Head movements punctuate their sentences more emphatically than other gestures. Arabs, on the other hand, use both hand and head gestures liberally. Some of their illustrators are identical to those used by Americans; others are surprisingly different. When Arabs shake their head from side to side, the message being sent is "yes" not "no." To communicate "no" nonverbally, they tilt their head upward and lightly click their tongue.

Admittedly these variations from the common American head-shaking and nodding illustrators are not the norm. Most Europeans communicate "yes" and "no" nonverbally in the same manner we do. My South American husband not only shakes his head while saying "no," he reinforces it with a side-to-side wag of his index finger. Sometimes, in a social group, he'll use only the finger wag to send me a private message. Usually that means I'm stuck with the verbal task of declining gracefully!

Affect Displays Communicate Emotion

Affect displays, the third category of kinesic behaviors, are primarily message-bearing facial expressions, although postures offer important supporting cues. The message they convey is a person's emotional mood and/or reaction.

More spontaneous than emblems or illustrators, displays of affective states are less under our conscious control. Consider, for example, the spectators at an individual athletic or other competition. All of them have their favorite contestants. They watch the performance intently, silently praying that it will not be marred by error. Tension builds until one competitor emerges victorious. If a TV camera focused first on the competitors and then in instant replay on the spectators, we could probably identify which competitor each spectator was supporting. The facial expressions and complementary postures and body movements of the spectators were not consciously intended to communicate to others, but they do. In situations such as this, affect displays can give us away, as they did Eliza Doolittle while she watched the Ascot opening day horse race among the cool, unemotional British gentry in Lerner and Loewe's *My Fair Lady*.

Affect displays may reinforce, augment, or even contradict verbal messages. It is possible for a good actor, either on or off the stage, to "put on a mask" and convince others by conscious and continual attention to his behavior. The challenge, of course, increases as the discrepancy broadens between the actor's personal emotions and those of his desired character. Many people are not convincing actors. They may manage to verbalize desired responses but cannot always make their face conform. To repeat the caution given earlier, every communicating cue available must be considered and decoded in context.

Putting too much credence in the messages conveyed by affect displays may be highly misleading, if the research of Ernst Beier is accurate. Beier and his associates asked several different persons to act out six emotional states before television cameras. The moods requested were anger, fear, seductivity, indifference, happiness, and sadness. After videotaping, the subjects were asked to view their tapes and revise or eliminate any portions they felt were inaccurate. In the judgment of the subjects, then, the resultant portrayals were accurate presentations of the desired moods.

When the videotapes were played to large audiences to see if they could decode the moods intended, Beier discovered that most senders had successfully projected only two of the six moods. The particular moods varied from sender to sender, but generally speaking, the researchers were surprised at the amount of misinformation sent by the subjects. Their intentions and self-images were surprisingly out of harmony with the behaviors as decoded by others. Beier records two extreme examples of discordance. One girl, who tried like everyone else to portray six different moods, was judged to be seductive in each case. Another sender, who also tried her best to convey the six moods, was decoded as being angry every time.[4]

The implication seems clear. It is not only advisable but imperative to consider all cues in context. We may want to make others like us. We may try to show them the most pleasant, agreeable face we can, but the message we intend may not be the one received.

When reduced to its lowest terms, the problem is twofold. One half lies with the sender, who may encode misinformation or send insufficient information no matter how sincere or fake his or her emotions may be. Beier's senders were, admittedly, not trained actors, nor were their moods recorded as they spontaneously occurred. Yet it must be remembered that they viewed and approved the recorded portrayals.

The other half of the problem is the receiver. He or she may be preoccupied and only paying partial attention. Or perhaps the receiver is predisposed by his or her own emotional state or earlier experiences to misread the cues. Ineptitude at sending or decoding affect displays is not a cardinal sin, nor does it make a person less human.

Researchers have devoted much time and effort to studies of affect displays. Unfortunately their findings have not been conclusive, partially as a result of the many factors involved in the encoding-decoding process, partially as a result of the differing methods of research employed. They do, however, agree that some emotions are easier to communicate than others.

After several studies, one team of investigators concluded that there were eight principal emotional categories conveyed by facial expression:

happiness, surprise, fear, anger, sadness, disgust, contempt, and interest.[5] Another writer agrees but adds two more — bewilderment and determination.[6] This may seem like a very short list, considering how many emotional states could be named.

But try this experiment right now. Make your face display disappointment. Imagine that you failed to get a position you wanted desperately, a position that will never again be available to you. You're absolutely crushed. Go ahead, droop your shoulders and your chest. Droop even the arches of your feet if that helps. Do everything you can think of with your body to nonverbally communicate disappointment. Are you satisfied with your portrayal?

Good. Now try another one. This time let your face reflect extreme fatigue. Imagine that you've just finished the longest, most comprehensive exam you've ever taken. You're not afraid that you failed, but you're entirely drained. Again, let your whole body follow the mood. You're thoroughly exhausted. Got it?

Now consider the two portrayals you've just finished. They were the results of two, quite different moods, but do you honestly think a person observing you could have accurately identified your moods without knowing anything about the situations that caused them? Probably not, even if that person knew you very well. Our bodies reflect our moods through affect displays, but to decode the meaning accurately, an observer must respond to more than that limited set of cues.

My Fair Lady's stereotypical presentation of the English gentry watching the Ascot races, "the immobility of their faces and bodies registering their abiding disdain from any emotional display" (act I, scene 7), brings into focus another aspect of the display of affective states — its variation from person to person, from family to family, and from culture to culture.

As any mother will tell you, there is recognizable variation between the display of emotion of any two people, even if they are children of the same parents. One child will burst into tears at the mildest reprimand. Another may stiffen and refuse to cry even if spanked. If, however, we compare the affect displays of the children of one family with those of another, unrelated family, the differences become even more obvious. Unfortunately, we do not simply note these differences, but we use them as the bases for value judgments. Instead of saying, "They display their anger readily," we conclude, "They're always looking for a fight." We don't simply observe, "Their emotions are inscrutable," but judge, "They're an insensitive lot." When we consider entire cultural groups and compare the affect displays of our own society with those of a foreign group, the differences become so obvious as to affect our decoding process.

Facial expressions do not vary greatly in kind from one society to another. Persons as widely separated as Borneo and rural America have accurately matched pictures of persons displaying the eight emotional categories mentioned earlier with a list of those emotions.[7] The cultural differences lie in which emotions are permissible to display socially and to what degree that display is appropriate.

Most Americans do not display their emotions easily, if compared to southern European, Latin American, or Middle Eastern culture groups. In the United States, for example, showing one's anger publicly is not considered respectable behavior. We don't even like to disagree openly. When socially well-trained Americans visit countries where bargaining and haggling over the price of common items is standard behavior, they often report feeling cheap and undignified by lowering themselves to such pettiness.

If an American president or state governor announces a policy we oppose, our appropriate course of action is clear. We immediately let our congressmen, senators, and legislators know of our disapproval so that the system of checks and balances may work to offset the executive decision. If that doesn't work, we set out to find and support a worthy opponent, who can defeat him in the next election. Only in cases of extreme frustration with the system, do we resort to public marches and organized demonstrations.

Many of my Latin American friends have speculated that the system of government that works so well in the United States wouldn't last a decade in Central or South America. Why? Simply because their culture does not produce people who will refrain from expressing their emotions openly. What red-blooded Latin American, full of righteous indignation, is going to sit down quietly and write a letter, they ask. Instead, he's going to take to the streets, display his discontent vociferously, and find others who support his anger. One thing will lead to another and before long there will be mob action and another revolution. I make no claim to understand political science, but knowing their people as I do, I'm inclined to feel they're probably right.

When Jacqueline Kennedy appeared in public in the days immediately after her husband's death, Americans openly admired her composure, her poise, her regal bearing, her lack of tears or any other sign of the grief she must have felt inside. Had she broken down, the nation would have understood, but she didn't; and for that she was greatly admired and respected. In other parts of the world where expected public demonstrations of grief are loud and ostentatious, the behavior of the president's widow was almost beyond comprehension. "Doesn't she feel anything?" asked the common people. "She'll suffer later for stifling her emotions," observed their psychologists. "Typically American," wrote sympathetic journalists.

Yet by comparison to some cultures, American behavior is far from cool. When John McEnroe has repeatedly expressed disgust with the officials at the Wimbledon tennis championships, London newswriters have been quick to condemn his unbecoming displays. Americans who have watched the tournaments have not been particularly surprised at his outbursts. The officials have made some questionable calls. The American McEnroe, who has no right of appeal, has been understandably frustrated.

The cool reserve of the British upper class has frequently been caricatured and satirized, but their control of affect displays is very real. Perhaps the best recent example of this occurred during the summer of 1982 when Queen Elizabeth II awakened at three one morning to find an unknown male intruder in her bedroom. According to authorities, the queen reacted in a calm way and for about ten minutes chatted quietly with the man who sat on the foot of her bed. When he asked for a cigarette, she told him she had none in the room but would get some for him. She used that opportunity to summon a palace footman outside of her door. The queen was reportedly "unharmed and unruffled by her ordeal," and the intruder, a thirty-year-old vagrant who had previously been caught stealing wine from the palace, was not beheaded, or thrown in the dungeons, or even charged with breaking and entering until thirty-six hours later.[8] How typically British!

The English-speaking world is not alone in practicing reserve. The Japanese, like many other Orientals, are also taught not to let their true emotions be seen. As children, Japanese are taught to show happy faces to their friends and neighbors so as not to bring them pain or sorrow. Well-bred Japanese never subject their friends or colleagues to tales of woe regarding their family illnesses, personal difficulties, or private griefs. In fact, they will probably never mention them.

To lose control of one's emotions among refined Japanese will produce a reaction that causes the subject deep shame and humiliation. All extremes are rejected, not only grief and sorrow but anger, frustration, contempt, jealousy, joy, and even love. To hug or kiss in public is considered totally inappropriate. In airports and depots, Japanese have been observed to turn away from offenders in disgust or embarrassment. A Japanese father or mother leaving or greeting his or her family will pat the children on the head and without physical contact bow to his or her spouse, who will bow in return. More intimate displays are reserved for the privacy of their home.

When Jimmy Carter became President, his ever-ready smile became his best known quality. Many Americans couldn't believe he could smile sincerely so frequently. However, long before Carter left Georgia, Ray Birdwhistell had noticed and studied the varied frequency of smiles in different parts of the country. He concluded that of all Americans, those in the Southeast smile by far the most. Those in the Great Lakes states smile the least. In New England, cultural upbringing teaches that restrained smiles show polite reserve, while in the South children are taught that a smile denotes hospitality and good manners.⁹ Thus people from Carter's section of the country did not question his smile; to them it was familiar. But in the North unsmiling Americans viewed it with suspicion and hostility.

In the United States, parents often play games with their toddlers, beating them soundly, "so they'll learn to lose gracefully." Children beyond the age of five who pout or cry when they're beaten in fair competition are taunted by jeers of "cry baby" and "sissy" from their peers. At Little League games, coaches and parents have been seen to yell cruelly at boys who seem even close to tears when they're ruled out or guilty of a fielding error. Anger and disgust are acceptable substitutes, but unhappiness must never be seen. Tears of sadness may be accepted from girls under other conditions but not in athletic competition. "If you're big enough to play, you have to be big enough not to cry" seems to be the rule.

In July 1982, American television audiences got their first opportunity to watch the World Cup soccer finals. The semifinal game matched France against West Germany, two tough, talented teams. At the end of regulation time, the score was 1–1. After a thirty-minute overtime, it was 3–3. The winner was to be decided by a penalty contest in which each team was allotted five kicks with no one but the goalkeeper allowed to interfere. France had scored three and Germany two of their kicks when the French goalkeeper successfully batted down the German Uli Stielike's kick. Stielike collapsed to his knees on the grass, held his head in hands, and cried!

Then Didier Six kicked for France and the German goalkeeper managed to keep him from scoring. Six walked glumly back to his teammates. Then *he* fell to the ground in tears! From coast to coast, American viewers exclaimed, "Did you see that?"

The West Germans won the game by scoring all of their remaining kicks while the French missed yet another, but for Americans the climax was not the Germans' hard-earned victory but the discovery that in World Cup soccer, big boys cry!

In the United States, the equal rights movement has drawn much attention to the old standard that women may acceptably display their emotions but that men should not. Men and women alike have asked, "What's wrong with men expressing sympathy, fear, or sorrow honestly and openly?" But in practice how do the teenagers in your community treat boys who cry where others see them? Do they act the same toward similar displays from girls?

In Iran, men traditionally display emotions that Americans consider feminine. Men are acceptably emotional and are expected to rely on intuition instead of logic. They weep easily and are given to impulsive behavior. Women, on the other hand, are expected to maintain control and remain practical. Americans are accustomed to look for this strength of mind and logic in men, not women.

In the display of affective states, as in all other nonverbal communication, sexual and cultural variations prevail.

Regulators Control Speech

Regulators, the fourth category of kinesic behaviors, are those body motions that monitor and control verbal communication. They provide the feedback necessary to let us know whether we are being understood and accepted. They inform us when clarification or repetition is necessary and when we can proceed. They let us know when our listeners desire to speak and when they have completed their verbal contributions.

Regulators are sent and received without conscious awareness. Nevertheless, they are learned behaviors, assimilated subconsciously as we learn to speak. Proof of this lies in the fact that they differ slightly from one culture to another and from one spoken language to another.

Whether sitting in class listening to the discussion, talking with their families, or visiting with friends, peoples' bodies are constantly providing others with information regarding their communication successes and failures. Many American speech regulators are subtle eye movements and head nods, but some are movements of the limbs and torso or entire body postures.

When people are interested in us and what we have to say, they tend to square their bodies to face us as directly as possible. They stand relaxed with their arms hanging loose. One hand may rest on a hip or their thumbs may be hooked in their pockets as they listen. If seated they may incline their bodies toward us or actually move forward on their chairs so as not to miss a word. As we speak they will look at us intently, focusing on our eyes, mouth, and face with peripheral vision of our arms and body.

When others agree with what we are saying, they will continue to display interest and will nod, smile, or make little "hmm"ing sounds from time to time. An interesting phenomenon noted by kinesic research is that people in groups frequently imitate the posture of those with whom they agree. These congruent postures may be mirror images or exact duplications of the postures or gestures of others. For example, if we tend to agree with a person who has both hands on his hips, we may place our hands on our hips as well. If we note the person who expresses our views putting all of his weight on one foot and crossing his arms, we too may shift to that posture. Such congruent behavior is frequently seen at conference tables where one, two, or more postures may become prevalent as discussion progresses and individuals take sides. If we watch a group from the time it forms, it is often possible to identify the leaders or dominant persons by noting which persons set the position that others assume. The fact that several persons in a group demonstrate congruent postures does not necessarily mean anything; but if they change from one congruent posture to another almost as if on cue, that behavior frequently indicates togetherness and mutual support. Other contextual clues will provide the necessary evidence to confirm or refute the assumption.

As other people listen to us speak, they decode, weigh, and evaluate our words. Their kinesic behaviors provide us with ample cues that our words are being processed thoughtfully. Listeners may stroke their chin, touch their nose, furrow their eyebrows, or rest their chin on one hand or fist. Two other gestures that are frequently used while trying to understand are rubbing one's head with the fingertips back toward the jaw and the index finger pointing along the cheek.

When people are unsure of themselves, they may rub their eyes or ears, pause to adjust their glasses, or respond with their mouth partially covered by one hand.

If we are alert, we should be able to see when our listeners are anxious or uncomfortable with the course of the conversation. They may rub their neck with one hand or place the hand in the hair at the back of the head. Others may fidget or play with a pencil or a fold of clothing. They may tug at their collar, clench and unclench their hands, or wipe their palms on their jeans. Cues such as these should warn us to proceed with caution. Perhaps we need to explain the reasoning behind our conclusions or ask the other person to voice his or her reaction. Unless we do something, these cues of discomfort will turn to signs of opposition.

When people disagree with us, their bodies usually display that fact. They frequently shake their heads from side to side, narrow their eyes, and set their jaw. These movements may be done quite subtly or in a defiant manner, depending upon the persons and the situation involved. Crossed arms often indicate that our listeners are on the defensive, especially if they lean back in their chair and clench their fists beneath their arms. Once our listeners assume such positions, our words are all but lost.

Another way of losing an audience is through disinterest and boredom. Again we should be able to recognize the nonverbal signs, so that we might do something to remedy the situation. When people lose interest they will break eye contact with us, look down for inappropriate periods of time, and look around the room or at the ceiling. They will change posture frequently—lean their elbows on a desk or table and rest their head on an open hand, turn their bodies 45 to 90 degrees away from us, or slouch back in their chairs. Bored people may also doodle, drum their fingers, tap their feet, or swing one foot rhythmically. When they begin checking the clock or their watch, and straightening up their possessions, termination is clearly desired.

There are other signs too that people use to let us know they want to turn their attention to something else. Some may simply try to make themselves comfortable while enduring the ordeal. Those who hope to terminate the communication situation will fidget, stretch their legs, look away frequently, shift their posture to one of readiness, and if not heeded, they may stand and/or walk away.

One of the less obvious functions of nonverbal communication is to let us know when a person plans to continue speaking or is ready to yield to another in conversation. Kinesic cues are highly important in helping us take turns smoothly.

Some turn-yielding cues are very obvious. A speaker will ask us a direct question or gesture to us with an open hand sweep similar to throwing us a frisbee. Most cues, however, are much more subtle and occur in clusters. When we are ready to yield our turn, we usually lock eyes momentarily with the person whom we expect to speak next. More important, however, seems to be the degree of rise or drop of the vocal pitch incorporated into our final spoken sentence. An extra high rise of pitch will mark a turn-yielding question, or a deep falling pitch will punctuate a terminal statement. At the same time, our heads and eyelids will rise or fall slightly, and arm and hand gestures will cease after a final parallel rise or drop.

When we wish to keep the floor, we employ a number of nonverbal turn-suppressing cues. We avoid meeting the eyes of others, keep our hand and arm gestures flowing, and maintain a straight head position. We may pass over the ends of sentences and questions without letting our vocal pitch rise or fall significantly.

Getting a nonstop speaker to throw you a turn-yielding cue, particularly in a large group, may take time and a full bag of nonverbal aids. Let's imagine you've been listening for some time, sitting back with your legs and arms crossed. Your first move would probably be to uncross your body parts and lean forward. This would communicate your desire to become involved. Next you might turn slightly to face the speaker more directly and try to catch his eye. If that doesn't work, you might be forced to maintain that posture a little longer, nodding or shaking your head a bit more noticeably as you listen to his words. You might at the same time vocalize your "hmm"ing sounds a bit louder as you agree or disagree with his statements. Usually this is sufficient to get him to throw you the needed cue. If he doesn't, you have a choice of subsequent actions. You might politely lean back for a few minutes and then start the whole process once again, or you might begin your own arm and hand gestures and interrupt vocally when he pauses for breath.

All of this is usually done subconsciously and may seem beyond belief when described in detail. Take time for people-watching. It's enlightening and often entertaining as well.

Students who make an announcement over the public-address system from their school office for the first time often find the experience unnerving, even if they are excellent speakers. They desperately miss human feedback. Without anyone in the broadcast booth, they have no idea of how they are progressing, how their words are being received, or even if they are being received. Speaking before television cameras in a studio without a live audience can raise anxiety levels even higher, even among experienced public speakers. Communication via the telephone removes the possibility of visual feedback. But we may be totally unaware of how important it is to hear someone at least reveal his continued presence and reception with occasional words and grunts, until we try to communicate unmemorized material with no feedback at all.

Because of their upbringing in a different culture, some people provide nonverbal feedback that we misinterpret. The results can be painful for both senders and receivers.

Take, for example, the Vietnamese who came to the United States as refugees. I have been told that children in their culture are taught to maintain constant eye contact while being addressed individually by a person in authority. To show humility and no desire to attack or defend themselves, they are trained to stand and fold their arms over their chest. Imagine, then, the miscommunication when an American teacher first found it necessary to scold a Vietnamese child. Instead of shying away into his chair and hanging his head in shame, the well-trained immigrant child stood erect, crossed his arms tightly, and stared the teacher squarely in the eye.

A similar situation involving different cultural training occurred in New York between an American high school principal and a Puerto Rican girl. The girl was suspended from classes because, when accused of wrongdoing, she looked at the floor and wouldn't meet the principal's eyes or even look at him. He promptly concluded this was a clear sign of guilt. Not until the punishment had been imposed did he learn that in Puerto Rico a nice girl, a good girl, does not meet the eyes of an adult. Refusing to do so is a sign of respect and obedience. Both the Vietnamese and the Puerto Rican child behaved exactly as they had been taught was proper. In each case the American adults understandably misinterpreted the cues.

American students from black communities have frequently complained that white American teachers, counselors, and employers insult them by talking down to them. Harvard professor Frederick Erickson investigated the problem and offered this explanation: Because the black students do not give a speaker the same nonverbal feedback that white students do, white teachers think that they don't understand. While receiving instruction, a white student will nod emphatically and murmur "uh-huh." Blacks nod almost imperceptibly or say "mhm," seldom both. As a result of this difference in feedback, speakers from purely white American cultures tend to overexplain to blacks, thereby insulting them by treating them as seemingly incapable of understanding the first time.[10]

Clearly, people-watching by persons educated in the field of nonverbal communication is more than just an enjoyable pastime. Its possibilities for improved interpersonal communication are only beginning to be felt.

Adapters Overrated as Communicators

The final category of kinesic behaviors is called adapters, bits of body movement that are performed with no intent to communicate. As the name implies, these motions are enacted as adaptive efforts to satisfy needs, perform actions, handle emotions, manage social contacts, and accomplish a variety of other tasks needed in daily living. Adapters are carried out when we are in private or out of the public eye. Under public scrutiny, they are sometimes modified or partially suppressed. For example, in private we can scratch wherever we itch until the itch is gone. We can yawn, pick our nose, belch stomach gases, or cry until our emotions are spent — but not in public.

Most adaptive behaviors develop in childhood. Some are learned by imitation, others are innate. Some innate behaviors draw the attention of others, who teach us to modify them in socially acceptable ways. Thus when others are present, we may momentarily touch our nose, or other parts that itch, and fidget uncomfortably but never satisfy the urge to scratch. We will stifle a yawn or burp and perhaps substitute displays of anger for tears.

Many popular books and articles on body language emphasize these bits of behavior and their significance far beyond the justification of scientific study. A series of cautions, therefore, is in order.

There are hundreds, perhaps thousands, of facial expressions possible. The forehead, eyebrows, eyes and eyelids, nostrils, chin, cheeks, jaw, mouth, and lips all can move independently and in many ways. The possible combinations are almost limitless, especially given the human differences existent. Any attempt to interpret them all is doomed to failure. The most that can be done is to offer generalized descriptions of the various components of a facial expression.

The absurdity of any attempt to label precisely was illustrated clearly as early as the 1920s when Russian filmmaker Kuleshev cut into his narrative sequences to insert reaction shots showing a man's face. Viewers interpreted the emotion registered on that face differently depending upon what scene it followed.

In addition to reflecting one's body size and structure, the postures a person characteristically assumes when sitting or standing communicate much about that person's attitude toward himself and his relationship to the people and world around him. Kinesic research has shown that geographic and cultural environment is an equally powerful force in determining one's postures. To judge the meaning of a given posture by considering only one of these factors might result in serious error.

For example, the European male's manner of crossing his legs when seated may seem effeminate to some Americans. In Europe, men characteristically cross their legs at the knee, stacking one knee above the other. American males rest the lower thigh or ankle of one leg on the knee of the other in what has been called the *figure 4 position*. Even some American women assume this figure 4 position when wearing slacks or jeans. Many Europeans consider the American way boorish for men and lesbian behavior in women.

The way a person walks reflects age, general health, mood, social status, and ethnic culture, any one of which, if changed, might make a notable difference. In chapter 1, we considered the differences in walks of black American, white American, and French males. The walk of some women has led men to judge their life-style and availability. Occasionally the men are right, but many American women from Hispanic neighborhoods have been erroneously evaluated and some have had to physically defend themselves from men who interpreted their walk as a nonverbal invitation.

I tend to be a rather outgoing person. I find it easy to talk to strangers and never miss an opportunity to greet people I know. At home, in the midwestern states, this behavior has always been an asset, so naturally I continued it when I traveled. Shortly after I started dating my husband in Bolivia, he quietly but clearly informed me that I should not be so quick to greet the men I met on the street. I couldn't imagine why not, especially if I knew them fairly well. My husband patiently explained that in his culture a virtuous girl or woman will never speak to a man until he has spoken first. To do so is to label herself as easily available. It wasn't easy to change a habit practiced from childhood. My behavior was no longer conscious, but semiautomatic, and holding back was as difficult for me as for a driver not to react when a traffic light turns green.

Actors, especially mimes, and artists, particularly cartoonists and caricature artists, have long been trained as observers of kinesic behavior. The time has come, however, for an examination and understanding of body language to be a part of the liberal education of every man and woman.

Activities

1. Using the library, research the stylized gestures, postures, and facial expressions that were part of the elocutionary movement popular at the turn of the century. These kinesics were used then by orators and actors. Today they are sometimes used when staging old melodramas.

2. Research the sets of standardized gestures used by one of the following: water skiers, basketball referees, baseball umpires, football referees, television and radio technicians.

3. While watching a movie on television, turn off the sound. Can you tell what is going on by the actors' kinesic behavior? Do you think the kind of movie it is makes any difference?

Plan and carry out an experiment of your ability to understand a movie or television program without sound. Have a friend watch the show naturally while you watch a silent version. Compare notes.

Or, as a class, watch a film or video tape without the sound track. Discuss what happened. Then rewind the film or tape and watch it again, with sound. Discuss.

4. Develop a study comparing male and female kinesics. Limit your study to one cluster, such as postures while seated at classroom desks. Compile a list of specific features to be compared. Then carry out your study using at least ten males and ten females, both randomly selected. Be sure all subjects are from a similar age group and ethnic background.

An examination of the way people walk, for example, might note such specifics as posture, length of step, movement of hips and arms, stiffness of knees and spine, heaviness of tread, position of head, and rhythm of movement. When comparing walks, ask repeatedly: Are all these differences caused by body size and structure?

5. Compare the walks of white teenage males to an equal number of black teenage males. Again work out a set of specifics to be examined and compared.

6. Pickpockets can usually spot strangers in a city. What details do you think they look for?

Demonstrate how you would walk through a strange neighborhood if you wanted to convey a message of fearlessness. If you wished to indicate that you pose no threat.

7. Have several members of the class randomly select one of the following to demonstrate for the class. Can the rest of the group identify the behavior?

Walk as if
—you know you look sharp
—you think you're ugly
—you're crossing the stage to get an award
—you're with someone you're proud of
—you're on your way to class
—you're trying to impress a group of the opposite sex
—you want to pass someone but not be seen
—you're trying to sneak in late

—you want to annoy the people downstairs
—you're late for class but afraid to be caught running

Using a static pose, sit as if
—you're in a boring class
—you're having a job interview
—you're posing for a portrait
—you're having breakfast alone
—you're trying to think of a good speech topic
—you're in a movie theater
—you're putting medication on your zits
—you're waiting for the dentist
—you're in your favorite class
—you're dining in an elegant restaurant

8. Design a mini-experiment to test the relative communication power of spoken words vs. kinesic illustrators when used together. Give identical directions to each of a series of subjects. You might tell them to look for someone in the second room to the left, but via gesture indicate that the room is to the right. Watch where they go. Which language speaks louder?

9. How do cartoonists show facial expressions? All that is really needed are two dots for eyes, two lines for eyebrows, and a third line for a mouth.

Your library may have books with further suggestions. Try your own hand at capturing cartoon expressions of happiness, surprise, fear, anger, sadness, disgust, contempt, interest, bewilderment, and determination. Show your cartoon faces to your classmates to see if they identify the intended emotional states.

10. With two or three classmates, play emotion charades. Prepare a set of cards, each listing an emotional state or attitude. Each player, in turn, is to draw a card and express the emotion cited by using facial expression alone. If the other players can't identify it accurately after one guess each, the sender is to strike a static pose using the entire body to convey the same emotion. A player earns ten points for each emotion identified after facial expression only, five points for facial expression augmented by static pose. The first player to reach thirty points wins.

11. Adaptive behavior is frequently modified when others are present. For example, how would you act if you were (1) at home alone and genuinely frightened, (2) with a member of the family and genuinely frightened, (3) with someone whom you wanted to think you were frightened? Demonstrate.

12. Pantomime the drinking of
—very hot chocolate or coffee
—a small glass of bitter medicine

— vintage wine
— cool water after a sports activity
— very sweet, syrupy punch
— sour grapefruit juice
— highly carbonated cola

13. If such a person is available in your area, invite a trained mime to perform for your class.

If not, try to obtain a film of a mime performance. World renowned French mime, Marcel Marceau, made an outstanding film series produced by Encyclopaedia Britannica Education Corporation in 1975. The series, titled *The Art of Silence: Pantomimes with Marcel Marceau,* has thirteen filmed performances ranging from seven to seventeen minutes in length. The films may be rented individually or as a set from the University of Iowa, Audio Visual Center Media Library, C-5 Seashore Hall, Iowa City, IA, 52242. Contact that source for individual titles and performance descriptions.

Another good film is *The Mime of Marcel Marceau,* produced by the Learning Corporation of America in 1972. This twenty-three–minute overview of Marceau's work may be rented from Iowa State University, Media Resources Center, 121 Pearson Hall, Ames, IA, 50011.

14. Develop and present an original pantomime or practice and present a professionally written pantomime for your class.

15. Watch the slide-tape program *Personal Communication: Gestures, Expressions and Body English* and discuss it with your class. The program is available from its 1974 producer, Center for the Humanities, Inc., Communications Park, Box 1000, Mount Kisco, NY, 10549-0010.

Notes

1. Paul Ekman and Wallace V. Friesen, "The Repertoire of Nonverbal Behavior: Categories, Origins, Usage, and Coding," *Semiotica* 1 (1969): pp. 49–98.
2. These and many other international emblems reported in chapter 3 are described in Desmond Morris, *Manwatching: A Field Guide to Human Behavior* (New York: Harry N. Abrams, 1977).
3. Ray L. Birdwhistell, *Kinesics and Context: Essays on Body Motion Communication* (Philadelphia: Univ. of Pennsylvania Press, 1970), p.81.
4. Ernst G. Beier, "Nonverbal Communication: How We Send Emotional Messages," *Psychology Today,* October 1974, pp. 53–56.
5. Paul Ekman, Wallace V. Friesen, and Phoebe Ellsworth, *Emotion in the Human Face: Guidelines for Research and an Integration of Findings* (Elmsford, N.Y.: Pergamon, 1972), p. 45.
6. Dale G. Leathers, *Nonverbal Communication Systems* (Boston: Allyn and Bacon, 1976), p. 24.
7. Ekman et al., *Emotion in Human Face,* p. 147.
8. Associated Press reports, 12 July 1982.
9. Birdwhistell, *Kinesics and Context,* p. 30.
10. Flora Davis, "How to Read People Better," *Woman's Day,* 8 March 1977, p. 134.

4

Eye Behavior

THAT THE EYES COMMUNICATE clearly and effectively is no great twentieth century discovery. For hundreds of years literature has been enriched by vivid descriptions of eyes sending messages to thousands of persons, both real and fictitious. The English language includes dozens of common phrases such as "shifty eyes," "steely eyes," "bedroom eyes," "bug eyes," "knowing eyes," "piercing eyes," and "an evil eye." We've all heard of "a dirty look," "a hurt look," "a burning glance," "a sideways glance," "an icy stare," and "a stare that pins you to the wall." Eyes have also been known to "shoot daggers," "look right through" a person, and "melt into the eyes" of another.

Yes, writers have contributed much to draw our attention to the power of the eyes. Women from the days of King Tutankhamen through modern times have used makeup to draw attention to the messages sent by their eyes. Twentieth century females no longer use drops of belladonna to enlarge their pupils, but a majority of them do use one or more of the modern varieties of ancient beauty aids — eye shadow, eye liner, eyebrow pencil, and mascara. Thousands of others wear what they consider flattering eyeglass frames. Some even change their apparent eye color with contact lenses.

Current research has shown that women were not mistaken in trying to enhance their eyes with belladonna. (Students of Romance languages will recognize that word as meaning "beautiful woman.") Eckhard Hess recently conducted studies in which men were presented with several pairs of female portraits. Each pair was identical except that in one photo the eye pupils were constricted; the other had been retouched so that the subject had large dilated pupils. The judges consistently assigned more favorable attributes to the women portrayed with large pupils and more negative personal characteristics to those with small pupils.[1]

Researchers of nonverbal communication have remained unaffected by the language of romantic novelists and employ their own terminology for eye behavior. The phrase *eye contact* is commonly used to refer to mutual locking of eyes. The scientists' preferred term, however, is *mutual gaze,* which refers to two interactants looking at one another's face including the eyes. The reason for this preference is the difficulty in identifying the precise object of a person's visual attention at distances of more than one meter. The term *gaze,* then, refers to a person's looking behavior, which may or may not be directed at another person.

You May See, But Must Not Look

In human interaction, there seems to be an important, though unstated, distinction made between looking and seeing. Looking is psychologically active behavior. The eyes are clearly focused on every part of the subject with intent to decode. Looking has been paralleled to spying upon a subject. The woman who told police, "He undressed me with his eyes," obviously felt that her person had been violated by the perpetrator's gaze.

Seeing, on the other hand, is passive behavior psychologically. Girls who wear bikinis to the pool want to be seen. In fact, they'd probably be hurt if the right young men didn't notice, but men must not look, or spy, on them. That would be less than acceptable behavior. A man who sees a girl does not prolong his gaze, but takes her in in a sweeping glance or two or three.[2]

American eye behavior in public settings is highly predictable and has been recorded by several trained observers.[3] When we encounter others on the street, in stores, offices, cafeterias, and other places where we have no intention of initiating conversation, we practice what has been called *civil inattention.* We see them but certainly do not look or stare at them.

We must respect the humanness of others but never intrude upon their privacy. To do this, we avoid catching the eye of strangers or looking at them for more than a fleeting glance. Sometimes this is difficult, especially when a stranger is dressed in an uncommon manner, is physically unusual or handicapped, or seems to be someone famous. Adults may go out of their way to steal a second glance. Children are often told, "Don't stare. It's not polite."

Elevator behavior is a perfect example of our deliberate and polite inattention to strangers. We step in, see the others inside, and immediately turn around to face the door. As we ride together, we avoid conversing and looking but stare at the ceiling, look at the floor, read the inspection tag, or watch the floor numbers flash.

If by accident our eyes do catch the eye of a stranger, we must hold that mutual gaze for a few seconds while we smile as an indication of trust and good will. A longer look would communicate disapproval, suspicious intent, or a desire to speak.

During a convention in a Chicago hotel, I was riding alone in an elevator when the door opened and television actress Sally Struthers stepped in. I couldn't restrain my gaze and had to flash my good-will smile before turning my eyes back to the floor numbers. Before we reached the lobby, another woman entered, and she too found her eyes betraying her good manners. Finally, as the elevator stopped, she blurted out, "You *are* Sally Struthers, aren't you?" When Miss Struthers nodded, she added as if to explain her rude behavior, "Excuse my staring, but you're more beautiful in real life than on the screen."

Eyes Control Encounters with Strangers

Strict though unstated rules of gaze also control our eye behavior as we meet and pass others on the street, in shopping centers, and in airports. Urban white Americans will avoid mutual gaze once they've reached definite recognition distance (approximately sixteen to thirty-two feet). Within this zone, they will only steal a glance at strangers but must greet friends and acquaintances or risk offending them. However, residents of small towns and urban blacks are more likely to greet friends and strangers alike.[4]

Avoiding the eyes of a stranger or breaking the mutual contact after a good-will smile indicates no desire to communicate. Establishing and locking mutual gaze indicates an open channel for communication. We try, therefore, to catch the eye of clerks, waitresses, and other strangers in service occupations, for we trust that mutual gaze will bring them to us for vocal communication. Experienced contribution solicitors and religious fanatics in airports and shopping centers often pull us into a communication situation without our realizing how they did it.

Their technique is based on the assumption that good manners and unwillingness to offend will keep us from dismissing them without speaking after mutual gaze has been established. They will catch our eye while we are still twenty or more feet away and then lock in, pulling us toward them and communication by mutual gaze. They may not move until we are about eight feet from them, but then they'll physically move in. Not a word will be said until we are vulnerably close, less than three feet away. Then it's too late.[5]

Under normal conditions involving strangers, we continue our civil inattention approach until we are about eight feet away from them. At that point, we signal in which direction we intend to pass by using a quick glance and slight inclination of the head in that direction. Then we turn our eyes downward. Erving Goffman, author of *Behavior in Public Places,* calls this a "kind of dimming of lights" while passing.[6]

This formula works so well that athletes employ it to fake out the opposition as they move upfield or up court. They will send all the appropriate signals of intent to move in one direction but then abruptly move the opposite way.

Human Reactions to Stare Conditions

We've all been involved in stare-down contests at one time or another. For children it's a contest of endurance and will, for only the strong can persist without feeling intimidated or breaking up in nervous laughter.

Any gaze longer than ten seconds with no intent to communicate further is likely to induce irritation if not real discomfort in the subject of the stare. Among primates, stares will cause fight or flight behavior. Human beings are not quite so direct in their reactions, but investigators from Yale University have shown that gazing steadily at a person will significantly increase his or her heartbeat, among other things.[7]

In another, frequently duplicated study, investigators posing as ordinary pedestrians and motorcycle riders stared at automobile drivers stopped for a red light. When the light changed, drivers subjected to such stare conditions crossed the intersection significantly faster than did those who had not been stared at.[8]

Children and members of physically identifiable minorities have often described being subjected to another type of stare—the stare that seems to look right through them as if they were not there. In stores and restaurants, for example, they may be clearly visible but patently ignored by those who thus practice discrimination. This is the slightly unfocused stare we reserve for nonpersons. Unprejudiced people use it while watching animals in a zoo. But many so-called refined persons have been seen to use it on servants, lower-ranked employees, students, apprentices, public servants, golf caddies, bellhops, and hired hands.

The Functions of Eye Behavior in Conversation

In normal two-person conversation, eye behavior remains highly predictable although it takes on a whole new set of functions. We do not gaze at others all the while we talk or listen to them, nor do we look away the entire time. Normal percentages of gaze will vary with the sex, personalities, and cultural background of the speakers, the topic, the setting, and several other factors; yet the functions of the eyes provide a predictable behavior pattern.

Five functions have been identified through varied investigations: (1) regulating turn taking, (2) monitoring feedback, (3) signaling thought, (4) expressing feelings, and (5) communicating the nature of the interpersonal relationship.[9]

As speakers, we begin a conversation by establishing mutual gaze with our listener, then we break away. At the end of a comment, we look again to check for listener feedback or to give a turn-taking cue as explained more fully in chapter 3, "Kinesics." If we do not reestablish mutual gaze, it is a clear signal that we mean to retain the floor for further speech.

As listeners, we look at a speaker finishing a comment to indicate that we desire to speak. Averting our gaze declines that opportunity. Sometimes a declined turn results in the speaker smoothly adding to a previous statement or asking a direct question. At other times, awkward silences follow. When gazing at one another has greatly diminished, the time has come to terminate the conversation.

Continually evasive eye gaze by others serves as an indicator that they would prefer to withdraw from our company. Sometimes they are simply shy and, as a result, uncomfortable with us. Their eyes, therefore, look everywhere but at us. However, we are never sure of their shyness. Perhaps they dislike us or are bored. Persons with "shifty eyes" that regularly glance away from us have the same unnerving effect. Occasionally the direction of their glance provides a clue to their preoccupation or preferred setting. After a short time, we're more than happy to let them go.

As we engage in conversation, we also use our eyes to monitor our partner's interest, understanding, and acceptance of our words. The extent of gaze afforded us serves as an indicator by which we judge attentiveness, and varied facial expressions combined with gaze provide the feedback we seek.

Studies have shown that both speakers and listeners look away more when considering thought-provoking questions and formulating responses. As their concentration turns inward, they seem to prefer to reduce visual stimulation. Not only do they avert their eyes, but they fail to focus on whatever it is that stands in their new line of sight.[10]

As indicators of emotion, the eyes function in tandem with the rest of the face to show surprise, fear, anger, disgust, happiness, sadness, and a myriad of other feelings. Eyes can also threaten, reproach, hate, frighten, ignore, plead, seduce, or love. These emotional states are conveyed not only by the physical appearance of the eyes and face but also by the duration and fixation of the gaze.

In its final function during conversation, eye behavior communicates to each partner the other's evaluation of the nature of their relationship.

According to research findings, if we consider the person with whom we are communicating to be of moderately high status, our gaze and mutual gazes will be maximized. If the person is of very high status, gaze and mutual gazing are moderate. And for low status people we employ minimal gaze.[11]

If we are dependent upon our conversation partner, our gaze will also tend to be longer and more frequent. We also gaze more at people we like, although we sometimes turn a cold stare on those we dislike.

Many writers and researchers have turned their attention to behavior of the eyes during courtship. The age-old idea of men or women "making eyes" at someone with whom they wish to establish a more intimate relationship is supported by scientific investigation. Engaged couples were found to have increased mutual gaze; and among men and women attempting to develop intimacy, longer glances and reciprocated glances were prevalent.[12]

One of the most interesting selections on this subject was written as advice to single women by Helen Gurley Brown in the book *Sex and the Single Girl:*

> Flirting is mostly just looking. Ready for a quick flirting lesson?
> Select a man at a restaurant table. (Somebody in the dentist's waiting room will do just as well. Place isn't important.) Spotted him? Look straight into his eyes, deep and searching, then lower your gaze. Go back to your companions or magazine. Now look at him the same way...steadfastly, questioningly. Then drop your eyes. Do it three times and you're a flirt! (P.S. You will have made him very happy.)
> Want to flirt some more?
> A man is talking to you, nothing very personal. Look into his eyes as though tomorrow's daily double winners were there. Never let your eyes leave his. Concentrate on his left eye...then the right...now deep into both. Smooth operators never take their eyes off a man even when a waiter spills a tray of drinks. This look has been referred to rather disdainfully as "hanging on his every word." It was good in your grandmother's day and it's still a powerhouse![13]

Other Factors Affecting Gaze Behavior

As stated earlier, the percentage of gaze and mutual gaze occurring in a given interaction situation is determined by more than the five functions already examined.

The sex of the participants is perhaps the most dominant of these factors. Whether speaking, listening, or sharing silence, women look more than men. According to one study, females, over the course of a conversation, average approximately 15 percent more time gazing at their partners than do their male counterparts. On every scale—gaze frequency, duration, and reciprocity—women surpass men.[14]

The personalities of the communicators also affect their gaze behavior. Persons who through unrelated psychological tests were judged to be extroverted gazed more frequently and for longer time periods than did those judged to be introverted.[15] Another study discovered low gaze frequency and duration in persons also ranking low in self-esteem on other tests.[16]

A third, highly complicated research project showed that many persons who were guilty of cheating tried to avoid mutual gaze; but others, who were equally guilty, employed mutual gaze to a high degree even after being accused of cheating. The gaze behaviors of these subjects were then correlated with results of personality tests measuring Machiavellianism (the tendency to use cunning and shrewdness to achieve a goal without regard for how unscrupulous the means might be). Persons rating high in Machiavellianism were found to have much higher gaze frequencies than were low Machiavellians.[17]

So much for the belief that a person can't tell a bold-faced lie and still look you straight in the eye. Some people can't. Some can. But when you meet those who can, beware! There's no telling what else they might be capable of doing to get what they want.

A person traveling from one part of the United States to another will notice dialectical differences in the English language. Standards of eye behavior also differ in persons raised in different parts of the country. A woman from Georgia, for example, told a writer, who was assigned to a seat beside her on a flight to New York, that she disliked that city because of the indifference people there displayed toward one another. "Moreover," she said, "I don't especially enjoy not being looked at and being made to feel that I don't exist. Why, in the South, we take time to look at people and, as you know, to smile at them."[18]

One need not travel even that far to note "dialect" differences in eye behavior. In cities with large minority populations, differences have been found between one ethnic community and another within a few blocks of one another.

Studies set out to test the hypothesis that in conversational settings people gaze more as they are listening than they do while they are speaking. Researchers discovered that the hypothesis was indeed true among white American adults, but the reverse was true among blacks. While they are speaking, black adults look at their conversation partners more than while listening.[19]

When white American teenagers see behavior they consider weird, they frequently roll their eyeballs upward as if to say "Oh, no!" But when blacks talk about "rolling the eyes" they often have an altogether different behavior and message in mind. This display might also be a reaction to the unacceptable behavior of another person, but this time the message is not disbelief but hostility. This kind of rolling the eyes begins by staring at the offender without locking eyes. Then the eyes are moved in a low arc from one side to the other away from the offender. The lids are slightly lowered, and the entire display may occur so quickly as to be unnoticed, especially by whites.[20]

Still another factor affecting eye behavior is the topic of discussion in a conversation. If the subject matter is impersonal and easily discussed, eye gaze is increased. On the other hand, if the topic is intimate or difficult, thereby causing the interactants some embarrassment, shame, sorrow, or difficulty of expression, eye contact will be minimized.[21]

The final affecting factor is the setting of the conversation. As the distance between the communicating pairs increases, their eye gaze will also increase. It seems as though we attempt to offset large physical distances by psychologically closing the gap through mutual gaze.

Another way in which conversational setting might affect gaze is through its visual stimulation or lack thereof. If there are no attractive objects, people, or backgrounds to look at, gaze and mutual gaze will be increased. A visually stimulating environment, however, will decrease gaze behavior between the interactants.

Partner Reaction to Increased Gaze

A person's gaze and mutual gaze behavior in normal two-person conversation has been found to range from 10 to 80 percent of the total interaction time.[22] That range is wide, but as we have seen, a great number of factors affect human gaze patterns.

Judges reacting to extremes of normal gaze, however, see the differences as reflecting a sender's mood, intent, or disposition. Using film clips, investigators asked persons to evaluate speakers who looked at them either 15 or 80 percent of the time. The evaluators labeled 15 percent lookers as cold, pessimistic, cautious, defensive, immature, evasive, submissive, indifferent, and insensitive. The 80 percent lookers were judged to be friendly, self-confident, natural, mature, and sincere.[23]

Findings such as these underscore the extreme importance of establishing good eye contact during job interviews. Prospective employers usually take time to interview only those candidates whose applications show acceptable basic qualifications. In other words, when the interviews begin, all candidates have pretty much the same chance for employment. The great moment comes. You are called for an interview. It's too late to change your basic appearance, and all serious job-seekers will try to appear clean and appropriately dressed. To boost your advantage remember the labels applied to the 15 and 80 percent lookers in the study just cited. Then look carefully at that personnel official or prospective employer. Try for frequent mutual gaze. No one would suggest a stare-down contest, but you'll know when enough is enough. Glance away from his or her face for a few seconds but come right back. What have you got to lose?

Eye Behavior with Large Groups

"To begin our oral presentations today," I said, as my eyes swept the twenty-two bodies trying to make themselves invisible, "let's hear from...Carol."

"I knew it. I knew you'd call on me," Carol moaned. "I'm ready, but I knew when I walked in that I'd be first."

How did she know I'd select her to open an hour of student reports? To begin with, she came into the room after the other students had entered and taken their seats. She wasn't late, but the room was quiet. I was at the front, behind the podium, putting the date on the attendance slip. She took her seat quietly, looked at the clock, pushed her extra books under her desk, and opened her notebook in front of her. Then it happened—she looked up and our eyes locked for a fraction of a second. From that point on her fate was sealed!

Teachers' lesson plans may include possible questions, but never specify who will be called on to answer. To make that decision, we rely on immediate situation appraisal. Nonverbal cues tell us when a student is interested or daydreaming, thinking or bored, understanding or puzzled, knows what's what or doesn't have the slightest idea. Reading this feedback is essential to teaching success.

Over the years, thousands of high school students and university student teachers have stood before my classes. The poor ones saw all eyes looking at them and felt threatened. So they kept their eyes on their notes, looking up only to glance at the door, stare blankly out the window, or check the clock. Every time they looked up, dozens of students' eyes followed their gaze to the door, out the window, and at the clock. The message was lost somewhere in between.

Good, large-group communicators sweep the audience with their eyes, slowly and at regular intervals. They watch for faces that provide feedback, and from time to time pause for mutual gaze with individuals in the audience. Class comprehension and interest always improve under these conditions.

In a formal investigation, researchers manipulated the amount of speaker gaze during an informative seven-minute speech. Increased gaze caused the audience to judge the speaker more skilled, informed, experienced, honest, friendly, and kind.[24]

Another study compared speakers' eye gaze to audience ratings for sincerity. "Sincere" speakers looked at the audience 63.4 percent of the time, "insincere" speakers only 20.8 percent.[25]

Cultural Variation in Laws of Eye Behavior

The unwritten rules for eye behavior described in this chapter so far have referred to the English-speaking people of the United States. Even within these boundaries, we've noted, "dialectical differences" occur.

Outside of this country, especially among cultures whose ancestors did not strongly influence the American heritage, rules for gaze and mutual gaze are quite different. The Tuareg of North Africa, for example, seem to stare at each other almost relentlessly while conversing. Gaze dominates their other nonverbal languages, perhaps because they cover their entire bodies with clothes and veils—with the exception of their eyes. Arabs look either directly at the eyes or deeply into the eyes of their conversation partners.

The Spanish-speaking people of Mexico seem to be a humble people, for they lower their eyes more frequently than do other North Americans. The people who speak Spanish in South America, however, appear proud by comparison and look one another directly in the eye as they speak. Swedes look at their conversation partners less often than do the English (and most Americans) but for longer periods of time.

In the United States, if a woman looks at a man too long, she indicates by that behavior that he may speak to her. In Latin American countries, that same look from a woman would probably be a direct invitation to physical contact.

The "rules" governing the duration and frequency of gaze in some cultures are not as different as are those regarding at whom one may or may not look.

Anthropologists report that Luo men from Kenya may speak to, but must not look at, their mothers-in-law. In another part of Africa, an American teacher serving with the Peace Corps reportedly upset the tribal elders by insisting that her students look at her while in class. In that culture, children were not permitted to look adults in the eye. With no intention to offend, she had been promoting behavior that violated social custom.[26] The Mende of Sierra Leone make it a point to always look their conversation partner in the eye and are suspicious of anyone who averts his eyes. They believe that the dead reappear in human form but can be recognized because they cannot look a living person in the face.

When American women visit Italy or France, they are sometimes upset by the way men look at them. Instead of taking them in with a glance the way American men do, Italians and Frenchmen look for embarrassingly long periods of time, examining their body inch by inch. French and Italian girls, accustomed to such looks, must think American men are extremely cold.

Investigating the Case of the Dilating Pupils

The last, and perhaps least believable, phenomenon concerning eye behavior is strictly reflexive and occurs the world over. The pupils of our eyes, we all know, change in size. In dim light they dilate to allow more available light to enter the eye. In bright sunlight they contract to the size of pinheads. Under constant lighting conditions there is nothing we can do to change the size of our pupils, short of putting drops of belladonna or other chemicals in our eyes. Right?

Wrong. Since the early 1960s E. H. Hess has been studying changes in pupil size resulting from the visual stimuli being viewed. In one of his early experiments he showed five pictures to male and female subjects and noted their pupil size as they looked at them. The pupils of the males dilated more when shown pictures of female nudes. Females' pupils dilated more in response to pictures of a partially clothed muscle man, a baby, and a woman with a baby. It seemed as if the stimulus value of the picture determined the pupil reflex.[27]

Hess theorized that pupils enlarge when a person has positive feelings toward something and contract when there are negative feelings. Advertising firms in marketing research thought they'd found a gold mine. Wouldn't it be great to know the marketability of a package or product before investing in production? Further experimentation mushroomed. Homosexual males were shown pictures of males and females. Other subjects were asked to react to photos of political candidates, food, detergent packages, snakes, concentration camp victims, and dead soldiers. The results were not always clear or conclusive. In fact, some researchers discovered they were getting dilation from negative stimuli![28]

There seems to be no doubt but that pupil dilation is associated with emotional arousal, attentiveness, and interest, but it does not seem to be a valid indicator of attitude orientation (like vs. dislike).

So ad men have lost interest, but professional poker players still watch the pupils of the guys across the table, and it is reported that math teachers become suspicious of students with dilated pupils behind propped-up copies of *Basic Algebra*.

Activities

1. Collect advertising photos in which the models are looking directly at the camera, thereby meeting the eyes of the reader. What is the effect of this mutual gaze when the model and the reader are the same sex? Is the effect any different when the model and the reader are of different sexes? Why do advertisers use this technique?

2. Try breaking the unwritten rules of elevator behavior. When you enter, do not turn around immediately. Meet the eyes of first one person, then another, and another. How do they react? How do you feel?

3. Can you cause motorists to make jackrabbit starts by staring at them while they wait at a red light? Try it.

4. Stand beside a public telephone or drinking fountain but do not talk to or specifically look at those who approach. Does your presence seem to make any difference? Now change your behavior and stare directly at the faces of those who come toward you. Note their reactions and compare them to the people who approached under nonstare conditions.

5. Talk to a group of little children while standing over them. Then crouch down so that you are addressing them at their own eye level. Note any differences in their reaction to you.

6. Wear mirrored sunglasses as you move about a shopping center. How do you feel as you watch others? When you are talking to salespeople? How do others react to you? What do you think they're thinking about you? Do their age and sex make any difference? Does it matter if people are alone or with others?

7. Try to conduct a conversation without any visual feedback. Place four chairs close together, each facing a different direction. Now, with three classmates occupy these chairs and conduct a discussion without ever looking at one another. Discuss and report your reactions.

8. Try Helen Gurley Brown's formula for flirting. What happens?

9. Conduct a planned interview asking increasingly more personal (and possibly embarrassing) questions. Note the interviewees' eye behavior and kinesic reactions.

10. Play a round or two of Killer. Prepare a slip of paper for each class member. Label one *killer*; leave the rest blank. Let each student draw one of the slips. The person drawing the killer designation must eliminate others from the game by surreptitiously winking at them. The aim is to "kill" as many people as possible without being caught. When a "living" person catches the killer in the act, the game is over. However, if a self-appointed detective is wrong, he or she too is out of the game. Warning: This game requires a lot of mutual gaze.

11. Try a duplication of the Hess test. Show test subjects two copies of the same portrait, one with constricted pupils, one retouched to simulate dilated pupils. Ask which one they like best. Why? Be prepared for strange answers.

12. Collect quotations from famous writers regarding the power of the eyes. For example: "The eyes of men converse as much as their tongues." —Ralph Waldo Emerson. "He speaketh not; and yet there lies a conversation in his eyes." —Henry Wadsworth Longfellow.

Notes

1. Eckhard H. Hess, "The Role of Pupil Size in Communication," *Scientific American,* November 1975, pp. 110–12, 116–9.
2. Sandor S. Feldman, *Mannerisms of Speech and Gestures in Everyday Life* (New York: International University Press, 1969), p. 233.
3. Erving Goffman, *Behavior in Public Places,* pt. 3 (New York: Free Press of Glencoe, 1963), pp. 83–148; Edward T. Hall and Mildred Reed Hall, "The Sounds of Silence," in *Language: Introductory Readings,* ed. Virginia P. Clark, Paul A. Eschholz, and Alfred F. Rosa (New York: St. Martin's, 1972), pp. 459–70.
4. Hall and Hall, "Sounds of Silence," p. 462.
5. Ibid., p. 465.
6. Goffman, *Behavior in Public Places,* p. 84.
7. John Gibson, "Eye Contact: Do You Know Its Real Power?" *Family Weekly,* 16 November 1975, p. 22.
8. Phoebe C. Ellsworth, J. Merrill Carlsmith, and Alexander Henson, "The Stare as a Stimulus to Flight in Human Subjects: A Series of Field Experiments," *Journal of Personality and Social Psychology* 21(1972): pp. 302–11.
9. Mark L. Knapp, *Essentials of Nonverbal Communication* (New York: Holt, Rinehart and Winston, 1980), pp. 185–91.
10. Ibid., p. 186.
11. G. Hearn, "Leadership and Spatial Factor in Small Groups," *Journal of Abnormal and Social Psychology* 54(1975): pp. 269–72.
12. Knapp, *Nonverbal Communication,* pp. 188–90.
13. Helen Gurley Brown, *Sex and the Single Girl* (New York: Bernard Geis, 1962), pp. 74–75.
14. Ralph V. Exline, "Exploration in the Process of Person Perception: Visual Interaction in Relation to Competition, Sex and the Need for Affiliation," *Journal of Personality* 31(1963): pp. 1–20.
15. N. Mobbs, "Eye Contact in Relation to Social Introversion/Extroversion," *British Journal of Social and Clinical Psychology* 7(1968): pp. 305–6.
16. Knapp, *Nonverbal Communication,* pp. 191–93.
17. Ralph V. Exline, J. Thibaut, C. B. Hickey, and P. Gumpert, "Visual Interaction in Relation to Machiavellianism and an Unethical Act," in *Studies in Machiavellianism,* ed. R. Christie and F. L. Geis (New York: Academic, 1970), pp. 53–75.
18. Gerard I. Nierenberg and Henry H. Calero, *How to Read a Person Like a Book* (New York: Simon and Schuster, 1970), p. 140.
19. Knapp, *Nonverbal Communication,* pp. 184–200.
20. Kenneth R. Johnson, "Black Kinesics—Some Nonverbal Communication Patterns in the Black Culture," in *With Words Unspoken,* ed. Lawrence P. Rosen-

feld and Jean Civikly (New York: Holt, Rinehart and Winston, 1976), pp. 232–34.

21. Knapp, *Nonverbal Communication,* p. 199.

22. G. Nielsen, cited in Knapp, *Nonverbal Communication,* p. 184.

23. R. E. Klick and W. Nuessel, "Congruence Between the Indicative and Communicative Functions of Eye Contact in Interpersonal Relations," *British Journal of Social and Clinical Psychology* 7(1968): pp. 241–46.

24. S. A. Beebe, "Eye Contact: A Nonverbal Determinant of Speaker Credibility," *Speech Teacher* 23(1974): pp. 21–25.

25. J. Wills, "An Empirical Study of the Behavioral Characteristics of Sincere and Insincere Speakers" (Ph.D. diss., Univ. of Southern California, Los Angeles, 1961).

26. Judee K. Burgoon and Thomas Saine, *The Unspoken Dialogue: An Introduction to Nonverbal Communication* (Boston: Houghton Mifflin Co., 1978), p. 123.

27. Eckhard Hess and J. M. Polt, "Pupil Size as Related to Interest Value of Visual Stimuli," *Science* 132(1960): pp. 349–50.

28. Knapp, *Nonverbal Communication,* pp. 195–96.

5

Paralanguage

A MAN STANDS inside of a closed glass phone booth. You cannot hear a word he says, but you see his postures, gestures, and facial expressions. You *see* his *kinesics.*

Now imagine that you are on the other end of his telephone line. You cannot see any nonverbal communication, but you can hear more than his words. You can *hear* his *paralanguage.*

Paralanguage, sometimes called *vocalics,* includes all stimuli produced by the human voice (with the exception of the words themselves) that can be heard by another human. This includes widely divergent cues ranging from forceful articulation, screaming, and deep resonance to whining, monotones, and vocalized pauses.

For years, actors, comedians, and public speakers have realized the value of employing a carefully selected variety of vocal tones and pacing to effect the desired response in their listeners. But only recently have psychologists added this dimension to their analytical studies of human communication.

Multitudinous Vocalics Available to Speakers

One of the earliest systematic classifications of vocalic cues was developed in 1958 by George Trager. Learning the specifics of Trager's classification is neither necessary nor particularly useful for the layman. You and I can recognize the voices of relatives, close friends, and well-known television and film stars without being able to pinpoint the qualities that those voices display. On the other hand, an overview of Trager's components will

67

aid in understanding the wide range of vocalics possible and considered for analysis by scientists.

Trager's first primary category is called *voice qualities.* Under this heading, he includes such factors as pitch range, vocal lip control, articulation control, rhythm control, resonance, and tempo.

The second primary category, *vocalizations,* has three subdivisions. The first, *vocal characteristics,* includes such things as laughing, crying, giggling, snickering, whimpering, sobbing, yelling, whispering, mumbling, moaning, groaning, whining, and other ways in which a speaking voice can be characterized. The second subdivision is *vocal qualifiers*—the acoustic characteristics of intensity (overloud to oversoft), pitch height (overhigh to overlow), and extent (drawling to clipping one's words). Trager's final division is *vocal segregates,* which are sounds that speech teachers often call vocalized pauses ("um," "uh," snorts, clicks, and sniffs) and silent pauses.[1]

As any young lover can tell you, paralanguage can overrule the significance of any string of words. One's vocalics can make a simple declarative statement like "I love you" mean everything or nothing. The pitch, intensity, stress, tempo, and volume all play their part in the communication. What is said isn't half as important as how it is said.

In another situation, a person's paralanguage might clearly convey annoyance and a negative attitude toward the listener. Again the vocal cues play a dominant role in communication. They are the message, regardless of what is said.

There is no danger of interpreting paralanguage out of context, for paralanguage cannot occur without the context of speech.

Each spoken language has its own associated set of vocal qualities, inflections, rate, and rhythm patterns. Thus, contrary to popular opinion, it is impossible to judge the attitude and emotions expressed by a speaker of an unknown language simply by noting his vocalics.

Travelers have often noted volume variations between native speakers of different languages. Speakers of the midwestern or general United States dialect of English are particularly sensitive to this phenomenon since people of many cultures and dialects speak louder than they do. In the Mediterranean countries, speech is often at decibel levels that seem aggressive, offensive, and obnoxious to American ears. Loudness in the Arab world conveys a message of strength and sincerity. The Saudi Arabian shows humility and respect to a superior by lowering his natural volume.

Recently my aunt and uncle from Germany came to visit my mother, who owns a large dog that has been trained to respond to oral commands. In deference to her guests, who spoke no English, Mother spoke only German except, of course, when talking to the dog, a well-behaved indoor pet. On occasion, my mother had to leave for several hours, and my aunt and uncle were left alone with the dog. It may have been a German shepherd, but never before had it been addressed entirely in German. My uncle didn't have much success in communicating with the animal; but my aunt, being an alert observer of behavior, imitated my mother's intonation, stress, pitch, and volume patterns as she talked to the dog. They didn't always fit her German phrasings and sometimes would have sounded comical to a native German speaker, but the dog responded perfectly.

Albert Mehrabian, an American who has devoted much of his career to research in nonverbal communication, has written that only 7 percent of one's perceived attitude is verbally conveyed. The 93 percent nonverbally transmitted consists of 38 percent paralanguage and 55 percent facial cues.[2]

No two voices are identical although some are very similar. Our voices are the products of both heredity (our physical makeup) and our immediate cultural environment. As a result, our voices tend to sound more like other voices in the same community than like those miles away and more like voices within our immediate families than like those unrelated to us. Spectograms, machine-recorded voiceprints, have become very valuable in police detective work. But they are not as individualized as are fingerprints. In part, this is because a person almost never says the same thing twice in the very same way. A voiceprint made one day will not exactly duplicate the same person's voiceprint recorded another day, even though the words spoken are the same. Two different voices, then, might appear to be very similar. We've all known families wherein all brothers or sisters sound identical on the phone.

Researchers investigating paralanguage have focused on three types of information listeners frequently infer from vocalic cues: (1) an impression of the speaker's physical qualities, (2) an impression of the sender's dominant personality or character traits, and (3) an impression of the speaker's emotional state.

Paralanguage Communicates Physical Features

From the time we are born, we hear people talk. Just as we learn vocabulary and the rules of grammatical construction from hearing hundreds of examples, we formulate ideas regarding which voices belong to whom. Little boys have high-pitched voices, we generalize, but big men have deep, resonant voices. Sexy girls have breathy voices. Discontent women have shrill, strident voices. One by one the stereotypes grow — some accurate, some not.

Generally speaking, our judgment regarding an unseen speaker's sex is fairly accurate. Research has shown that we base our judgments on average pitch level, inflectional patterns, voice quality, resonance, and tonal complexity.[3]

Test subjects were also quite accurate in judging a speaker's age category, especially when the categories were quite broad such as 10–20, 20–30, 40–50, and 60–70 years old.[4] As people age, their vocal rate and flexibility change, and their pitch level drops. However, in elderly men the pitch level may rise again slightly.

. Height and weight judgments are possible only in broad ranges. Endomorphic and ectomorphic extremes appear to offer the best chance for accurate judgment. Whatever vocal stereotypes we've formulated for very thin and very obese people seem to be more dependable than those developed for muscular or in between types.[5]

When American speakers use standard English, few listeners, either black or white, are able to identify their race based on vocalics alone. However, if black speakers use black dialect, their race can be identified with regularity.[6]

In order to conduct experiments such as these to determine if, in fact, paralanguage alone is affecting a listener's evaluation of the speaker, three techniques are frequently used. The first, and simplest, is to have a variety of speakers deliver the same monologue. The second asks the speakers to recite the alphabet or say numbers so as to make the verbal message meaningless. Obviously, this will not affect some vocalic dimensions, but others, such as variation in pitch and rhythm, may be lost unless the speakers make a concerted effort to communicate attitude and emotion. A final method uses electronic methodology to filter out verbal content. The higher frequencies of speech, upon which word recognition depends, are eliminated mechanically by a low-pass filter. This electronic filtering technique admittedly may eliminate some vocalic cues as well.

Paralanguage Suggests Character Traits

Further experimentation has been conducted to see if, in fact, dominant personality and character traits can be identified by paralanguage alone. The most reliable judgments have been achieved in rating speakers as enthusiastic/apathetic, energetic/lazy, and good-looking/ugly, according to one study. Far less reliable were the ratings of introvert/extrovert, honest/dishonest, law-abiding/criminal, and healthy/sickly.[7]

The vocal patterns of one's first spoken language become so much a part of the way a person communicates that unless he or she learns a second (or third) language before the teen years, the new language most likely will be forever spoken with what is commonly called a foreign accent. Listeners who are unfamiliar with the first language of a speaker may be unable to identify which language patterns are affecting that speaker's use of English. A foreign accent of any kind, however, affects a listener's judgment of a speaker. In test situations, the voices of native speakers were judged more dynamic, more aesthetically pleasing, and more reflective of high sociointellectual status than those with foreign accents (in this case, Chicanos and Europeans speaking English).[8]

Regional dialects within the United States do not seem to lower a listener's value judgments of a speaker as much as do foreign accents. However, speakers with heavy New York accents were judged more dynamic but less sociable than those with a southern drawl. And those with midwestern dialects were labeled more competent and credible than persons with southern or New England dialects.[9] The perceived dialects clearly reinforced existing regional stereotypes.

Accuracy in judgment of speakers' occupations varies from study to study, with trained speakers, such as preachers and actors, most often accurately identified.[10] Listeners have proven to be surprisingly accurate, however, in their ability to judge a speaker's social class or status from vocal cues alone. Speakers have been rated upper, middle, or lower class and as having high school or college educations after sometimes incredibly short (10–15 second) speaking times. Even when speakers tried to put on airs, their true status was identified better than 60 percent of the time when compared to independent measures of status for those speakers.[11] Human beings clearly pick up identifiable vocal cues from their dominant environment.

Another factor that can be communicated by paralanguage is the speaker's attitude toward the subject or person being addressed. Friendliness, hostility, superiority, submissiveness, sincerity, and power have all been identified as communicated far oftener than can be attributed to chance.[12]

In all research related to the perception of personality traits inferred from paralanguage, the stereotypes in the minds of the listeners were considered dominant factors in determining their judgments. In almost every study, the listeners agreed with one another's conclusions more consistently than their conclusions agreed with the subjects' true personalities as defined by other tests.[13]

Paralanguage Helps to Judge Emotion

Clearly kinesics provides strong cues regarding a speaker's emotional state; but when we cannot see a person, we often can tell whether he's joyful or unhappy, angry or anxious by more than the words he speaks. Volume, pitch, rate, and vocal characteristics frequently convey emotion. However, it has been discovered that humans vary greatly in their ability to encode and decode emotion via vocalic cues.

At Columbia University in New York City, Joel and Lois Jean Davitz assembled eight American native speakers of English to serve as subjects and thirty judges to evaluate their vocal presentations. Each subject was asked to repeat the alphabet ten times, each time expressing a different emotion. To help the subjects create the desired emotional states, ten cards describing emotionally laden situational contexts were given them, one before each sample was recorded.

An analysis of the judges' identifications clearly supported the thesis that feelings can be communicated reliably by content-free speech. However, the speakers varied from 23 percent to 54 percent accuracy in their ability to communicate the desired emotion. (Ten percent accuracy would have been attributable to pure chance.)

The emotions communicated and their percentage of accurate identification were as follows: anger, 65 percent; nervousness, 54 percent; sadness, 49 percent; happiness, 43 percent; sympathy, 38 percent; satisfaction, 31 percent; love, 25 percent; fear, 25 percent; jealousy, 25 percent; and pride, 21 percent. Again, chance expectancy would be 10 percent accuracy. Commonly confused were the emotions of fear and nervousness, fear and sadness, love and sadness, love and sympathy, and pride and satisfaction.

The judges, too, varied in their ability to correctly identify the emotions that had been encoded. The most accurate judge was correct 49 percent of the time; the least accurate, only 2 percent.[14]

In real life, fortunately, judgments do not have to be made on paralanguage alone. The verbal component provides a context that makes precise distinctions much easier. And if we can also see the speakers to observe their other nonverbal behavior, the totality of their encoded messages is readily available.

Vocalic Cues Effect Attitude Changes

In addition to helping us judge the character traits, attitudes, and feelings of those who speak to us, paralanguage may change the way we respond to what they tell us. Two studies have proven this to be a fact worth consideration.

The first study involved alcoholic patients and their doctors. Recordings were made of nine Massachusetts doctors' voices as they discussed their experiences in dealing with newly arrived alcoholic patients. Thirty student judges from Harvard-Radcliffe and MIT then rated the doctors' voices on four scales: anger/irritation, sympathy/kindness, anxiety/nervousness, and matter-of-factness/professionalism.

An overview of the results of the study shows that the doctors' speech and tone of voice affected their success in referring alcoholic patients for additional treatment. In other words, what a doctor said to his patients perhaps wasn't as important as the way he said it. A dominance of anger and irritation in a doctor's voice seemed to have a negative effect. There was a significant negative correlation between voices judged to be particularly angry and their success in encouraging alcoholics to seek further aid. On the other hand, the more anxious a doctor's voice was rated to be, the more successful were his referrals.

The designers of the study discovered that the relationship between an angry tone of voice and a doctor's lack of effectiveness with alcoholics, "who may be especially sensitized to rejection," concurs with clinical and anecdotal patient reports. They speculate that patients interpret nervousness and anxiety in a doctor's voice as a sign of greater concern.[15]

A study following a somewhat similar design recorded the voices of eighteen mothers whose children had taken part in a twenty-seven–month infant study at Harvard University. This time the tapes were rated on five dimensions: anger/irritation, anxiety/nervousness, warmth, pleasantness, and emotional involvement (of the mother in what was being said).

The most significant results were the high correlations discovered between mothers' voices that were rated high in anxiety and anger and observed signs of irritability and insecurity in their children. There are, naturally, several possible explanations. The high correlations may be caused by external conditions affecting both the mothers and their children. The children's prior and continued display of such character traits, for whatever reasons, may have generated feelings of inadequacy and anxiety in their mothers, which were then reflected in their voices. Or, both the ratings and the children's behavior may be directly influenced by the mother's personality. An anxious mother may continually convey her anxiety and fearfulness to her children, who in turn become anxious, insecure, and fretful.[16]

In any case, it is clear that our reactions to paralanguage can begin very early in life and have significant effects on our lives.

Does Status Affect Skill in Paralanguage?

Before leaving this examination of paralanguage, let us consider one more conclusion, drawn by a university professor and research scientist specializing in nonverbal communication. Shirley Weitz, who is also the editor of a book of readings and research reports on the subject, introduces the section on paralanguage with this observation regarding human interaction between any two persons: In any communication setting "the more dependent member [of the pair] has the most to gain by being attuned to the other's emotional state and to the affective tone of the interaction. Thus," Weitz concludes, "women seem to be more sensitive to such cues than men, and blacks more so than whites."[17]

That women and blacks are more sensitive senders and receivers of paralanguage has been supported repeatedly by research that analyzes the results by sex and race.[18] Furthermore, in every culture where such findings have been noted, women and blacks have been raised in positions of secondary power. Has this dependent status caused them to be better users and interpreters of paralanguage? What do you think?

Activities

1. In novels and short stories with dialogue, paralanguage is often specified through verbs or modifying adverbs. How many different paralanguage-suggesting verbs can you think of to replace *said* in the following sentence? "You're impossible!" she (said).
How many adverbs can you add to this sentence to describe possible paralanguage variations? "It's time to go," he said _____ (-ly).

2. Tape record the voices of a variety of speakers. Let your collection represent all ages, both sexes, and all available ethnic groups. Edit them carefully and play them for your classmates. How many physical features can they identify accurately from voices alone?

3. Tape record your own voice speaking in a variety of ways (e.g., as if you were a child; an old man or woman; or someone frightened, nervous, excited, disappointed, etc.). Let your classmates listen to the results and for each variation complete the following sentence. The speaker sounds as if _____.
Discuss their conclusions. Did your voice communicate what you had hoped it would?

4. Try a number of paralanguage variations on your dog. For example, let your kinesics and paralanguage pet him while your words tell him what a miserable cur he is. Note his response.
Try giving your dog orders in a different tone of voice. If you usually demand, try begging and pleading. See how the animal responds.

5. Practice delivering the following sentence until you can convey at least ten different variations of meaning, both declarative and interrogative: "Tom loaned that bike to Jeff."

6. Pick a partner and try having a two-minute conversation using the words: "Ketchup tastes great on fresh cantaloupe." You may not add any other words. What messages did each of you communicate? Try to identify the specific changes in paralanguage that caused different messages.

7. With a partner or two develop a skit dramatizing a confrontation between two or

more characters. For example, imagine a school principal reprimanding an unruly freshman sent to the office. Portray a high-pressure salesperson trying to gain entrance to a home in order to show his or her wares or an unrelenting motorist trying to talk a police officer out of a traffic citation. Impersonate two shoppers both wanting to buy the same item from a sale table or a parent taking a child into a clinic for a shot that the youngster is determined not to have.

As an extra challenge, use content-free speech. Whenever you talk, use numbers or letters of the alphabet instead of words. Rely on paralanguage and kinesics to convey your message. Present your rehearsed skit before the other members of your class to see if they can identify the characters and the conflict.

8. Conduct a study of the communication of emotion by content-free speech in your class. Use the Davitz and Davitz methodology and compare your findings to theirs.

Notes

1. George L. Trager, "Paralanguage: A First Approximation," *Studies in Linguistics* 13(1958): pp. 1–12.
2. Albert Mehrabian and Susan L. Ferris, "Inference of Attitudes from Nonverbal Communication in Two Channels" in *Nonverbal Communication,* ed. Shirley Weitz (New York: Oxford Univ. Press, 1974), pp. 291–97.
3. Judee K. Burgoon and Thomas Saine, *The Unspoken Dialogue: An Introduction to Nonverbal Communicaton* (Boston: Houghton Mifflin Co., 1978), p. 151; Mark L. Knapp, *Essentials of Nonverbal Communication* (New York: Holt, Rinehart and Winston, 1980), p. 211.
4. Burgoon and Saine, *Unspoken Dialogue,* p. 149.
5. Knapp, *Nonverbal Communication,* pp. 211–12.
6. Ibid., p. 210.
7. Ibid., p. 207.
8. Burgoon and Saine, *Unspoken Dialogue,* pp. 182–83; Knapp, *Nonverbal Communication,* p. 209.
9. Burgoon and Saine, *Unspoken Dialogue,* pp. 182–83.
10. Ibid., pp. 155–56.
11. Knapp, *Nonverbal Communication,* p. 213; Burgoon and Saine, *Unspoken Dialogue,* p. 156.
12. Knapp, *Nonverbal Communication,* pp. 219–20.
13. Ibid., pp. 206–7; Burgoon and Saine, *Unspoken Dialogue,* pp. 164–67.
14. Joel R. Davitz and Lois Jean Davitz, "The Communication of Feeling by Content-Free Speech," in Weitz, *Nonverbal,* pp. 99–104.
15. Susan Milmoe, Robert Rosenthal, Howard T. Blane, Morris E. Chafetz, and Irving Wolf, "The Doctor's Voice: Postdictor of Successful Referral of Alcoholic Patients," in Weitz, *Nonverbal,* pp. 112–21.
16. Susan Milmoe, Michael S. Novey, Jerome Kagan, and Robert Rosenthal, "The Mother's Voice: Postdictor of Aspects of Her Baby's Behavior," in Weitz, *Nonverbal,* pp. 122–26.
17. Weitz, *Nonverbal,* p. 96.
18. Knapp, *Nonverbal Communication,* pp. 233–39.

6

Silence

Todd, a high school junior, is not into regular dating and has no interest in having a steady girl. But the prom is coming up and his friends have encouraged him to go. He decides to ask Michelle, whom he has taken out only once before, after a ball game with a group of friends. He finally telephones her and, after a couple of minutes of empty conversation, asks her to be his prom date. Michelle hesitates. The line is silent.

Poor Todd. Like a computer seeking an acceptable alternative, his brain ticks off the possibilities in lightning sequence: (1) She doesn't want to go with me to the prom or anywhere else and is deciding how to tell me so. (2) She was hoping someone else would ask her. She wants to say "no" but doesn't know if she should. (3) She already has a date for that night and is wondering what to do about it. (4) She wants to go but is too proud to admit that she can't afford a dress. (5) She doesn't like dancing. (6) Her folks frown on dancing. (7) Her folks have told her not to see me again. (8) She's been grounded and doesn't want to explain the details. (9) Her little sister is listening in on us. She's waiting for her to back off. (10) She thinks...

There's no question but that silence is a powerful communicator. Decoding its message, however, may be next to impossible unless the entire context is examined. The personalities and emotions of the people involved, their relationship to one another, the subject upon which their minds are focused, the place, the time, the culture, and the relationships between these factors and dozens of others—all affect meaning. This chapter will make no attempt to help you identify the meanings of the silences you may encounter but through examples will help you realize the wide range of possibilities.

76

Paralanguage Silences

Before going on, however, it is important to note that some silences accompany spoken communication while others are independent of verbal interaction. Whenever we speak, we include breaks between words, phrases, and sentences that last from milliseconds to minutes. Technically, these are extensions of paralanguage.

The shortest silence, called a *juncture,* is that speck of silence that lets us differentiate between "ice cream" and "I scream," between "at all" and "a tall," or between "night rate" and "nitrate." All languages have such small silences. In Spanish, it is juncture that keeps "Es un hombre" ("He's a man") from being "Es su nombre" ("It's his name").

Another paralanguage silence is a *pause.* We pause to punctuate or accent our words, to gain emphasis, or to give a message time to sink in. Comedians are masters in the use of the pause, spacing silence for maximum impact. Jack Benny once said that the biggest laugh he ever got was when he didn't say anything at all.

Many of our pauses are hardly noticeable when we converse face to face. This is because we fill the silence with facial expressions, gestures, eye movements, and other communicative nonverbal cues. On the telephone or a tape recording, they become more noticeable.

The last silences that accompany speech are called *hesitations.* Like pauses, they vary with human differences, the purpose of the verbalization, the degree of spontaneity, and the pressures of the social situation within which the communication takes place. When we hesitate, we are usually collecting our thoughts for the next phrase, decoding feedback, and reacting to emotion. We swallow, clear our throats, breathe deeply, and frequently emit vocalizations to help fill the space. The frequency, extent, and nature of hesitation silence is highly individualized.

When There's Nothing to Say

Interpersonal silences that are independent of verbal communication defy classification. One silence may occur because a person has no ideas to share at that moment. Another might happen because a speaker can't decide where or how to begin. One couple is so filled with love and contentment that they need not talk to share the feeling. Another refuses to speak out of hatred and intense negative feelings.

When we must face those whom we dislike and reject, most of us abide by the old adage,"If you can't say something nice, don't say anything at all." People also find themselves without words for someone who has deeply wronged them in the past. Innocent prisoners, who after a fair trial are judged guilty, may collapse into a silence of hopelessness. There are times that there is simply nothing to say.

Frequently misunderstood and misinterpreted are the silences of persons who tend to be shy and retiring. In a large group, Mary usually says nothing. She avoids meeting new people and seldom initiates conversation, even with old friends. She is strikingly beautiful and certainly not physically handicapped or mentally retarded, which in the eyes of some people might justify her reticence. I have heard acquaintances call her "stuck-up" and "snobbish." Those of us who know her better realize that her silence covers fear and anxiety and is her way of protecting herself against others. When she is forced to address a group, she is almost panic-stricken.

We have all turned silent at times when we have been in danger of saying something stupid or of making fools of ourselves by verbalizing our ignorance. In cases like these we hope that saying nothing will remove us from the attention of others and provide refuge.

The Negative Messages of Silence

At other times we have been so busy gawking that we have forgotten the norms of polite behavior. Unintentionally perhaps, we have looked too long at people we perceived as different in appearance, dress, or color of skin. Our gaze might have suggested an open channel of communication, but our subsequent silence was interpreted as rejection. Silence can very powerfully communicate prejudice.

Silence is often used as a weapon to hurt others. After Mark and Terri had an argument, Terri refused to speak to Mark or even accept his phone calls. She told her friends that she was punishing him for his behavior. Whether he felt punished or relieved, like Dagwood's boss, Mr. Dithers, when his wife Cora won't speak to him, only Mark can tell.

Members of minorities have also told of the humiliation and anger they have felt when prejudiced people refused to acknowledge their presence. Even when approached, some of these bigots would not speak and treated them like inanimate objects. Those who have not been recent victims of this weapon of silence may remember times when as children they were given the silent treatment by store clerks and other adults.

Perhaps the best example of silence as punishment has been reported as occurring from time to time at the U.S. Military Academy at West Point. In cases where a cadet has been exonerated for an honor code violation by the officers in charge but was still guilty in the eyes of the cadet corps, "The Silence" has been sentenced upon him by his classmates. "The Silence" as practiced at West Point was an extreme form of ostracism. A victim was forced to room by himself and eat alone at a table for ten. He was not permitted to take part in class activities and no other cadets would associate with him or even speak to him, except on official business.[1] Many cadets could not endure those conditions and dropped out of the academy.

In 1971 the corps sentenced a second year cadet to this ostracism. (His name is being withheld intentionally for the author feels he has suffered enough.) He was too proud, and at the same time humiliated, to tell the folks back home, even his parents. Instead he endured the silence for two more years, until he graduated in 1973. When his ordeal became public, West Point authorities, bombarded by criticism, officially abolished "The Silence." The victim, who continued to be ostracized by other academy graduates throughout his five-year mandatory tour of military duty, was unimpressed by the official abolishment. "You can't legislate social conduct," he told a news reporter. "You can't compel someone to associate with someone else. You can't tell someone to talk when they don't want to."[2]

Silence as Emotional Response

When we are very angry, silence plays several roles in our behavior. First, we may be simply too angry to talk. So much of our attention and emotion is focused on the situation that our minds cannot formulate sentences. Secondly, we may wisely choose to count to ten, to give ourselves a chance to cool down and think before we speak. Finally, we may decide to use silence as a defense against further attack or to punish the attacker. The feelings that frequently follow anger—resentment, disgust, defiance, and hate—use silence to build barriers that frequently last even longer.

Confronted by a big dog bounding up to check him out, three-year-old Robin breathed irregularly, opened his eyes wide, but was too frightened to utter a sound. Movies and television programs are also built around stories of persons so terrorized by thugs that they are afraid to notify the authorities or even tell friends who could help. In cases of extreme fear, silence is not uncommon.

The silence of defeat is well-known to athletes. The lack of locker room chatter and the quiet bus ride home after a disappointing loss occur worldwide. When the opponents' tactics have been unfair or the officiating bad, speech is not difficult. But when we've tried our best but been beaten in a fair contest, who wants to talk?

Silence is also the language of love. Even when sexual arousal is not the objective, lovers do not always need to speak to communicate. One couple, whom I watched during a transcontinental flight, traveled from Miami to Chicago without saying a word. They looked at one another frequently, smiled, and entwined their fingers, but conversation never occurred. They were obviously happy just enjoying the experience together. At times like these, we may remember past words and experiences, and we may fantasize or plan for future words and experiences, but current talk would break the spell.

Many humans are also quiet when they are sad. At times of mourning, people who are otherwise talkative frequently observe long periods of silence. The hurt, the memories, the bleak future are too personal, too intense to talk about. Combat soldiers and ex–prisoners of war seldom want to speak of their experiences upon return to civilian life. The pain of remembering clearly enough to tell others is just too great.

When we wish to show reverence or respect for others, silence is also the rule. At weddings and funerals and in churches, hospitals, libraries, and courtrooms, we are quiet unless asked to speak.

Silence in Which to Think

Sometimes we observe silence simply because we want to concentrate. If we desire to listen carefully to another person, if we expect to hear something significant, we will not talk and will barely move so as to improve our auditory capabilities. If we wish to evaluate what we've heard, if we want to decide upon an appropriate response, we may pause far beyond normal. If we want to create something original or work out a plan mentally, we may find progress difficult unless we and our surroundings are silent. For this kind of thought, we may screen out undesirable noise by playing music or turning on an air conditioner. Some people have even bought an audio device that produces *white noise,* a steady stream of sound without melody or rhythm. Its message is silence.

The periodic human need for solitude usually includes a search for silence. This is the silence we enjoy while watching a sunset, the stars, or the sea. We go to the woods for peace of mind and an opportunity to tune in to ourselves, to reflect, to think. For centuries monks and religious hermits have respected silence as a means to contemplation and meditation. Silence complements the privacy of our thoughts.

Variations on the Theme of Silence

Even silence is not used the same by all people the world over. The Gbeya people of the Central African Republic indulge in silence freely and frequently as part of normal interpersonal communication. There the people never speak while they eat, especially if guests are sharing their meal.

All conversation must wait until a time after dinner. Gbeyans will visit people who are sick but never say a word. Silence communicates their concern and friendship to those who are ill and doesn't encourage them to waste their strength speaking.[3]

A visitor to Scotland's Shetland Islands, where the pace of life is slower than in the rest of the United Kingdom, noted that these islanders tend to maintain long pauses between speakers in social groups. As the women knit together or a family sits around its kitchen fire watching the flames, one person will offer a comment. Several minutes might pass before a second person adds a thought. A third won't speak until several more minutes have passed. When men form the social group, they will pass the time smoking and tending to their pipes, spacing conversation in the same manner.[4]

When a new worker joins us on the job, we usually try to make him or her feel a part of the group. Strangers who join Apache work groups may not be spoken to for several days while their coworkers watch them work and check them out, so to speak. Only after this time has passed will they speak.[5]

During the early stages of courtship, Apache men and women speak very little. Only after several dates will they engage in a lengthy conversation. For the men this reticence is often attributed to self-consciousness. The women are explicitly taught not to talk too much. Silence in a woman is considered a sign of modesty and feminine virtue.[6]

In many world cultures throughout history, women have been expected to observe silence when their husbands die. In cultures as widely scattered as an African tribe in Kenya, the aboriginal Australians, and an Indian tribe in California, widows have observed silent mourning periods of up to two years.[7] In some cases whispering was permitted when speech was absolutely necessary. Other groups developed elaborate hand signing systems to substitute for words.

A final use of silence is employed in Arab nations. Because people in this culture live in such close proximity to one another and seldom use enclosed places for privacy, they achieve solitude by simply not speaking. No one is upset if another is quiet; no one wonders what's wrong. It is simply understood that at times a person needs to shut off the rest of the world and be alone.[8]

Activities

1. Can you remember a time when you were the victim of the silent treatment? In a two or three page paper, recreate the experience for your readers. Try to make them feel the way you did.

2. During several one-on-one conversations with friends, consciously avoid responding in any way to what they say. Do not smile, nod, or comment while the other is speaking. Note the verbal and nonverbal measures various people use to get you to react.

3. Read the poem "Silence" by Edgar Lee Masters (see Appendix). Note the various kinds of silence he has known.

　　Write an original first-person essay titled "I Have Known the Silence of _____." Explain the situation that gave rise to silence in your case.

　　Or, write a poem on an aspect of silence you have experienced.

4. Read and discuss Marianne Moore's poem "Silence" (see Appendix). Is there a contradiction between the message of the first quotation and that of the second? Explain. What does the inclusion of the closing line mean to you?

Notes

1. Eileen Keerdoja, "Silent Treatment," *Newsweek,* 8 August 1977, p. 11.
2. Associated Press news release, Fort Benning, Ga., October 1973.
3. William J. Samarin, "Language of Silence," *Practical Anthropology* 12(1965): pp. 115–19.
4. Erving Goffman, *Behavior in Public Places*, pt. 3 (New York: Free Press of Glencoe, 1963), p. 103.
5. K. H. Basso, " 'To Give Up on Words': Silence in Western Apache Culture," in *Language and Social Context,* ed. Pier Pavlo Giglioli (Baltimore: Penguin Books, 1972), pp. 71–73.
6. Ibid., pp. 73–74.
7. Sir James George Frazer, "The Silent Widow," vol. 3, chap. 17 of *Folk-Lore in the Old Testament: Studies in Comparative Religion, Legend and Law* (New York, 1927), pp. 71–81.
8. Edward T. Hall, *The Hidden Dimension* (Garden City, N.Y.: Doubleday and Co., 1966), p. 159.

7

Tacesics and Stroking

TO ALTOGETHER TOO MANY AMERICANS, interpersonal touch means one of three things — greeting, hostility, or sex.

This is truly unfortunate, as anyone will tell you after studying *tacesics,* touch in human communication.

The human sense of touch is one of the first senses to develop. Even within the womb, the unborn child feels the warmth, pressure, and rhythms of its mother's body. Its first sensations at birth are tactile ones, and jarring sensations they are — the cold air, the doctor's firm hands and metal forceps, the new textures and pressures that stimulate its skin surface.

For many years in American hospitals, the umbilical cord was cut and the infant immediately whisked away to be bathed, weighed, and measured. In many hospitals today, the newborn child will be placed on the mother's stomach where it may lie for a while but not long enough to cool down. There the mother may touch it for the first time, even before the umbilical cord is cut. After the mother is delivered of the afterbirth and made comfortable and the baby is clean and wrapped for warmth, it may be returned to her for early contact and bonding. Sometimes infants are even allowed to room in with their mothers rather than be kept in the sterile environment of the hospital nursery.

In the first hours together, communication between the mother and child is entirely tactile. The mother is not always overwhelmed with maternal love and may be almost afraid of such a tiny human, but she wants to examine her child, count its fingers and toes, and touch its body.

The baby's sucking movements begin minutes after birth, long before the mother's milk begins to flow. But the colostrum, which is available from the mother's breasts, is also a valuable substance for the infant. Nowadays some babies are put to their mother's breast immediately after birth, before being wrapped in blankets.

Touch Deprivation and Abnormal Development

Why all this recent emphasis on contact? And what is bonding all about? Doctors have learned that if an infant is to grow and develop normally, it is essential that it be given plenty of human contact.

Until about 1920 the death rate for well-fed infants under one year of age in warm, hygienic foundling institutions was almost 100 percent.[1] Medical science couldn't explain the cause of death and therefore called it *marasmus,* from the Greek word for "wasting away." Conditions did not begin to change until Dr. Fritz Talbot of Boston visited a children's clinic in Germany where he saw a fat old woman carrying a baby on her hip. When Talbot asked the clinic director who the woman was, Dr. Arthur Schlossmann told him, "That is Old Anna. When we have done everything medically we can for a baby, and it is still not doing well, we turn it over to Old Anna, and she is always successful."[2]

By the late 1920s several hospital pediatricians were beginning to provide mothering for their charges. Infants were brought to their mother's room for several hours a day whether or not the mother nursed them. Dr. J. Brenneman, who had previously served in an old-fashioned foundling home where the mortality rate was almost 100 percent, proclaimed that in his hospital every baby should be picked up, carried around, and mothered several times a day. In New York City's Bellevue Hospital the death rate for infants fell from 55 percent to under 10 percent after mothering practices were instituted in the pediatrics ward in the mid 1930s.[3] The cure for marasmus was TLC—tender, loving care.

A documentary film entitled *Second Chance* recounts the story of Susan, a twenty-two-month-old baby who was left in a large children's hospital by her parents.[4] Upon admission she weighed only fifteen pounds (the weight of an average five-month-old baby) and measured twenty-eight inches (the average height of a ten-month-old). She could not talk or even crawl. Whenever people approached her, she withdrew and cried. The doctors who examined Susan found no birth defect or physical causes for her severe physical and mental retardation.

Three weeks later a social worker contacted the parents, who had never come to see the child. Both parents were well educated, but neither really cared about children—or Susan. Susan didn't like to be held and preferred to be left alone, according to her mother, who admitted to not wanting to care for her anymore.

Susan's case was diagnosed as "maternal deprivation syndrome."

The hospital staff gave Susan as much attention as their schedules would allow. They held, fed, rocked, and played with her. A volunteer substitute mother was called in for six hours a day to provide continuity and a single person with whom Susan might develop a bond.

Two months later Susan's development was still far behind others of her age, but in that time she had grown two inches and gained six pounds. She was affectionate and no longer afraid of people. She had learned to crawl and walked while holding on to people and furniture. The loving touch and care of others had made the difference.

Interestingly enough, children who are not cuddled, caressed, hugged, and touched in a secure, loving way seem to bear the scars of this deprivation all their lives. A baby can sense if a mother's touch is nervous, angry, or insecure, and this too can affect normal development. In addition to walking and talking later than the norm, children who had had little physical contact during infancy more often displayed social maladjustment, speech difficulties, learning difficulties, allergies, and eczema. Many schizophrenic children were also found to have been deprived of handling as babies.[5]

As a result of his own studies and those of others, neuropsychologist James W. Prescott concluded that "deprivation of body touch and body movement which differ from the senses of sight, hearing, smell, and taste is the cause of a number of emotional disturbances which include depressive and autistic behaviors, hyperactivity, sexual aberration, drug abuse, violence, and aggression."[6]

Touch Needs and Training

The need for tender, loving care doesn't go away after infancy. Children show their desire to touch and be touched in hundreds of ways daily. Bedtime behavior is a perfect example. Little children know that if they delay getting undressed long enough, Mommy or Daddy will usually help them into their nightclothes. Then follows the "tuck-me-in," "listen-to-my-prayers," "I-need-a-drink," "tell-me-a-story" routine. Some children even have their parents trained to lie on the bed beside them until they fall asleep. And, of course, a bad dream or a clap of thunder will send them scurrying to crawl into bed with Mother and Dad.

Even school-age children need to be hugged, cuddled, and touched. Many bruises and scrapes that "need a Band-Aid," really need only the TLC that accompanies its application.

Yet as children grow, we Americans, little by little, convey the message that touching oneself and others is wrong or sinful. We must keep our bodies covered, never look, and not touch, for (as everyone knows) touching leads to sex. When one adult touches another, children see reactions of embarrassment, displeasure, and guilt, and they internalize these reactions. Even their mothers, who always touched them more than their fathers did, don't embrace or kiss them in public anymore.[7] And if they do, older children and adults tease or otherwise embarrass them.

Most other cultures are not as restrictive, ritualized, and punitive in their tacesic behavior as we are in the United States; and as a result of ethnic background variations, not all American families are the same, but elementary school children slowly get the same message.

Investigation shows that even in their own peer groups, touch decreases noticeably between grades one and six. The same pattern continues into junior high, where children were found to touch same-sex peers only half as much as they did in the primary grades. The only exception to this rule was among black children in all-black schools.[8]

Middle-school children are known for their roughhouse behavior. They push and shove, poke and punch, pull hair and wrestle, and generally act rowdy with one another. Could this be a way of acceptably getting and giving the physical touching they can't attain any other way?

A popular bumper sticker asks, "Have you hugged your kid today?" This seems to indicate that the benefits of physical touch are not unknown in America, and indeed, research tells us that we are touching each other more now than at any other time in our nation's history.

Emotionally disturbed children have been found to respond well to physical stroking and rhythmic slapping. Sidney Simon reports that children who receive enough nonsexual hugs and affection engage in less drinking of alcohol, less drug abuse, less sexual promiscuity, less thumb sucking followed by less cigarette smoking, and less compulsive eating of junk foods. They also tend to be more secure in their own decisions and less vulnerable to peer pressure.[9]

Touch Behavior among Adults

Because we know that people often become uptight, anxious, and uncomfortable when touched, we generally keep our hands to ourselves. Some teacher-education classes regularly tell prospective teachers not to touch their students either for punishment or encouragement. Not long ago in-service sessions in integrated schools warned teachers to avoid touching black students at all times.

As a result of our cultural training, males are more hesitant to touch males than females, and females are more hesitant to touch males than members of their own sex. Women touch and are touched more than men, probably as a result of the fact that little girl babies beyond the age of six months are allowed and encouraged to spend more time touching and staying near their parents than are boy babies. Between ages fourteen months and two years, girls also were found to receive many more physical signs of affection than boys.[10]

Sadly enough, some of the people who need affection the most are seldom touched by people who are not forced to do so. Able Americans were found to interact at greater distances with persons who have deformities, handicaps, and debilitating illnesses. We also tend to avoid touching members of races other than our own.[11]

American Touching Rituals

While the potent effects of the laying on of hands are acknowledged in the history of many religious groups, most of our nonsexual touching today is cold and highly ritualized. Ministers and priests touch a person's head in blessing or baptism. Athletes engage in physical contact as part of the sport and to encourage and congratulate one another. Couples touch while dancing.

Many of our touching rituals are associated with greeting or leave taking. The handshake is thought to be only about one hundred and fifty years old. It was preceded, however, by the hand clasp, which dates back to ancient Roman times. A study of persons in an American airport showed that 60 percent of them touched in greeting or saying goodbye. More frequent and longer physical contact was observed in people saying goodbye than in those greeting one another.[12]

But even our leave-taking embraces reflect our anxiety and fear of being misunderstood. Sidney Simon describes our greeting and goodbye hugs as "chest-to-chest-burp" hugs. We embrace chest to chest but then pat one another on the back like babies needing to be burped. Simon feels this reduction of the other person to infant status helps us neutralize the touching behavior.[13]

Americans, hungry for touch, turn to licensed touchers. Barbers and hairdressers, manicurists, masseurs and masseuses help us overcome the stress in our society by offering the physical contact we desire. The evening backrub given all hospital patients has long been recognized as therapeutic for more than bed sores, and the relief offered by chiropractors and chiropodists might not be as great if their treatments were administered by machine.

The Satisfaction and Messages of Touch

There is a satisfaction and comfort available through touch that can be acquired in no other way. Desmond Morris provides the following illustration. When we are anxious and fearful, we might prefer a hug or squeeze of the hand from a loved one, but in the absence of family and friends, we accept a don't-worry pat from our doctor or pastor. If the situation offers no human comforters, we might press a dog or cat to our cheek. Or, finding ourselves completely alone, we might feel more secure hugging the bedclothes around ourselves. In the absence of all security options, we still can hug, clasp, and embrace our own body in a variety of ways.[14]

The messages that can be conveyed to another person through tacesics are many. A sender's methods of touch may vary in pressure, duration, frequency, and location of contact as well as in the part of the body used to transmit the message. In a study of touching between adults, most recipients interpreted pats as expressing friendliness and playfulness, and strokes as showing sexual desire. All other squeezes, brushes, and such were ambiguous in their meaning.[15] Sadness, love, grief—all may use similar touch or caresses. Under conditions of extreme emotion and close interpersonal relationships, we usually employ touch as part of our communication with others.

We can touch to express desire for friendly relations, to show affection, empathy, or consolation. In fact, most of us find it hard to comfort persons overcome by sorrow, grief, or terror without touching them. Touching an arm or hand can express commitment, sincerity, or good will. Fortunately, it is not usually necessary for touch to communicate independent of other systems. An otherwise ambiguous physical contact can be clarified by words, a meaningful gaze, and appropriate facial expressions.

A hand on the shoulder or back might also be a sign of dominance, as it is when a police officer puts a hand on a suspect. However, that touch of superiority might also communicate a supportive concern between a teacher and student, doctor and patient, pastor and parishioner, or manager and worker.

There's no avoiding the fact that touch also conveys sexual desire. For adults, sexual intercourse is the ultimate of tactile experiences, and sexual arousal is elicited by touching behaviors. Yet it is obvious that not every man who might touch a woman or vice versa has sex in mind. It does appear, however, that some lonely and unhappy people seek sex as an attempt to make some sort of touching contact.

The final type of message conveyed by tacesics is hostility. Neuropsychologist James Prescott's study of four hundred primitive cultures led him to observe that cultures displaying a lot of physical affection and touch toward infants also have lower incidences of theft, murder, rape, and physical punishment. Those cultures that deprive infants of satisfying tactile interrelationships have high rates of adult violence.[16]

Prescott concluded further that cultures with low touch behavior for infants still may have low violence rates if premarital sex is tolerated. High correlations were found between the punishment of premarital sex offenders and practices of slavery, wife purchasing, fears of castration, theft, exhibitionist dancing, sexual mutilation, and killing of enemies.[17]

Naturally it's not completely accurate to consider one condition the cause of the other. High correlations may be the result of a common cause or may occur as a result of completely unrelated forces. In these cases, however, Prescott and other psychologists seem to feel the relationship is significant. People who have always felt unloved and unloveable may well be those who resort to violence. Perhaps they unconsciously want to retaliate against an uncaring world. Perhaps they have a twisted belief that any physical contact is better than none at all. Perhaps they simply have not internalized values of human worth. Psychologists may pursue the reasons.

Touching in Other Cultures

Examination of touching behavior in other cultures also gives us a better understanding of our own. Americans are generally a nontactile people; but the English, English Canadians, and Germans are reported to touch one another even less. In Japan, tacesic behavior is estimated to be only half that practiced in the United States.

This is not to say that Germans or even Japanese are cold and unloving to their children. Within the family and with close friends, hugging is common behavior at bedtime and before departures in Germany; and German men frequently nudge or pat one another in social interaction. Handshaking and other ritualistic touching is also widely practiced. In Japan, a great deal of body contact occurs between mothers and their children. An entire family may even bathe together until a child is about ten years old. Then there is a sudden break in tacesic behavior.

The French, French Canadians, Italians, southwest Asians, Russians, Spanish, and Latin Americans are, on the other hand, more tactile in their relationships than Americans. When greeting, Frenchmen kiss one another on the cheeks; in the Middle East men may kiss each other's beards. Most other tactile cultures also have greeting rituals more elaborate than a simple handshake.

Everybody loves a baby. Even American politicians will stop to kiss a rosy-cheeked cherub if it's not too tiny. In some cultures babies are carried on their mother's back or in a slinglike device over the shoulders. There the babies are in constant contact with their mother's body, feeling her warmth and rocking with the rhythms of her activities. Other cultures place infants in small cradles or strap them to a board, which is kept within sight of the mother but away from her body.

For years American infants were carried in their parents' arms, but today most babies are tied into plastic seats to be carried or set off to one side as the mother goes about her daily activities. Research may discover that the increased use of these infant seats will change the character of our children more than did the change from rigid time schedules to demand feeding practices.

In Spain and South America, female friends and relatives often walk down the street arm in arm, or with one woman holding the other's arm as if to guide her. Men will not commonly touch each other as they walk along, but in conversation one man may touch another on the arm to emphasize a point or put an arm around the shoulders of a friend.

The sight of two men hand in hand in the United States would elicit snickers and knowing glances among bystanders. In the Middle East this is a common sight among male friends who are decidedly not gay. Students from that culture studying in the United States and aware of the American interpretation of this practice told one investigator that they had been embarrassed on occasion by newly arrived friends from home who had insisted upon holding their hands.[18]

Americans may never accept behavior as foreign to them as men holding hands, but the popularity of sensitivity groups and personal growth seminars is increasing body awareness. One indication of the changing attitudes can be seen in thousands of churches across the country. One denomination after another has included in its service a sharing of God's peace, requesting congregation members to turn and shake hands with those all around them. Perhaps some day we can go so far as to touch others in a nonritualistic way without their wondering about our sexual interests.

Accepting Nontactile Strokes

One interesting extension of our touching behavior is the conditioned substitution called stroking.

Conditioned behavior means that one stimulus is associated with and ultimately substituted for another to elicit a given response. In the classic conditioning of Pavlov's dog, Dr. Ivan Pavlov regularly presented a dog with food, which caused the dog to salivate. Every time he presented the food, however, Dr. Pavlov also rang a bell. After repeated food-bell stimuli combinations, the bell was rung, but the food withheld. The dog was so conditioned to receiving food when he heard the bell that his salivary reflex was triggered by the bell alone.

Children are conditioned in much the same way. While mothers rock and caress their infants, they talk and sing to them. Little by little, the babies are conditioned to accept their mother's verbal comfort for her tactile embrace. "It's OK, dear. Mommy's here" is just as calming as her physical touch. Other stimuli are also substituted for tacesics. A favorite blanket or stuffed toy has reassured many a child. The rhythms of music are accepted replacements for the mother's rocking and cuddling.

By the time children are of school age, the conditioning is sufficient to allow them to accept nontactile strokes from others as well as their parents. A smile, a word, and a nod can be substituted for some of the physical strokes they received as babies. Before long, much of their hunger for tacesics is replaced by recognition hunger. This is not to say that the substitution is complete, but to a great extent other stimuli will satisfy.

Some people need more stroking than others. The girl who hangs all over her boyfriend clearly needs a lot of stroking to feel secure. The same is true of many entertainers.

Stroke Exchanging Rituals

Just as physical touching can transmit many messages, nontactile strokes also encode a variety of meanings. Sometimes the intent is simply to recognize the other person's existence. Many of our ritualized greetings do just that and little more. We really have no desire to know the state of others' health or their emotional outlook when we greet them with "How are you?" Both parties understand that it's just part of a stroke-exchanging ritual.

Psychologists who have developed and explored this field of human interaction call their work "transactional analysis." These analysts report that the number of strokes we give in a ritual exchange is frequently related to the length of time that has passed since we last saw the other person. If it has been only a few hours, a simple "Hi" might suffice. If an entire summer vacation has passed, a few more strokes are in order.[19] For example:

A: "Hi."
B: "Hello, there."
A: "How are ya doin'?"
B: "Just fine."
A: "What you been up to?"
B: "Same old stuff. What's new with you?"
A: "Not much."

B: "Kinda hot, isn't it?"
A: "Sure is!"
B: "Well, gotta be going. Good to see you."
A: "Me too. See ya later."
B: "Have a good day."

No sincere interest has been shown by either party. No information has been communicated, but both parties feel a little better for having been addressed by the other.

Positive and Negative Strokes

Strokes can be either positive or negative depending upon the message conveyed. If the message is "You're OK," the stroke is said to be positive. Examples of positive strokes are compliments regarding one's appearance, performance, behavior, or judgment; expressions of affection or appreciative feelings; information regarding one's competencies; or even attentive listening. Some positive strokes take the form of increased eye contact, smiles, nods, or approving vocalizations. Others are expressed verbally.[20] A question may give more strokes than a statement if the question requests advice or asks for a sincere opinion or evaluation. For example, the classmate who asks "Do you think Roy's is a good place to eat after the homecoming dance?" gives you more strokes with that question than with the statement, "We're debating whether to eat at Roy's or The Silver Spur."

A stroke may be negative too. Angry and cold vocal tones, frowns, scowls, knitted brows, and reduced eye contact all communicate "You're not OK." Sometimes a cold stare does the same thing, as does that unfocused look that says you're a nonperson. Lack of attention from someone you expect to recognize you communicates as clearly as a verbal discount.

Discounts are those strokes that diminish, humiliate, tease, degrade, or ridicule. Laughing at others and name-calling are similar negative strokes.[21] Such discrediting is common fare in television situation comedies. We laugh when others are cut down; but when we're on the receiving end, it's hardly funny. Some people use put-downs while they're with a group because they think others will consider them clever or entertaining. Unfortunately, it often works at the expense of the poor soul who is the butt of the discount.

"Sticks and stones may break my bones, but names can never hurt me," children chant at their tormentors. Most adults will admit that those words are not really true. Even the English language suggests the actual relationship between tactile and nontactile strokes. The word *feeling* is used as frequently to refer to an emotional state as it is to the sense of touch. Both can be sources of contentment or pain.

Activities

1. In a public place such as a restaurant or shopping mall, find a place from which you can observe others inconspicuously. Count the number of times you see people touch others in a one-hour period. Note the sex and approximate age of each pair.
   Try the same experiment in a bus station or airport. Compare the results.

2. Violate the usual norms of touch with your friends. For example, try putting your arm around someone as you talk and holding it there. Note the reactions.

3. Record and analyze the verbal strokes you give and receive in the next few days. What "rules" seem to be followed unconsciously?

4. In television situation comedies, humor is often at the expense of the personhood of another. Put-downs, discounts, and sarcasm may cause an audience to laugh, but in real life such psychological aggression can be damaging to relationships and the development of confident, happy persons.
   To help you become aware of these negative strokes and their effects, watch three TV sitcoms, tabulating the put-downs used and noting what was said each time. After the programs have finished, examine your notes and consider the possible effects of such discounts if used in day-to-day interpersonal relationships.

5. Read John Steinbeck's "The Leader of the People," a section of his book *The Red Pony* (available in most public and school libraries). What kinds of strokes are given by each of the characters? What kinds do they receive?

6. Read the Jean Mizer story "Cipher in the Snow" (see Appendix) or watch the 1973 film of the same name based on her award-winning story (available for rent from Iowa State University, Media Resources Center, 121 Pearson Hall, Ames, IA, 50011). Discuss its message in light of what you've learned about silence, tacesics, and stroking.

7. Read and discuss David Ignatow's poem "Two Friends" (see Appendix). Explain your understanding of the author's choice of title, the form of the poem, the lines, and the central idea. Do you agree with the poet?

Notes

1. Ashley Montagu and Floyd Matson, *The Human Connection* (New York: McGraw-Hill, 1979), p. 112.
2. Ibid., pp. 113–14.
3. Ibid.
4. *Second Chance* (Nutley, N.J.: Hoffman-La Roche Laboratory), film.
5. Ashley Montagu, *Touching: The Human Significance of the Skin* (New York: Harper and Row, 1978), pp. 205–6. See also Mark L. Knapp, *Essentials of Nonverbal Communication* (New York: Holt, Rinehart and Winston, 1980), pp. 148–49; Lawrence B. Rosenfeld and Jean J. Civikly, *With Words Unspoken* (New York: Holt, Rinehart and Winston, 1976), p. 122.

6. James W. Prescott, "Body Pleasure and the Origins of Violence," *The Futurist* 9(1975): pp. 64–74.
7. See overview of research in Judee K. Burgoon and Thomas Saine, *The Unspoken Dialogue: An Introduction to Nonverbal Communication* (Boston: Houghton Mifflin Co., 1978), pp. 67–71.
8. Ibid.
9. Sidney B. Simon, *Caring, Feeling, Touching* (Allen, Tex.: Argus Communications, 1976), pp. 91–101.
10. Burgoon and Saine, *Unspoken Dialogue,* pp. 67–71; Knapp, *Nonverbal Communication,* pp. 147–53.
11. Burgoon and Saine, *Unspoken Dialogue,* p. 180.
12. Knapp, *Nonverbal Communication,* p. 150.
13. Simon, *Caring, Feeling,* p. 82.
14. Desmond Morris, *Intimate Behaviour* (New York: Random House, 1971), p. 214.
15. T. Nguyen, R. Heslin, and M. Nguyen, "The Meaning of Touch: Sex Differences," *Journal of Communication* 25(Summer 1975): pp. 92–103.
16. Prescott, "Body Pleasure," pp. 64–74.
17. Ibid.
18. O. Michael Watson, *Proxemic Behavior: A Cross-Cultural Study* (The Hague, Netherlands: Mouton and Co., 1970), p. 105.
19. Eric Berne, *Games People Play* (New York: Grove, 1964), pp. 36–40.
20. Muriel James and Dorothy Jongeward, *Born to Win: Transactional Analysis with Gestalt Experiments* (Reading, Mass.: Addison-Wesley Publishing Co., 1971), pp. 46–50.
21. Ibid., pp. 50–55.

8

Proxemics

WHAT DO TYPICAL MODERN TEENAGERS have in common with song sparrows, Grimm's three bears, and the Sioux Indians at the time of Custer's massacre?

Give up?

All become more than a little ruffled when outsiders encroach upon things and places they consider theirs. *Territoriality,* as such behavior is called, is a basic concept in the study of animal behavior, but it can be applied just as well to what Desmond Morris has called the naked ape — mankind.[1]

That specialists in nonverbal communication should use terminology from zoology is not as unusual as it seems. All studies in nonverbal behavior are cross disciplinary. In fact, no college or university is known to have a department of nonverbal communication studies. Research and courses regarding its varied aspects have been found in other departments from *a–z*: anthropology, architecture, biophysics, business administration, child development, criminology, environmental planning, marketing, mental health, organizational management, psychiatry, psychology, physiology, rhetoric, sociology, speech-communication, and zoology, to name the most important contributors.

Zoologists have proven that no living creatures are truly born free, nor can they live free. Each species has its own rules of territory, within which it is held by its own and other species, by the need for food, shelter, a place to raise young, and a place to avoid danger.

Anyone who has kept pets or other animals will know that each species finds its place to sleep (not always the place its owner has chosen), its place to eat or hunt for food, and its nesting place to bear and raise young.

Squirrels, rabbits, and other small animals usually live out their entire life in the same rural or suburban neighborhood. TV programs like "Wild Kingdom" frequently show the capture and relocation of wild animals whose territories are endangered by encroaching civilization or natural disaster. The difficulty of relocation is underscored for us by oft-told stories of dogs finding their way home from rural areas or new owners. As if more evidence were needed, birds return to the same nest and feeders season after season, even though their migration patterns take them thousands of miles away to another home territory. If an animal's territory is invaded or usurped by an enemy, it will threaten, attack, and if necessary, fight for its territorial rights.

Territoriality and Human Behavior

People aren't really any different from animals about territoriality. They too claim territories that they will protect when threatened by invasion.

On the national level, most Americans feel all fifty states are ours. Should they be attacked or invaded, we'd want to fight back in defense. Where our borders are flanked by oceans, we proclaim a three-mile limit that may not be occupied by unauthorized oil rigs, ships, and other seagoing vessels.

Neighborhood groups form in our cities. Some build makeshift clubhouses or take over a restaurant or other place of business. A few terrorize others in defense of their turf. Younger children form play groups and plot out their ball diamonds in empty lots or playgrounds. Retired people claim specific park benches as theirs.

Now let's look at your home territory. First there's your room or at least your part of it, your closet and dresser drawers, your seat at the dining table, your record player, your bike, and additional possessions that others may use only with permission. If you ride to school, there's your seat in the car or school bus.

At school you have your locker, your desk in each classroom, your lab station, your customary seat in the library, your group's cafeteria table, its auditorium assembly seats, and its bleacher section at home football and basketball games. Many of these places were not assigned to you, but you and your friends consider them yours just the same and return to them regularly.

When you go out in the evening with your friends, there's your loop of streets, your place to stop, and your favorite restaurant table.

Your parents have their territories, too, that are closed to others without permission. At dinner they have their chair at the table. Later they occupy their easy chair in the living or family room. Dad may have his den or workshop. Mother may prefer to keep friends and relatives out of her kitchen. In some families Dad drives to work in his car and Mother to work in hers. Upon arrival, they park in their place before reporting to work at their desk or station or before covering their beat or territory.

Your sister may have a fit over anyone touching her diary, reading her magazine, or even expanding into her half of the closet. She begs regularly for her own telephone.

Some things become ours because we are members of the same family. When your little brother has an argument with the neighbor kids, he dares them to touch his house or even cross the line into his yard.

On Sundays you sit in your pew at church. When you visit Great Aunt Martha at the retirement home, she's seldom in her room but in her chair in the solarium. No, she didn't take it there with her, but it's hers nevertheless.

Desmond Morris points out that *hairy* apes and other animals leave their scent marks on and around their territories. Naked apes do the same thing by putting signs and photographs on their doors and desks, vanity license plates on their cars, and decorations and pictures inside their lockers and on their walls or otherwise personalizing their territories.[2]

To show dominance and ownership, humans also employ kinesic symbols. They lean against their cars and put their feet up on their furniture. No one would think of putting his feet up on the desk of another, but when it's his desk in his office—why not?

In many cases our need for physical privacy isn't as important as the desire that others respect our territorial rights. As children we enjoyed the feeling of security we got inside of tents we built by draping old sheets or blankets over clotheslines, furniture, or whatever support was available. Our pets and best friends might be admitted, but no grownups! Almost all of us had private places—a hidden corner of the attic room, a depression among the gnarled roots of a tree with low-hanging branches, a small clearing under dense foliage or among thick bushes near the creek. There we played, imagining that no one else had ever occupied that place before us.

Cultural Variation Regarding Open Space

But American culture trains us to appreciate open spaces. Thus we build our homes with mirrors, picture windows, and unbounded yards to give us the feeling of spaciousness.

Latin Americans build high, impenetrable walls around their yards, decorating the area between the house and the wall for their own pleasure. Beautiful flowers, statuary, and walks may fill the area; but whenever I am inside the first floor of such a home, I feel uncomfortable. The walls block my view of the neighborhood and cast depressing shadows across the room.

How much nicer are the upstairs rooms, flooded with light and permitting unbroken views of the city and perhaps the mountains beyond.

German homes, on the other hand, usually have their exterior walls built right up to the street, but their entrances are set back, often out of sight from the street. Between houses one will find a gate, behind which is a courtyard, or well-groomed *Hof,* leading to one or more home entrances. To enter the gate of a Hof is to enter the German home. It may not be locked, as would be the Latin-American gate, but it frequently has a bell, and a visitor is expected to request permission to enter.

Inside an American home a closed door means one of three things: the view beyond is unsightly (a closet or a messy room), the occupants desire to conserve energy by not heating or cooling that room, or someone has closed it for privacy. Germans close all doors behind them automatically. They can't explain why except that it's neater that way.

German business personnel visiting the United States see our open doors in offices and businesses as indicative of an unusually relaxed and unbusinesslike attitude. Americans get the feeling that the German's closed doors conceal a secretive or conspiratorial operation.

When Americans want to be undisturbed or are angry, they'll enter a territory they consider theirs and close the door. Arabs, who dislike walls and doors and frequently use the word *tomb* for closed-in places, simply stop talking and turn their thoughts within. Even the English do not share the American's need to close oneself behind a door. English middle- and upper-class children are brought up to share rooms. Even the members of Parliament do not have private offices. Like the Arabs, they close out others without visible barriers when they need to concentrate or be alone emotionally.

In the United States, neighboring is common. Being a neighbor carries privileges, rights, and responsibilities that others do not share. As a result, we pick our neighborhoods as carefully as we choose our homes. In many parts of the world, you would not consider asking favors of, sharing with, looking out for the property of, or even chatting with strangers just because they live next door.

Yet we do not need Berlin-type walls to keep us apart. In Chicago, Ashland Avenue as clearly separated one community from another as did Ninety-sixth Street in New York.

Reserving Our Place

Another interesting phenomenon regarding our possession of territory is our use of markers to keep our places free from outsiders. To leave a coat, sweater, or jacket draped over a chair marks it as occupied and unavailable to others. In a library or classroom a notebook or an open book will convey the same message. In waiting rooms and cafeterias we may reserve our place with a package, umbrella, or briefcase, whereas at the beach or pool we save a chair with a towel or bottle of suntan lotion. Almost any personal item may be used as a marker. The important thing is that others see it as a marker, not a piece of litter. A newspaper or magazine may be an ineffective marker in some places, for people often leave them behind after reading them.

The effectiveness of markers to reserve territory has frequently been measured through carefully designed research. Lee Mohr investigated their use in a university library study hall during a period of high room density. Arriving early each evening, he placed four different types of markers about the room — a sport jacket, a notebook-textbook-pen combination, a neatly stacked pile of magazines, and a randomly scattered magazine pile. Then he moved to another table to watch what happened. Spaces identified as control areas (unmarked) were occupied well before the two-hour sessions ended. The average time before occupancy was twenty minutes. The sport jacket and notebook-pen combination kept their places vacant the entire two hours. Magazines neatly piled reserved a chair for an average of seventy-seven minutes, whereas scattered magazines kept another free for thirty-two minutes. (All magazines belonged to the library and were frequently left on tables by departing students.)[3]

An interesting discovery was that of the role of the person sitting beside the marked spaces. In all five trials with the scattered magazines, the potential invader asked the person seated beside the marker if that space was vacant. As a neighbor, he or she was held responsible for knowing the status of the territory. At first the "good neighbor" unknowingly protected the area by telling others that he or she thought the chair was taken. As time passed, doubts formed and were passed on to potential invaders. "Yes, there was someone sitting there, but that was over an hour ago and he may not be coming back." Interestingly enough, no one who saw the notebook and pen talked to a neighboring person. In the case of the jacket, a few people asked but left after good neighbors told them the chair was occupied.[4]

In a study conducted by students from one of my own high school language arts classes, a heavy sweater hung over the back of a chair during first period each morning and removed after school each afternoon kept one of eight library carrels unoccupied for three consecutive days. Students with differing free periods took turns watching the space. On the fourth day it was removed by a well-meaning library aide, who hadn't been informed of the experiment.

Three Types of Territorial Trespass

Intrusion upon one's territory has been found to take three different forms.[5] The first is *contamination* of the territory thereby rendering it unacceptable for our own occupation and use. In this case it's not so much the presence of others we reject but what they have left behind. Examples of this might be finding your mother's lingerie and hose hanging over the tub when you want to take a shower, discovering food particles on your silverware in a restaurant, or having to clean up droppings of a neighbor's dog from your lawn.

Violation is the unwarranted use by others of what we consider to be ours. The person whose poorly parked car encroaches upon the parking space that should be yours alone is guilty of violating your territory, as are the neighbors who play their stereo at full volume after midnight or the children who regularly cut across your yard on their way to school. The kitchen of the three bears was violated by Goldilocks.

The last type of territorial trespass, and the one that upsets us the most, is *invasion,* the physical presence of others with seeming intent to take over our territory. Goldilocks invaded the baby bear's bed! Other examples are your mother offering your room to house guests without consulting you, someone else taking your campsite while you spend an afternoon at the beach, or another student taking your seat in the library while you are at the stacks.

Human Reactions to Territorial Intrusion

Our reaction to the intrusion of others depends on several factors including our judgment of the violators' identity and intent. Were they friends, strangers, or enemies; little children, peers, or adults; high status persons or low status ones? Did they trespass knowingly or naively? Furthermore, was the trespass onto public or private territory? How was it accomplished? How long did it last?

Several investigators have reported how humans react to invasion. In his book *Personal Space,* Robert Sommer records a two-year investigation conducted by Nancy Russo in the study hall of a college library. All of Russo's subjects were women who had chosen seats with empty chairs across from them and to either side, which indicated their preference for solitude but made invasion relatively easy. Russo sometimes sat across from her subject, sometimes directly beside her. Occupying an adjacent chair and moving it to approximately one foot from the subject produced the quickest departures. There was no singular defense pattern employed by the subjects. Some students shifted postures; some tried moving books and materials toward the invader; others tried to move in the opposite direction. When these gestures failed or were ignored, the subjects eventually fled. After about thirty minutes, about 70 percent of them left the table. There was a wide variety of verbal responses to the invasion, but only one subject out of eighty asked the invader to move.[6]

Louis Forsdale, professor at Columbia University's Teachers College, tells of an unnerving experience that occurred in his own none-too-tidy office. He met a student at the office door, asked her to come in, and was shocked to have her take his seat behind the desk leaving him the chair on the other side. At first he thought perhaps she was playing a joke on him but soon discovered she was a sincere foreign student who simply hadn't been able to decipher the clues as to which was his side of the desk and which was hers. The top of the desk was cluttered, obscuring clues she might have noted there, and the chairs were of equal size, both padded and with arm rests. An American student might have responded to the clue that his chair was a swivel model and the guest chair was not or some other detail that she simply did not see.[7]

Perhaps the most puzzling case of invasion is that reported by Edward T. Hall in his book *Beyond Culture.* After having occupied the same room in a Tokyo hotel for about ten days, Hall returned one afternoon to find his room filled with someone else's clothes and personal items and his own missing. When he returned to the hotel desk for an explanation, he learned that during his absence he had been moved to another room because his original room had been reserved in advance by another party. Entering his new room, he found his clothes and possessions placed as if he had put them there himself. About three days later the hotel management moved him once again without notice. Hall's American upbringing told him that this was very shabby treatment, certainly not appropriate for a man of his status. Yet the rooms were equally pleasant, and his years of work dealing with cultural variation kept him politely quiet — except among friends and colleagues. Later while staying in a hotel in Kyoto, another Japanese city, he was not only moved to another room but to an entirely different hotel without being consulted.[8] It wasn't until much later that he learned an explanation for this behavior on the part of Japanese innkeepers.

To the Japanese, "belonging" is important to a person's identity. When a person is employed by a company, he "joins" the corporate body and his loyalty to the group and its products becomes very strong. To be a guest in a Japanese hotel means that you become a member of a large, mobile family. You belong. Many hotels even provide all guests with identical cotton kimonos called *okatas*. Each hotel has its own identifiable okata design. The fact that Hall had been moved was proof that he was considered one of the family. With family members a person can be relaxed and casual. It's not necessary to stand on ceremony. Unfortunately Americans do not like being treated as one of the family. Needless to say, Japanese hotels catering to Americans do stand on ceremony.[9]

Usually Americans are amazingly polite about respecting another's right of tenure in cases of territory. An investigation into this behavior was conducted by Ann Gibbs in a campus soda fountain where students had been observed to habitually occupy the same tables day after day. In a well-planned experiment, Gibbs approached persons who had been seated for various lengths of time saying, "Excuse me, but you are sitting in my seat." She discovered that persons who had been there for only short periods of time felt no rights to their chair and moved away. However, her invasion was strongly resisted by those who had been seated longer. In typical fashion, a short-term person answered, "Oh, all right, excuse me — I'll move," even though there were many other vacant tables in the area. On the other hand, when a person who had occupied a chair for twenty-five minutes was told "You're sitting in my seat," he replied, "No, I don't think so. I've been here for half an hour," and refused to move.[10]

Other studies show that invasions by persons of higher status are permitted but not intrusions by those of lower status. An employee's supervisor acceptedly entered the employee's office without knocking or asking permission, even while the employee was on the phone, a behavior considered unacceptable by a person of lesser rank.[11]

Students in my laboratory high school classes never object to my looking over their shoulder to check their accuracy and progress on a given assignment, but they sometimes object to university student observers doing the same thing and become downright hostile if their classmates "stick their noses in where they don't belong."

Many students also declare their bedrooms off limits to their brothers and sisters but will not object to a parent entering.

Proxemic Distances and Interpersonal Relationships

Territoriality is only one aspect of *proxemics,* the study of the way humans structure space. Another well-researched aspect concerns the distances we strive to maintain between ourselves and other persons. Each of us goes through life carrying about us a protective bubble known as personal space. That space shrinks or expands depending upon many factors, the most important of which is the relationship we permit between ourselves and others.

Edward T. Hall distinguishes four distances that he has observed used repeatedly by middle-class adults who are natives of the northeastern seaboard of the United States. The first is *intimate distance,* which ranges from actual touching to approximately 18 inches. Next is *personal distance,* extending from 1.5 to 4 feet. *Social distance* stretches from about 4 feet to 12 feet where the last zone, *public distance,* takes over.[12] Let us examine each of these zones more closely.

Intimate distance allows other persons so close to us that we share the warmth and scent of their bodies. The close phase of intimate distance is reserved for adults cradling children, lovemaking, comforting, and wrestling. The arms often encircle the other person and the smallest details are visible to the eyes. Vision may be distorted, however, by the eyes' inability to focus on close objects. Vocalizations often take the form of whispers.

The far phase of intimate distance (6 to 18 inches) keeps the head and torso out of contact with those of another person but allows the hands to reach out and touch. Except between adults and children, this distance is closer than is considered proper in public (unless, of course, the locale is unusually crowded as in a bus or elevator).

The close phase of personal distance (1.5 to 2.5 feet) still permits us to touch others — if we extend our arms. We can no longer feel another's body heat, but at times strong breath odors may be detected. Normally this is the far perimeter of colognes and perfumes. This is the distance a wife or fiancée may stand from a man in public. Everyone else is expected to maintain a greater distance.

At the far phase of personal distance (2.5 to 4 feet), one person can still reach another if both extend their arms. Beyond this we can no longer dominate another person physically.

Social distance also has two phases. When we interact informally with classmates and friends at a social gathering, we generally use the close phase (4 to 7 feet). Business transactions and other more formal conversations are conducted within the far phase (7 to 12 feet). Unlike intimate distances where mutual gaze is awkward, at social distance gaze is important and necessary. Office desks, restaurant tables, and business counters usually keep us at social distances. With physical barriers such as these, however, we sometimes allow others closer to us than we would without them.

The close phase of public distance (12 to 25 feet) gives us the protection of space generally desired between strangers. At that distance a threatening move would leave us an opportunity for escape or defensive action. We may lose details of others' faces and eyes at this distance, but we can still see and hear them without straining.

At the far phase of public distance (beyond 25 feet) certain adjustments must be made. Speech must be projected or amplified to be heard;

subtle facial expressions must be translated into larger gestures. This distance is, however, necessary to accommodate large audiences who come to see and hear public figures and stage presentations.

Other Determiners of Personal Space

When forced to share space with strangers, we are inclined to separate ourselves from them as far as possible. In a bus or train, we choose a seat that gives us the biggest space bubble possible. The same is true in airports, waiting rooms, and unfamiliar restaurants without hostesses to seat us. Sometimes the logic of this action is questionable. For example, we'll select a seat far distant from others in a nearly empty movie theater while there are dozens of seats available that offer a less distorted view of the screen.

The purpose for our being in a given place also affects our handling of personal space. When we join dense crowds at pep rallies or to see a public figure, we may let people crowd us to the point of leaving ourselves only six to eight square feet. In loose crowds, such as those gathered to hear outdoor concerts, we'll probably maintain at least ten square feet. These figures were determined by a journalist who found it necessary to estimate crowd size frequently. His figures were confirmed by aerial photographs.[13]

Robert Sommer and his staff tested student selection of seats in a low-density library study hall. When faced with long rectangular tables with three to five chairs on each side, students selected an end seat if their purpose was to be as far as possible from the distraction of others but a center seat if they wanted to try to keep the table to themselves and discourage others from occupying it.[14]

Even a casual observer will note that cafeteria chairs are frequently moved to allow additional persons to join a table designed for a lesser number, but chairs at library tables are almost never moved.

Police officers who must serve as interrogators are often advised to face the suspect directly and sit as close as possible with no table or desk between them. They are encouraged to move even closer as the questioning proceeds until one of the subject's knees is almost between the officer's knees. This invasion of personal space will help break down the suspect's defenses.[15]

William Leipold studied the way in which university students seated themselves when confronted with varying degrees of stress. As the students arrived for interviews requested by Leipold, they were met by another staff member who gave them either stress, neutral, or praise instructions. The stress directions were "We feel that your course grade is quite poor and that you have not tried your best. Please take a seat in the next room and Mr.

Leipold will be in shortly to discuss this with you." The neutral instructions read, "Mr. Leipold is interested in your feelings about the introductory course. Would you please take a seat in the next room." The praise directions began with a sentence telling the students they were doing very well in the course.

When Leipold came in, he recorded which seat the student had taken in relationship to his own and conducted the interview. The results showed exactly what he had hypothesized: Those given praise sat closest to Leipold's chair behind the desk while those given the stress instructions maintained the greatest distance. He also found that students whose scores in separate examinations showed them to be introverted and anxious sat farther away from him than did students shown to be extroverted and to have lower anxiety levels.[16]

Other studies, using different methods and standards, support Leipold's observation that introverts generally need more personal space than do extroverts.[17]

Investigation also substantiates the expectation that persons who like one another will converse at closer distances than those who dislike each other.[18] And people were found to maintain closer distances with their age peers than with those who were either noticeably younger or older than themselves. This was true even when the older person was a parent of the younger.[19]

The owners of popular nightclubs who keep the lights low and the music moderately loud in their establishments will tell you it's done for atmosphere. They may not know it, but that atmosphere allows much greater population density without their customers feeling crowded. Dim light and loud music cause our personal bubbles to shrink. We must move closer together to see and hear one another. Thus many more people can comfortably occupy a small space.

When crowds grow dense, a difference has been noted between the responses of men and women to the density. Large all-male groups confined in small spaces displayed negative reactions, becoming suspicious and hostile toward one another. Women, under the same conditions, became pleasant and intimate.[20] It seems that being "crowded" is not determined so much by actual population density as it is by each individual's perception of the conditions.

Cultural Variation in Personal Space

Although factors such as sex, age, personality, and attitude affect the distance we place between ourselves and others, our cultural backgrounds are perhaps more constant determiners of personal space in a conversational setting. Studies of cultural "dialects" in proxemics within the United States have not been as common as one might expect. Nevertheless, one investigation found that whites stood closer together while speaking than did blacks. When whites spoke with blacks, however, they maintained greater distance than when speaking with other whites.[21] Navajo and Zuni Indians were discovered to prefer greater personal space than whites, and American Jews desired closer distances.[22]

On the international level, differences in comfortable conversation distance become obvious quite readily. Nations are frequently classified as having contact or noncontact cultures. When compared to persons from noncontact cultures, members of contact cultures interact at closer distances, while facing one another more directly, engaging in more mutual gaze, touching more frequently, and speaking more loudly. Included among the contact cultures are the Latin American, southern European (most notably French and Italian), and Arabian. Oriental cultures (especially Chinese, Japanese, Thai, and Filipino) and northern European cultures (German, Dutch, Scandinavian, and English) are considered noncontact, as are the North American (United States and Canadian) and Australian.[23]

In places where representatives of varied cultures interact regularly, as they do at the United Nations, persons from a noncontact culture are often seen being backed across the room during a conversation with someone from a contact culture. The Latin Americans or Arabs continually move in to what they consider a comfortable conversational distance, and the Germans or Canadians back away to a distance where they feel more at ease. As the dialogues continue the interactants slowly move across the room or down the hall.[24]

Not only do people from noncontact cultures prefer to be farther apart while they speak, they are also inclined to stand in line while waiting their turn. Americans think it's only polite to stand behind one another to enter a bus or train or to wait for service in a post office, bank, or box office.

Many busy financial institutions and post offices in the United States have tried to improve efficiency by building attractive entry routes similar to the design in Figure 1. Such enforced lines guarantee that no one will be delayed by a slow customer ahead. Upon reaching the head of the line, a person is waited upon by the first available clerk.

At large American tourist attractions, similar gates have been built to guarantee orderly entrance by large crowds and to permit more people to wait in small areas. The English use the phrase *to queue up* to identify their standing-in-line behavior, which is practiced regularly in their culture even without enforcement. In Latin America, however, I've never seen a group standing in line. It was particularly surprising to see seemingly humble

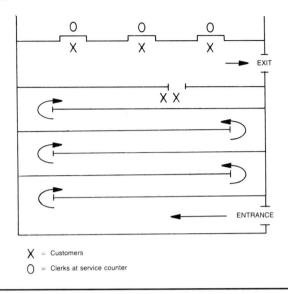

X = Customers
O = Clerks at service counter

1

Christians all pushing their way to the front of a church to receive communion at the same time.

I have never learned to accept the pressures of the crowd. Generally, I prefer to return at a less busy time or to wait and be the last served. At theaters and concert halls, my husband tucks me into a safe corner to wait while he bucks the crowd to buy our tickets. After we had visited the Inca ruins at Machu Picchu, I refused to push my way onto the train for the return trip to Cuzco. As a result, the conductor proclaimed the coaches full before we were aboard. We had to wait twenty-four hours for the next train. Believe me, the next day I pushed and shoved as hard as anyone.

An interesting sidelight to the American standing-in-line behavior is the observation by movie-theater managers that the distance between people standing in line differs depending upon the kind of movie they expect to see. Sommers reports an interview with a suburban theater owner who said his lobby held only one hundred to one hundred and twenty-five people when they were waiting to buy tickets for a film rated G or GP. "The patrons stand about a foot apart and don't touch the person next to them." But for an R- or X-rated film, about three hundred to three hundred and fifty persons stood in the same space. "Those people stand so close to each other you'd think they were all going to the same home at the close of the show."[25]

When Physical Space Is Not Available

Sometimes the number of people occupying a given locale (population density) makes physical separation from others impossible. At times like those we protect our personal space by psychologically isolating ourselves and perceiving others as nonpersons. Giving people the same status as things or furniture denies that an invasion could occur. When doctors and nurses discuss a patient's diagnosis and treatment across his or her bed, they isolate themselves by making the patient a nonperson. Parents and their friends who cannot escape the responsibility of child supervision sometimes treat children the same way, as if they weren't capable of hearing and/or understanding. Other persons who are frequently accorded nonperson status are food servers, custodians, taxi drivers, and live-in servants.

In subways, elevators, and other high-density locations, we often treat all strangers as nonpersons. We lower our eyes and freeze as a method of minimizing possible invasion of our personal bubble.

On the highway, our automobiles become natural extensions of our person. We desire the same freedom from invasion of personal space around us there as anywhere else. Of course, space is more clearly needed as insurance against injury. A car length for each ten miles per hour is commonly recommended. To travel side by side with another car on a four or more lane highway isn't particularly dangerous. Yet having anyone in that position very long makes us anxious and uncomfortable.

Because the personal space bubble has been extended, being inside of a car can make us feel more powerful and less human, however; and we may behave in ways uncharacteristic of us under other conditions.

Proxemics as a Clue to Status

To a stranger visiting the United States for the first time the process of discovering who's who in America can be truly mystifying. Status clues that communicate so loudly in other parts of the world often mean nothing here.

A candidate named Washington has no better chance of being elected than one named Smith. A part-time file clerk may dress no differently than a university dean. A salesperson working on commission may drive the same model car as a second generation millionaire. The home of a hospital bookkeeper and a construction worker might be appraised at the same value as one belonging to a lawyer. The parish priest and the owner of the XXX movie theater may play golf at the same club. A third-shift factory worker may display more cash than the owner of an oil well. So if family names, clothes, cars, home value, affiliations, and ready cash don't indicate status in America, are there no recognizable clues?

Yes, there are ways to identify persons to whom Americans ascribe status and persons who claim it for themselves, but the clues are obvious only to those who know our culture well. One of those clues is the way Americans use and apportion space. Persons whose roles place them physically above others are generally of higher status within that group. A judge's bench raises him above the rest of the courtroom, as does the professor's podium in a lecture hall and the pastor's pulpit in a church. The most important people at a banquet sit at the head table. Offices on the top floor are occupied by executives. The financially wealthy build mansions on hills (not in the valley) and live in penthouse apartments high above the rest of the city dwellers.

In a place of business, the desk of an American of higher rank is not in a huge room among the others but in a private office. The president's office is larger than the vice-president's, which is larger than the division manager's. A change in responsibilities that gives a tenured employee a 20 percent salary increase but a 20 percent smaller office would probably not be considered a promotion. A sure indication of status in one's place of employment is an assigned work area that is larger and more private than the work space of others.

Offices in American business firms are often laid out quite differently from those in Europe or Japan. In Europe, desks are most commonly placed near the middle of the room. Authority flows outward from the center. In American offices, desks are placed near the walls, leaving the center open for traffic and interaction with others. In an office complex, the power most frequently flows from a larger, more private corner office with windows facing two directions.

When they move to conference rooms, those in leadership roles usually select seats from which everyone in the room can see them. At a rectangular table this will probably be the head or the foot of the table.

Interesting facts were gathered in Chicago through systematic observation of experimental jury sessions that were not actual court cases. Each panel of twelve experimental jurors was ushered into a jury room containing a rectangular table with five chairs on each of its long sides plus one at the head and one at the foot. Their first task was to elect a foreman. A person seated at the head or foot of the table was most often chosen for that role.[26]

Surprisingly, when the sessions were over and the jurors were asked to rate each other's contribution, they regularly indicated that the people in the head chairs made the most significant contribution.[27]

Was all this pure accident? Probably not, say the researchers. The jurors voted for one of the persons at the end of the table because of the "intrinisic propriety" of the chairperson being at the end of the table and the likelihood that electing someone else would be taken as a personal rejection of the person seated there initially. Examination also revealed that the initial choice of seats was not random. The end positions were more often chosen by people from a higher economic class—proprietors and managers—than could be attributed to pure chance. It appears as though the jurors took a good look at the person at each end of the table and selected as their foreman the one they judged to be of higher status.[28]

Seating Preferences at Tables

Let us assume that the setting is a school cafeteria open to students during their free hours. You and a friend of the same sex enter the room and find only two tables vacant—one round, one rectangular. There are six chairs around each table in the positions shown in Figure 2.

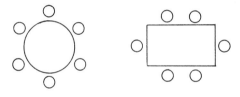

2

Now let's insert a set of possible reasons you entered the room:

1. To converse. You simply want to visit a few minutes before class.
2. To cooperate. You want to study together for the same exam or work out a difficult math problem.
3. To coact. You each have to study for a different exam.
4. To compete. You want to compete against each other to see who will be the first to solve a series of puzzles or a Rubik's cube.

In Figure 3 are sets of possible seating choices. For each of the purposes listed above, select a seating arrangement in which you would feel comfortable. Do this before reading the next paragraphs. Then you'll be

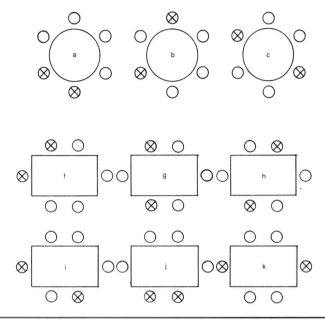

3 (From the book *Personal Space: The Behavioral Basis of Design* by Robert Sommer, © 1969 by Prentice-Hall, Inc. Published by Prentice-Hall, Inc., Englewood Cliffs, N.J.)

able to compare your choices to those found by researchers.[29] Choose seating arrangements for both the round and the rectangular table.

When the seating is for conversation, 63 percent of those polled chose *a* at a round table; 46 percent chose *g* at a rectangular table, while 42 percent preferred *f*. They explained their choices by pointing out the advantage of proximity and ease of eye contact in these positions.

For cooperation, 83 percent selected position *a* for a round table and 51 percent selected *j* at a rectangular one. Side-by-side seating was seen to be advantageous for sharing things.

For purposes of coaction at a round table, 51 percent preferred *c*. No single seating arrangement was chosen by a majority for a rectangular table: 43 percent of the respondents chose *h*; 32 percent chose *g*. Greater distance was a deciding influence for all respondents. Students who selected the kitty-corner position, *h,* cited the advantage of being able to stare off into space without being distracted by seeing their friend.

When the object was competition, 63 percent chose round table arrangement *c*. For rectangular tables, 41 percent selected *g* and 20 percent *h*. Those who chose face-to-face arrangements said this stimulated competition. They wanted to be able to see how the other person was doing without actually looking at his or her work.[30]

Classroom Seating

Most classrooms for American elementary and secondary school children haven't had the desks fastened to the floors for at least thirty years. Nevertheless, most rooms still have their straight rows of student desks (with light entering from the left) undisturbed except for cleaning.

In Price Laboratory School at the University of Northern Iowa, the school in which I teach, seating arrangements are constantly being changed depending upon the subject matter and the instructional methods involved. For several years I have asked my students to express their views regarding their comfort in each of the possible settings in Figure 4.[31]

The students' responses showed that the subject matter is not an important factor in determining their views, but teacher's instructional methods are of primary importance.

Settings *d* and *b* were judged desirable for classes in which student interaction was dominant. Foreign language learning was frequently cited as a situation in which the instructional methods matched these seating patterns. However, many students indicated that the twenty-four students suggested by the drawing were too many for interaction classes.

The settings labeled *a* and *e* were judged unacceptable for classes in which teachers talked to the group frequently. Students want to be able to see the teacher as he or she speaks, and seeing one's classmates instead can be a distraction. On the other hand, setting *a* was seen as useful for temporary small group discussions, which many teachers use to encourage brainstorming and wider participation. Setting *e* would be fine for a class in which independent study or laboratory work was practiced.

The choice between *e* and *f* appears to depend on the personality of the student more than on the teaching method employed. In laboratory and independent study situations, some students appreciate having a teacher check on their work whenever he or she passes by. Others find this distracting and would prefer to go to the teacher when help is needed or feedback desired. The students are quick to point out, however, that lazy, disinterested, or insecure children might not get the help they need if they have to seek out the teacher.

Settings *c* and, to a lesser degree, *b* were definitely preferred for classes in which teachers frequently use the blackboard or ask students to watch a projection screen or television monitor. Students pointed out what educa-

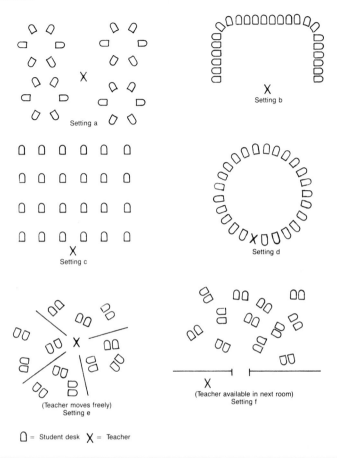

Setting a

Setting b

X
Setting b

Setting c

X
Setting c

Setting d

X
Setting d

(Teacher moves freely)
Setting e

X
(Teacher available in next room)
Setting f

◻ = Student desk X = Teacher

tion experts readily admit: In the typical class, the teacher talks almost half of the time. Therefore, students generally agree that setting *c* is comfortable for them. Everyone can see the teacher, and the teacher is able to make eye contact with them. This, they say, is more important than interaction with their classmates.

An intensive study concerning the effects of straight-row seating was conducted by Raymond Adams and Bruce Biddle, who observed sixteen different teachers in thirty-two classes ranging from grades one through eleven. Their findings were consistent for all teachers, grades, and subjects. The students across the front and down the center participated more than did those along the sides. Those in the back corners participated the least.

This center-of-the-room action zone existed despite the fact that "none of the seating procedures used by the teachers deliberately selected pupils for placement in the center-strip locations."[32]

Studies by Robert Sommer and his staff confirmed these findings and produced the percentage of participation numbers shown in Figure 5.[33]

X

57 %	61 %	57 %
37 %	54 %	37 %
41 %	51 %	41 %
31 %	48 %	31 %

5   (From the book *Personal Space: The Behavioral Basis of Design* by Robert Sommer, © 1969 by Prentice-Hall, Inc. Published by Prentice-Hall, Inc., Englewood Cliffs, N.J.)

Sommer notes, however, that student environmental preference should be taken into account. Student interest and location interact to determine classroom participation. When given a choice of seats, interested students are inclined to sit where maximum visual contact with the teacher is possible. Thus in classes where students select their own seats, the action at the front is more pronounced than in those where the students are seated alphabetically or in another arbitrary fashion.[34]

Life-Style and Building Design

Architects and engineers have done a pretty fair job of designing schools for study, libraries for reading, churches for worship, restaurants for dining, and stores and shopping malls for sales. But function isn't the only consideration in designing a building or room and furnishing it. The life-style of the future occupants is also important.

Dormitory directors will tell you that college students' rooms are the center of activity. Even when study libraries are provided, most students prefer to study in their room. They socialize in each other's room and seldom use the floor lounges except to watch television programs. In dorms that permit students to have their own television sets, students will more likely watch a friend's set than the one in the lounge. The only lounges used frequently are those on the street floor where members of both sexes meet to visit.

College students like to personalize their rooms and rearrange them to fit their needs and interests. In the newer dormitories, built-in furniture makes this very difficult to do. The reason that chests, beds, and desks are built-in, however, is purely financial. Low-interest building loans are available to cover the cost of a dormitory structure and all items permanently installed in it. Detached furniture must be financed separately.[35] So economic considerations, not student needs, determine dormitory room design.

In these rooms, few students find their desk the most comfortable place to read—and a high percentage of a college student's study time is spent reading. Nevertheless, few dorms provide each resident with a lounge chair. Most students sprawl on their bed to read.

As declining student numbers reach the college level, some schools are considering converting dormitory space to other uses. At the same time, the need for housing for the elderly is on the increase in most cities. Wouldn't it be logical to select the dormitories farthest from the campus center and rent their rooms to ambulatory senior citizens?

The answer is "no!" As anyone who has worked in or frequently visited a retirement home knows, its residents do not like to feel confined to their rooms. They socialize in the dining room, in game rooms, and in craft rooms. Some just sit quietly in a dayroom, library, or solarium. These people move to a retirement home from multiroom homes and apartments and have no desire to be cooped up in a single cell.

In the 1960s and 1970s public housing built for low-income families replaced ancient tenements and slums in many cities. Some of these new buildings were high-rise structures that showed no consideration for the families that would live there. Mothers complained that they could not adequately supervise their children ten stories below. Stores, supermarkets, and community services were often miles away and public transportation scarce. An out-of-order elevator—which is not uncommon when children are frequent operators—meant carrying babies and groceries up hundreds of stairs. Hallways and elevators were hard to keep secure from bullies and muggers. Today many of these buildings stand vacant.

Another conflict of building and life-style was reported by a woman who had lived all of her life in old two-story houses with nearly a dozen small rooms. When she and her husband were finally able to afford their dream home, they built a house with cathedral ceilings, an open balcony, and lots of glass on exterior walls. She never felt "at home" there. She longed for a place to get away from everyone and everything else. She missed the privacy and security she had felt in small, closed rooms.

To be comfortable, a structure must fit the family life-style not only in degree of open and closed space but in appropriate space for favorite activities. If your family piano is not just a piece of furniture but an instrument that is played for an hour or more each day, it must be placed where it will not interrupt other activities. And how about your television viewing habits? What hours are prime time for your family? What other activities are apt to occur in the house during these hours? Is there space for both?

Does your family like to have guests? If so, what do you enjoy doing with your guests? If you frequently invite them for dinner, you need adequate dining space apart from the kitchen if possible. If you play cards, there must be a comfortable spot for a card table or two. If you simply like to chat, is there a place where the seating is comfortable and distances are appropriate for good interaction? The recommended arc for comfortable conversation in a home is about eight feet;[36] and remember, people prefer to sit where they can face one another, rather than side by side. The best seating arrangement for conversation is far from ideal for television viewing.

Even the most expensive interior decorator cannot make your home comfortable for your family unless you let him or her know your habits and life-style. The most beautifully coordinated colors and textures in designer-book arrangements may be appropriate for only a designer book!

Figures 6 and 7 suggest two ways the same family room might be arranged. The design of Figure 6 offers opportunities for maximum communication. All seats in the room face one another. Even the person working at the desk is involved with whatever else is going on in the room. Closeness is emphasized. Traffic patterns cross for togetherness and com-

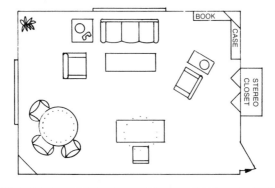

6   Family room arranged for maximum interpersonal communication.

munication even during individual activity. Hanging lamps descend over the game table and desk. Large table lamps stand on the end tables. The light sources blend together to create unity. There is no television set in the room. Instead, the closet contains a stereo set, which is heard through the speakers in the upper right and lower left corners of the room. A plant stands in another corner, causing no visibility problems. Even a telephone caller is brought into the middle of the room. The phone is placed near the sofa and lounge chair, on an end table for easy reach and comfortable seating. The door is hung so that it swings out and anyone entering can see everyone else and be seen by them. There's no escape from others in this room.

The same family room is arranged in Figure 7 for privacy and peaceful coexistence. The room is almost visibly divided into four "stations": (1) desk work, (2) television viewing, (3) reading, listening to stereo, and (4) games and activities that need space to spread out. All stations are self-contained so that there are no crossing patterns. There are no overhead lights or overlapping of light circles. The lamps on the tables and desk illuminate only that station. The furniture is placed so that it is difficult to see others in the room, thus discouraging communication. The telephone, placed on the desk, deters the long, easy conversations encouraged by a lounge chair and suggests a more businesslike attitude. The position of the plant provides a screen for station 3. The stereo set is located in the end table within station 3, and a single speaker is placed behind that table. A headset is available for private listening. The closet contains games and materials for station 4. The door to the room has been changed to swing inward so that a person entering will not be as likely to disturb the people already in the room.

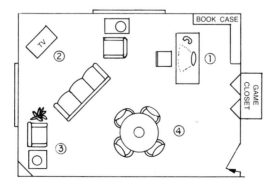

7   Family room arranged for privacy and peaceful coexistence.

To a visitor entering either of these rooms, the proxemic message is clear. The ways people manipulate space and react to it form a distinct nonverbal language complete with rules of grammar and usage. Proxemics is used the world over with culture creating dialectical variations. Like so many other methods of nonverbal communication, it has power that is only beginning to be recognized.

Activities

1. At a restaurant, move your water glass to a spot that invades your companion's part of the table. Next slide over your silverware and dishes. Note the reactions you get with each step.

2. Upon entering an uncrowded library or lunchroom, sit at a table with several people you don't know. Move in; try not to leave a lot of space between yourself and them. Note their reactions.

3. In an uncrowded waiting room, theater, bus, or lunch counter, sit immediately adjacent to a person already seated. Do not talk to him or her but sit as close as you can. What verbal or nonverbal reactions occur?

4. Walk behind the counter in a store, library, or office (perhaps to dispose of something in a wastebasket, which you'll usually find there). Watch the reaction of the person on duty.

5. Watch the eighteen-minute animated film *The Hat—Is This War Necessary?* (McGraw-Hill, 1967), which may be rented from ROA Films, 1696 North Astor Street, Milwaukee, WI, 53202. Discuss the real and symbolic consequences of accidentally invading another's territory.

6. With unsuspecting friends of both sexes, begin a conversation at the normal standing distance. Then gradually move in to invade their personal space bubble. As you talk, inch closer and closer. Observe the nonverbal and verbal reactions. At what point do most people step back? See if you can get people to back up more than once. Do males react the same as females? How do you feel as you do this?

7. Upon entering a classroom or school bus, take a seat normally occupied by another student. If you are told "That's my seat," simply answer "I know." Do not move unless specifically asked to do so. Note results.

8. With a partner for moral (and possibly physical) support, enter the school cafeteria, auditorium, or gymnasium and take seats usually occupied by another group. Note reactions.

9. At home, sit down for dinner in a chair usually taken by another member of the family (preferably one smaller than you are).
   Or in the living room or family car, take a seat normally occupied by an adult member of the family. Note reactions from all family members.

10. Upon entering a library, take the seat of someone who is at the stacks. Note the reaction.

11. Walk up to someone who has recently entered and taken a seat in the library (or at a lunch counter) and tell him or her, "Excuse me, but you're sitting in my chair." See if people move for you as they did for Ann Gibbs.

12. Note where various classmates tend to sit in each course. How do their seating preferences match their personalities as you know them?

13. For a class in which students have chosen their own seats, make a seating chart. On it, tally the number of times each person participates. What do your notes tell you about seating and interaction patterns?

14. If you live in an apartment building, note which tenants communicate with others and when. Are there any proxemic influences at work?

15. Design a two-person bedroom for maximum personal communication. Rearrange the same room for privacy and peaceful coexistence.

16. Watch the twelve-minute film *Invisible Walls* (University of California, 1969). This award-winning film records a research project in which trained actors with clipboards approached shoppers to ask their reactions to the new shopping mall where the film was made. In reality, the purpose of the study was to note the shoppers' reactions when the actors invaded their eighteen-inch personal space. The film may be rented from the University of California, Education Media Center, Berkeley, CA, 94720.

Notes

1. Desmond Morris, *The Naked Ape* (New York: McGraw-Hill, 1967).
2. Ibid., p. 184.
3. Robert Sommer, *Personal Space: The Behavioral Basis of Design* (Englewood Cliffs, N.J.: Prentice-Hall, 1969), pp. 53–54.
4. Ibid.
5. These forms of trespass were first distinguished by Stanford M. Lyman and Marvin B. Scott, "Territoriality: A Neglected Sociological Dimension," *Social Problems* 15(1967): pp. 236–49.
6. Sommer, *Personal Space,* pp. 35–36.
7. Louis Forsdale, *Nonverbal Communication* (New York: Harcourt, Brace, Jovanovich, 1974), p. 90.
8. Edward T. Hall, *Beyond Culture* (Garden City, N.Y.: Doubleday and Co., 1976), pp. 58–61.
9. Ibid., pp. 64–65.
10. Sommer, *Personal Space,* p. 52.
11. Ibid., p. 19.
12. Edward T. Hall, *The Hidden Dimension* (Garden City, N.Y.: Doubleday and Co., 1966), pp. 116–25.
13. Herbert Jacobs, cited in Sommer, *Personal Space,* pp. 27–28.

14. Sommer, *Personal Space,* p. 49.
15. Ibid., p. 28.
16. Ibid., p. 30.
17. Ibid.
18. Judee K. Burgoon and Thomas Saine, *The Unspoken Dialogue: An Introduction to Nonverbal Communication* (Boston: Houghton Mifflin Co., 1978), p. 94.
19. Ibid.
20. J. L. Freedman, J. Klevansky, and R. R. Ehrlich, "The Effect of Crowding on Human Task Performance," *Journal of Applied Psychology* 1(1971): pp. 7–25.
21. F. N. Willis, "Initial Speaking Distance as a Function of the Speaker's Relationship," *Psychnomic Science* 5(1966): pp. 221–22.
22. S. Fisher and S. E. Cleveland, "Cultural Differences in Boundary Characteristics," in *Body Image and Personality* (New York: Dover Publications, 1968), pp. 277–97.
23. O. Michael Watson, *Proxemic Behavior: A Cross Cultural Study* (The Hague, Netherlands: Mouton and Co., 1970) pp. 62–118. See also Hall, *Hidden Dimension;* Edward T. Hall and Mildred Reed Hall, "The Sounds of Silence," in *Language: Introductory Readings,* ed. Virginia P. Clark, Paul A. Eschholz, and Alfred F. Rosa (New York: St. Martin's, 1972), p. 463.
24. Edward T. Hall, *The Silent Language* (Garden City, N.Y.: Doubleday and Co., 1959), pp. 160–61.
25. Bob Ellison, "If the Movie Is Comic, Sex Is OK, in Suburbia," *Chicago Sun Times,* 15 January 1967, sec. 3, p. 4 (quoted in Sommer, *Personal Space,* p. 29).
26. Fred L. Strodtbeck and L. H. Hook, "The Social Dimensions of a Twelve Man Jury Table," *Sociometry* 24(1961): pp. 397–415.
27. Ibid.
28. Ibid.
29. Sommers, *Personal Space,* pp. 61–63.
30. Ibid.
31. These arrangements were suggested by a study done by Fred C. Feitler and two associates. See "Teacher's Desk," *Psychology Today* 5(September 1971): p. 12.
32. Raymond S. Adams and Bruce Biddle, *Realities of Teaching: Explorations with Videotape* (New York: Holt, Rinehart and Winston, 1970), p. 50.
33. Sommer, *Personal Space,* pp. 117–18.
34. Ibid., pp. 116–17.
35. Ibid., p. 135.
36. Burgoon and Saine, *Unspoken Dialogue,* p. 96.

9

Chronemics

"Time is a river."
"Time's only a rule."
"Time is money."
"Life is time's fool."

"Time means y'hafta wait."
"Time is a line."
"Time's the grim reaper."
"Life's rhythms are time."

"Time is for city folk."
"Time's a paradox."
"Time is our life."
Listen, "Time talks."

ASK A HUNDRED PEOPLE the meaning of time and you'll get a hundred different answers. Every one of the "definitions" in the rhyme opening this chapter actually was given by a different person. Time isn't the same for a poet, a child, a merchant, a physiologist, or a retired farmer. But whoever you may be and wherever you live, your perception and structuring of time and your reactions to it affect your relationships with others. In this respect, as Edward Hall writes, "Time talks."[1] The word *chronemics* is used in the field of nonverbal communication to refer to these message-laden aspects of time.

Most white Americans think of time as a line, a road, or a river that extends from the unknown region of the past into the unknowable future. We embark upon this river at birth and are carried along until death pulls us under. We move through time. Its current propels us along.

In the Greek culture, people are more likely to figuratively describe themselves as stationary. Time moves up behind them, overtakes them, and goes on to become the past.[2]

Some cultures, including those of several American Indian groups, have little concept of the past or the future. They are concerned with "felt time," the immediate present. Clocks and calendars are not culturally significant.[3]

Time and Human Orientation

People differ in their orientation to time. Here in the United States are individuals who are past oriented, groups with present orientation, and other people oriented toward the future.

People who are past oriented see events as cyclical. They look to the past as a guide for modern living. Situations and occurrences in the past offer lessons from which we can learn. Keeping copious diaries and souvenirs are indicative of a person's past orientation, as are his or her retelling of old happenings.

Orientation to the present means living for today. Mistakes, people, and events of the past, no matter how pleasant or painful, are *gone*. The challenge for these people is to handle current situations as they arise. The past is best forgotten, and it's futile to worry about the uncertainties of the future. In the United States, black and Chicano cultures frequently produce present-oriented people.

Future orientation emphasizes the fact that tomorrow is inevitable. We are constantly moving ahead. Planning and anticipation, therefore, become important. Puerto Ricans tend to be future oriented, but middle-class, white Americans are decidedly more so. Everything that's done today is completed with an eye to the future. Today may be a drag, but tomorrow...

A Sense of Time

Formally we speak of time as years, seasons, months, weeks, days, hours, minutes, and seconds. But informally, we consider time in relationship to other things. "It's *almost time* for the bell to ring." "That assignment will take *forever*." "Please write him *one of these days*." "We'll stop for a coke *later*." Or "I'll take the dog out *after a while*." In cases like these, the meaning of the time phrase is usually clear to both the sender and the receiver.

Time is not always perceived as passing at the same rate of speed. When we are busy, happy, or enjoying good company, "time flies." But when we are doing a tedious task or are bored, it "crawls along." If we are lost in thought, time is more likely to "stand still." Studies done in England indicate that our body temperature also affects our sense of time. When the body temperature falls below normal, time appears to pass more quickly. If we have a high fever, time seemingly passes more slowly than normal.[4]

In the United States, where seasonal changes greatly affect the angle at which the sun strikes the earth, people rarely develop any skill at judging the time of day without a clock. In La Paz, Bolivia, (16° south latitude) some people show an impressive ability to tell time by simply looking at the length of the shadows around them. My mother-in-law's maid was an Aymara Indian from the high plateau where neither money nor clocks were common. In learning city ways, she had integrated the new concepts with her childhood knowledge. When we went shopping together, she would frequently state the time, although she never wore a watch. She was never off by more than five minutes.

Some people need a clock to tell time during the day but can tell themselves to awaken at any hour during the night and do so. Tests under controlled conditions show that if they know the time before they go to sleep, they can awaken within a minute or two of a preset target time. According to Dr. Charles Tart, who conducted the experiment, no single stage of sleep preceded the awakenings.[5] More research is needed before it will be possible to theorize why this faculty for self-awakening appears in some people but not others.

Have you ever been on vacation, out of touch with your usual schedule, and lost track of time — forgetting even whether it was Wednesday or Thursday? Retired persons whose life-style allows every day to seem like every other day quickly lose track of the date and the day of the week. In nursing homes, therapists encourage them to remember such details, calling it part of reality orientation. To be honest, the patients don't have much use for this information, but their knowing it makes relatives, friends, and staff members think their mind is sound.

Finding the Best Time

Sometimes it's called timing, that ability to choose the most advantageous time to do or say something. Consumer market reports suggest the best months for buying everything from shoes to furniture, from household linens to motorcycles. Human physiologists tell us the best time to eat proteins and carbohydrates or to take certain medicines. Farmers' almanacs recommend the best time to plant, fertilize, and cut back vegetables, flowers, and bushes. But when is the best time to apply for a job, to request money from your parents, to report bad news, or to ask your heartthrob for a date?

Let's begin by looking at the worst time. A social telephone call between 11:15 P.M. and 7:50 A.M. is seldom appreciated. The lower tolls on long distance calls placed at 11:01 P.M. or 7:51 A.M. make them understandable and, therefore, acceptable. But local, nighttime calls have a sense of irresponsibility or urgency that most of us don't want associated with our messages.

When people are very busy, they don't like to be bothered by interruptions that require thought or time for attention. Therefore, it is not recommended to ask your mother what she thinks is wrong with your bike while she is rearranging the garage. Nor should you remind your dad that he promised to help you with your biology project while he is cleaning out the gutters under the eaves. Naturally her presence in the garage and the sprouting seeds he's throwing out bring related thoughts to your mind—but keep them there.

Merchants, managers, and proprietors who are approached during rush hours by persons seeking employment might find it easiest to say they're not hiring. They don't welcome special requests or ad salesmen then either. Professional door-to-door salespersons avoid mealtimes for their calls—a practice that might well be noted by students selling magazines, candy bars, or Girl Scout cookies.

There's never a good time to drop a bomb. But some times are better than others to report that you've wrecked something, lost something, or flunked something. When business and professional persons have unpleasant announcements to make to their employees, they often schedule them to be made on Friday or payday. Why? Because they hope the impact of the news will be partially offset by the anticipation of the weekend or the forthcoming pay envelope.

Advance notice, sometimes called lead time, is important to Americans, but the rules regarding the best amount of lead time are also hazy. If someone invites you too early for a social engagement, you may mistakenly think it's an elaborate affair, learn later of other events you regretfully will have to miss, or, heaven forbid, forget the date entirely. On the other hand, if you are not invited until the last minute, you may wonder if the inviter is so egotistical as to think you would cancel anything in order to accept, if your open calender is being taken for granted, or if you were invited only after someone else had declined the invitation. The success of our messages, be they requests, invitations, announcements, or replies, might often be improved by attention to timing.

Americans' Schedules and Punctuality

If Benjamin Franklin was speaking only metaphorically when he said "Time is money," millions of Americans today don't seem to know it. We talk about money and time using the same verbs: We *make* it, *find* it, *buy* it, *earn* it, *save* it, *waste* it, *spend* it, and *lose* it.

Our way of life also supports the equivalency. We treat every minute like a precious commodity, living by schedules, following the same efficient routine day after day.

Children quickly learn that the day follows a program. There's breakfast time, toilet time, Mr. Rogers time and Sesame Street time, play time, and lunchtime. Then there's quiet time, outdoor time, dinnertime, bath time, and perhaps story time before bedtime.

When American children reach the age of responsibility, the initiation rite consists of the gift of a watch.

Student schedules are controlled by the clock. Whether a concept is clear, a question answered, or an experiment finished—when the bell rings, students must drop one subject and move on to another. Extracurricular activities are as time bound as classes. Special lessons, religious instruction, and family obligations fill other time blocks.

Most American workers are expected to observe working schedules. Over half are paid by the hour. They punch a clock when they arrive on the job, take lunch and coffee breaks according to plan, meet deadlines and rate schedules, and punch out when their shift ends. After-work time is regulated by personal appointments, store hours, social engagements, and entertainment and television schedules. If the morning paper or the evening meal is fifteen minutes late, we may have to go without it for the day, our schedules are so tight.

To reward ourselves for months of timetable servitude, we schedule a vacation in which we must submit to plane and bus schedules, guided tour hours, and motel checkout times.

We are so clock bound that every year people complain about the switch to daylight savings time. Since our activities are determined more by clock time than by the actual hours of daylight, a change in that clock is disturbing to many. Dairy farmers who want to take advantage of summer evening daylight activities discover that their cows won't advance their internal clocks to comply with the wishes of the majority of the people living in the United States. Therefore, farmers are frustrated by cows that won't adjust, and cows are upset by farmers who push them to do so. If clock time were not so important, no adjustments would be necessary.

For official business along the East Coast between middle-class Americans who are not on intimate terms, the expectations of punctuality and tardiness are very strict. Edward Hall points out that when a person is five minutes later than the preset clock time, a slight apology is in order. After a mildly insulting ten-minute period, a full apology is required. Being fifteen minutes late requires not only an apology but an explanation as well. A half-hour tardiness is downright insulting.[6]

Researchers Leslie Baxter and Jean Ward asked eighty-four secretaries what their impressions would be if someone arrived fifteen minutes early, on time, or fifteen minutes late for an appointment. Prompt arrivers were considered most competent, composed, and sociable, but not very dynamic. Late arrivers were regarded as highly dynamic but low on competence, composure, and sociability. Early arrivers were judged even less favorably. They were rated low on dynamism and only moderate on the other three qualities.[7]

The "Dialects" of American Punctuality

By comparison to those along the Atlantic seaboard, the clocks in the Old South and Far West are far less exact and more approximate. The people are more relaxed in their attitudes toward punctuality. Greater deviations are permissible from the preset hour before judging a person discreditable. In Utah, on the other hand, Mormons practice promptness to an extent unknown anywhere else in the country. They are almost never more than a minute late and generally try to be a little early.[8]

The subculture of the urban blacks regards time in a highly lax manner. They call it "street time," for it revolves around the activities of the street, not the hours of a clock. When you live on the street, things happen in sequence, but there's no concept of being late. Work isn't something that begins at a given moment; it's what you do at your place of employment. Middle-class blacks often chide other blacks for their tardiness, calling it "CPT" (Colored People's Time) as opposed to the exactness of "WPT" (White People's Time). A black mother, for example, might tell her son to pick her up at "five WPT, not CPT," meaning precisely at 5:00.[9]

In Hawaii, the native Polynesians prefer the same approximate, relaxed way of handling time. They call it "Hawaiian time" as opposed to the demanding exactness of mainland America. This they dub "Haole time" after the life-style of early missionaries to the islands. To be told "We'll see you at eight Hawaiian time" means sometime around eight, whenever convenient. But "We'll see you at eight Haole time" means you have an appointment for exactly 8:00.[10]

Many American Indian cultures are far less clock bound than the rest of the people in the United States. Sioux Indians are said to have no words in their language for *late* or *waiting*. Their traditional life-style simply made them unnecessary.[11] Pueblo Indians might tell you an event will occur "when the time is right." They make no attempt to explain what that means, but you can be sure it is not now.[12]

Being "On Time" Elsewhere in the World

In northern Europe, the people are exact and precise about time, much like Americans on the East Coast. The northern Germans and Swiss are particularly punctual. (Their world fame for accurate watches and clocks was not caused by accident.) There are time "dialects" in Europe, however. The Laplanders, for example, are much more casual about promptness. People in industrialized cities, be they Stockholm or Milan, are more concerned about clock time than those whose lives are tied to agriculture or to the tides of the ocean. Generally speaking, the inhabitants of southern Europe are less concerned about being on time. Like the people of the Old South, they live in a more relaxed manner, not treating tardiness as a catastrophe. In Italy, for example, television stations make no effort to begin their programs on the hour or half hour. One program is run until finished, and a new one begins with no concern for clock time or schedules.[13]

Few people in the world, however, are less exact in their handling of time than are Latin Americans. Mexicans, who by their geographical proximity to the United States are frequently exposed to our emphasis on punctuality, call their time "hora mejicana" and ours "hora americana." In South America, most people know no other way of living and never explain or apologize. To my upper Midwest sensitivity, their lack of respect for clock time is almost unbelievable.

La Paz, Bolivia, where I have lived for several months at various times, is a cosmopolitan capital city of over three hundred thousand. Stores and businesses there open when their proprietors arrive and close when they decide they've done enough business for one day. Dinner time, at noon, is a time for everyone to go home to eat and always means locked shop doors for at least two hours. No two business establishments keep precisely the same hours.

Movie theaters show a *matinee* about two o'clock, a *tanda* about six-thirty, and a *noche* about nine o'clock. The exact time depends upon the projectionist's arrival and assessment of the audience. If the theater is not yet full and people are still milling about, they'll wait a little longer.

Student tardiness is no big problem; for their teachers, who often instruct classes in more than one school, are seldom on time.

Public transportation is regular—every quarter hour, every two hours, or whatever—but no one would presume to assign clock times to the schedule. They probably wouldn't be valid the next day anyway. In the dozen or so times I've said goodbye to others, or myself taken international flights leaving their large, modern air terminal, not one plane has left on time. The earliest was two and a half hours late; the latest twenty-seven hours. (A mountain storm had dropped two inches of snow on the runways, and they had to wait until it melted.)

One of my early experiences occurred on *El Dia del Indio* (The Day of the Indians), a festival recognizing the many original Bolivians, who live throughout the country. Representatives come to the capital from hundreds of miles away, over mountains and nearly impassable roads, to sing and dance in the pageant, which is held in the municipal soccer stadium. All of the posters and the tickets, which we purchased in advance, said it would begin at 2:00 P.M. Since no seats were reserved, and only part of the stadium was shaded by a roof, we arrived at 1:50 and found excellent seats. The program began at 3:32!

On another occasion, after I should have known better, I accepted a 7:00 P.M. date with a young Bolivian. In the afternoon preceding my date, my friends (both American and Bolivian) made plans to attend a concert of the National Symphony Orchestra scheduled for 8:00 that night. I wanted to hear the concert, but there was no way of communicating with my date before he arrived. Seven o'clock came, and passed. Naturally I was ready to go. 7:15...7:30...7:45... (In Spanish the words *to wait* and *to hope* are the same, *esperar.* I've often wondered about the significance of that fact.) At 7:55 my friends were ready to leave for the concert. I suddenly decided to join them. I told the maid she could tell my date, if he ever arrived, that I'd waited an hour and had decided he wasn't able to come, before I had left for the concert. She met my gaze for a split second longer than usual but quietly agreed.

We arrived in time for the opening number, at 8:28. At intermission time you can imagine who was waiting for me in the lobby, not apologetic, but angry. In order to avoid an international incident, I left with him and missed the remainder of the concert. The trouble with him was me!

Years later, after I'd married a Bolivian, my sister-in-law invited us to a family dinner at 5:00 on a Sunday afternoon. My husband chose the same day to take me to a park in the suburbs of the city. We had a delightful afternoon and it was 4:45 before I realized how fast the time had passed. I insisted that my husband take me home immediately so that I could bathe and change my clothes for dinner. He sighed and gave in. Despite his many assurances, I was more than a little upset when my watch said 5:30 and I was still waiting for the water to heat for my bath. At 6:30 we arrived at my husband's sister's home.

Then it was her turn to be upset. We were the first guests to arrive and had caught her in the kitchen with the maid. She hadn't begun to bathe or change her own clothes for the occasion. At 5:00 her roast duck probably would still have been alive!

The cultural adjustment is no easier for Latin Amerians coming to the United States. In fact, it may be more painful. In the years before I married, I shared my American home with a Bolivian student attending the University of Northern Iowa. She had been in the States only a month or so when she told me she'd been invited out for Friday night. I didn't press her for details, and she didn't offer them. That Friday we had an early supper, but then lingered at the table for conversation. When we finally got ready to wash the dishes, I told her she didn't have to help, if she wanted the time to get ready for her date. She assured me that she had plenty of time to do both. At 7:40 she began washing her heavy, almost waist-length hair.

At 7:55 the doorbell rang. Her friend, in the manner typical of first dates in America, had shown his enthusiasm by arriving five minutes early. I spent the next hour and a half sharing my knowledge of "hora latina" with this confused and uncomfortable young man, while my housemate finished washing and drying her hair. The next day I had to spend another half hour trying to explain his behavior to her.

Human Physiological Rhythms

The last way in which time can affect our interpersonal communication is the same in all cultures. The lives of human beings, like those of all other living creatures, are controlled by a number of physiological rhythms. In other words, our bodies do not function in the same manner at all times. Some of our biological systems are geared to cycle every ninety to one hundred minutes; some cycle once a day; others approximately once a month or a year.

Medical science has long been aware of these rhythms which are identified by Latin names. *Circadian* rhythms have cycles of approximately twenty-four hours (*circa* = about + *dies* = a day). Shorter cycles are called *ultradian* (*ultra* = going beyond or more than once + *dies* = a day). *Infradian* is used to identify cycles with periods longer than a day, such as a week (*infra* = lower or less than once + *dies* = a day). *Circamensual* cycles are *about* + *a month* in duration; *circannual* describes cycles of *about* + *a year*. Each of these cycles is worthy of closer examination and further explanation.

To begin with the shortest, the ultradian cycle is frequently about ninety to one hundred minutes in length. Given only enough food to satisfy, our stomachs contract approximately every ninety minutes. Research subjects viewed through a one-way glass were noted to engage in oral behavior every eighty-five to one hundred minutes, reaching for something to eat, drink, or smoke.[14] When we must concentrate or study for long periods of time, it becomes obvious that our alertness and concentration peak once in about each one hundred minutes. About halfway through that time we pass a point of maximum drowsiness and feel the need for a break. That same cycle is the culprit when we find ourselves dead tired on the road or with guests but forty-five minutes later, when we finally get to bed, wide awake and unable to sleep.[15]

You may not be aware of the fact unless you have a cold, but we do not breathe through both nostrils equally. Most people breathe through one nostril for two to three hours and then switch to the other since the resting nostril has tissues that are slightly engorged.[16] Another ultradian rhythm is the male sex drive, which fully recycles in an average of ninety minutes, more or less, depending upon the age and sex habits of the individual. While we sleep, our REM (rapid eye movement) dream cycles also recur on an average of once every ninety minutes.[17] There are other bodily functions too that have ultradian cycles, but their effects are obvious only to doctors with special recording devices.

In babies and children, most of these rhythms cycle more rapidly. No one needs to be told that young children can't stay alert as long as can older children or that the attention span of junior high students is shorter than that of adults! We're also well aware of children who complain that they're hungry less than forty minutes after finishing a meal.

Circadian Cycles in Humans

The circadian rhythm is probably the most obvious in humans, for it includes our sleep-wake cycle. However, many other bodily functions also cycle approximately once every twenty-four hours. Sensory acuity, blood sugar level, pulse rate, respiration rate, hemoglobin level, brain wave patterns, adrenal hormone level, amino acid level, and urine volume also rise and fall with circadian rhythm.[18]

Human body temperature and blood pressure tend to peak in the late afternoon and fall to their lowest in the early morning while we are asleep. Research has proven that the effects of many drugs vary with the time of day, a fact that is being used more and more in medical practice.[19]

Investigations show that our memories seem to be better in the morning than in the evening. Our perceptual acuity and capacity to perform tasks, on the other hand, seem to peak in midmorning and again in late afternoon.[20]

We are also least sensitive to pain in the morning, but this sensitivity grows as the day progresses. Most of us experience little peaks at noon and about six in the evening and are most pain sensitive in the late evening. Research also records higher measures of anxiety, stress, regression, depression, and other mood displays in the late afternoon than in the morning.[21]

Allergy sufferers are usually aware that sensitivity to pollen and other allergies peak in the evenings. Doctors are beginning to realize that allergy tests given in the morning may not accurately record sensitivity and that the time at which a medicine is taken will significantly affect its potency.[22]

For most women, menstrual periods begin between four and six in the morning. A few start between eight and noon. But after an adolescent's first irregular months, few women start their periods in the afternoon or evening.[23]

When women become pregnant, they display even more circadian rhythms. So-called morning sickness is worst when expectant mothers first awaken and their stomach has been empty for some time. For 60 percent, labor begins at night, the average peak being at three in the morning![24]

Some years ago, I taught the first semester of an American literature course at 8:00 A.M. each day. During the second semester, the class was scheduled at 4:55 P.M. With very few exceptions the same university students were enrolled in both classes — but how differently they behaved. Students who had never said a word early in the morning led class discussions when they were held in the late afternoon. Others, who asked questions and were generally good students in the morning, nearly failed the class held late in day. When I teased them about the changes in their personality, they informed me that I too behaved differently. In the morning I was very precise and matter-of-fact. In late afternoon I was more likely to show a little humor and let the class become informal.

Some people are larks and at their peak in the morning. Others are owls who find mornings totally unproductive and don't do their best until late afternoon or evening. Even within the same family, differences occur. One child may be a lark among five siblings who are owls.[25] Evidently they have physiological metabolism cycles and hormone level rhythms that are out of synchronization. This is not a condition requiring medical or psychiatric attention. Just a little understanding and a great deal of tolerance are needed.

Young people might do well, however, to consider the owl-lark aspect of their personality when choosing a career or lifetime occupation. Some people are perfectly suited to jobs with second shift hours. They are cheerful, comfortable, satisfied, and productive after going to bed at three o'clock and sleeping until eleven o'clock each morning. Not only factory jobs offer these hours but also careers in journalism, entertainment, and accommodations management. And let's not forget the support staff and technicians who work with newspaper and television reporters and commentators, theater and nightclub performers, and hotel and restaurant operators.[26]

Gastrointestinal disturbances, ulcers, and other physical and emotional problems are common among night-shift workers who do not live every day according to the sleep-wake cycle demanded by their job. Frequently they are mothers and fathers whose family life causes them to revert to a day-wake, night-sleep pattern on weekends and days off. The body can adjust to regular night-shift hours, but constantly having to readjust causes the series of symptoms associated with dischronia (*dis* = absence of + *chronos* = time).[27] The rotating shifts of airline personnel, flight controllers, transportation workers, and hospital staff members are even more disturbing to the human circadian rhythms.

Many of us have experienced temporary dischronia as a result of a long airplane flight crossing several time zones. When we arrived at our destination, our bodies were bewildered by the demands of the new environment. We had to eat, sleep, and be alert at times when our body simply wasn't ready to do so. The effects of jet lag, as this form of dischronia is popularly called, are both physical and mental. The only cure is several days without further rhythm disruptions and plenty of rest.[28] A good night's sleep is valuable for more than just the rest it provides weary bodies. It also provides for brain activity, nerve repair, and essential hormone secretions.[29]

Are you one of millions of Americans who regularly feels rotten on Mondays? If so, temporary dischronia may be the cause, despite the fact that you never flew anywhere. On weekends we typically stay up late Friday and Saturday nights and sleep in, if possible. We eat foods that we don't usually have, at irregular hours. Such practices throw our rhythms off cycle. When we attempt to return to the weekday practices, the result is "blue Monday."[30]

What's so upsetting about having a hamburger and Coke after an evening movie, you ask? Let's consider the hamburger first. That quarterpounder has protein, which stimulates the production of brain chemicals used in waking activities. Physiologists say the best time to eat protein is for breakfast, although our smell and taste cycles tell us later is better. Carbohydrates aid in the formation of sleep chemicals, but then you left half of the bun uneaten, didn't you? Caffeine—and there's plenty of it in cola drinks—can advance or delay biological rhythms depending upon when it's consumed. In the morning it delays rhythms; in the evening it speeds them up.[31] So there was your body, cycling merrily along until you threw a wrench in the gears!

For most people the internal clocks that regulate circadian rhythms are not synchronized to a 24-hour solar day, nor to a 24.8-hour lunar day.

Investigations show that the average is closer to 25 hours.[32]

To gather information like this, researchers have found volunteers to live in caves or isolation chambers free from all time cues. In Germany, at the Max-Planck Institute near Munich, luxurious underground apartments were prepared with heat and lighting that subjects could control; books, phonograph equipment, and musical instruments chosen by each volunteer; and a one-way telephone through which messages could be given to the research team. For three weeks each, eighty-five volunteers were thus provided with room, board, and solitude to spend as they saw fit. In return they had to phone in before they went to sleep, upon awakening, and at mealtimes. They also had to take their own pulse and temperature, take psychological tests, and collect all urine.

Subjects involved in these free-running experiments varied in their sleep-wake cycles. The shortest average cycle was 23.5 hours; the longest was 27 hours. In most cases subjects were surprised when they were told that their twenty-one days had passed. They had calculated it to be only twenty days or less. The average cycle for the eighty-five volunteers was 25.05 hours.[33]

The Body's Circamensual Cycles

Although our circadian cycles are more obvious, circamensual, or nearly monthly, cycles control our lives as well. The first extensive research of circamensual rhythms was conducted by two Europeans in the late nineteenth century. Working independently, Dr. Hermann Swoboda, a psychologist in Vienna, and Dr. Wilhelm Fliess, a physician practicing in Berlin, each collected data regarding the rhythms they had noted in their patients. Dr. Swoboda first published his findings in 1904, Dr. Fliess in 1906. Both observed that basic cycles of twenty-three days and twenty-eight days affect the mental and physical well-being of humans.[34]

Dr. Fliess hypothesized that the twenty-three–day cycle was a masculine rhythm affecting the physical condition of mankind. The twenty-eight–day rhythm he ascribed to feminine inheritance. Of course, every individual inherits both male and female sexual characteristics. Therefore, all humans have elements of bisexuality in their makeup.[35]

Twentieth century research has led to the conclusion that a twenty-three–day cycle marks physical strength, endurance, energy, and general well-being. During one half of the twenty-three–day period, a human's well-being seems to increase; during the other half it appears to decrease and we are more content to rest and recuperate. Instead of calling this the masculine cycle, modern writers refer to it as the *physical cycle*.[36]

The twenty-eight–day cycle was discovered years ago to mark the average female menstruation period, which probably led Dr. Fliess to associate all twenty-eight–day rhythms with femininity. Some women notice marked mood changes corresponding to their menstruation rhythm, but cyclic mood changes have been found to exist in most people, whether they realize them or not. These have been linked to hormones and, in turn, the nervous system.

The modern term for the twenty-eight–day cycle is the *emotional* or *sensitivity cycle.* At the top of the curve we tend to be more cheerful, cooperative, and confident. At the bottom, we're more irritable, easily frustrated, and apathetic.[37]

A third circamensual rhythm was first studied by Alfred Teltscher, an Austrian engineer and teacher. During the 1920s he studied high school and college students at Innsbruck and concluded that their performance fluctuated with a thirty-three–day rhythm. During part of that time they seemed to be more alert and accurate in their thinking. They could create, judge, and remember better and make better progress academically than they could sixteen to seventeen days later.[38] Further studies supported his observations and this rhythm came to be known as the *intellectual* or *cognitive cycle.* Some scientists think it is related to the secretions of the thyroid.[39]

Many readers are probably thinking, "Here they're called circamensual cycles, but they sound like biorhythms to me." Yes, such cycles are biological rhythms, but the term *biorhythm* has been avoided for one very important reason. For most people, it is associated with meticulous methods of charting curves based on one's birthdate. Many publishers, technicians, and computer programmers have earned money selling these aids to calculations; but according to modern scientists in the field, the curves generated by these means are no more scientific than palm reading.

Admittedly, both Dr. Swoboda and Dr. Fliess suggested calculating one's present rhythms by charting them from birth, but modern research doesn't show these curves to be accurate for most people.

As most women can tell you, their menstruation periods are not totally predictable. To begin with, twenty-eight days may be an average, but the typical range is twenty-four to thirty-two days. Furthermore, surgery, severe illness, and the prescription drugs that accompany them often throw their cycle into a new pattern. A stressful experience, such as an extreme change of environment, a broken love affair, or the death of someone close, can have the same effect. Isn't it logical, therefore, that a person's present curves are unlikely to match average rhythms that have been unchanged since birth?

A recent magazine article quotes Dr. Andrew Ahlgren of the chronobiology laboratory at the University of Minnesota in Minneapolis, one of the modern research groups studying biological rhythms. According to Dr. Ahlgren,

Biorhythms are uniquely individual. There is no single static "clock" regulating our lives. There are hormone clocks, nervous-system clocks, and even cellular clocks — a vast web of interlocking timekeeping mechanisms, all making continuous adjustments.

Anyone who says you can chart your biorhythms by your birthdate is trying to sell you something — and it *isn't* science.[40]

Circannual Cycles in Humans

People do not shed their heavy fur or give birth to young each spring, hoard food beginning in early fall, or instinctively hibernate or fly south for the winter. Nevertheless circannual cycles do exist in humans as well as in birds, fish, and other mammals. These rhythms affect our physical growth, our moods, and our health.

Many people experience a sudden restlessness, energy, and sense of well-being with the first warm breezes of spring. This often leads to flights of fancy, romance, and frivolous behavior. We even have a name for it — spring fever. The physiological cause is a rhythmic surge of adrenal hormones, which stimulate the neuroendocrine system.[41]

Persons living in areas where seasonal extremes force them indoors for several months are prone to attacks of "winter madness." Research has shown that this anxiety neurosis is related to winter calcium deficiencies, which are known to affect the parathyroid and thyroid glands, and thus, the entire endocrine system. In reality, the long winter nights are to blame. Sunlight is needed to form vitamin D, without which absorption of calcium from foods is retarded.[42]

Certain illnesses also seem to rise and fall circannually. Ulcers and asthma increase in the spring and autumn, allergies in the autumn.[43] Suicides and mental hospital admissions peak in the spring.[44] In the future, research may provide even more information regarding our biological rhythms, the way our life on this planet affects them, and the way they affect us.

For some people such knowledge is frightening. They feel entrapped and confined after learning about their life rhythms. In the proper perspective, however, understanding our biological ups and downs is not a burden to be endured but a tool that can be used to live a richer life.

Activities

1. Survey the meaning of being on time in your locale. Prepare a multiple-choice questionnaire asking people when they would actually arrive for various kinds of appointments and events — more than fifteen minutes before, fifteen minutes before, the stated clock time, fifteen minutes after, or more than fifteen minutes after.

Items should include both business and social engagements of varying types. Ask people of several age groups to respond. Tabulate the results.

2. Keep records to put you in touch with your circadian rhythms and to find out when you are at your peak physically, emotionally, and intellectually each day.

Keep track of your eating and sleeping habits for two weeks. Be sure to include between-meal snacks and naps. At approximately three-hour intervals, starting at eight in the morning and concluding at eleven in the evening each day, make a brief note of your levels of energy and strength, your mood, and your mental alertness. For most people there is a definite pattern that may be disrupted by changes in eating and sleeping habits.

3. Test your self-awakening ability. Set a time in the middle of the night for yourself and try to wake up at that time. Try it on at least three separate occasions.

4. Try calculating your biorhythms by one of the popularly available methods. Analyze its accuracy over the course of several weeks in light of your personal evaluations of your moods, intellectual power, and physical endurance and strength.

5. Keep a record of your moods each day for two months. Can you see a pattern or cycle? Remember, events may have a stronger effect than your emotional cycle.

6. If you are involved in sports, keep a record of your performance after workouts each day for two or three months. Rank yourself from one to five on such items as coordination, strength, quickness, and stamina. The daily average of these items should form a recognizable circamensual pattern. Look for it.

7. Write a poem or essay in which you compare time to something else. Think about the details of your analogy.

Notes

1. Edward T. Hall, "Time Talks: American Accents," in *The Silent Language* (Garden City, N.Y.: Doubleday and Co., 1959).
2. R. E. Porter, "An Overview of Intercultural Communication," in *Intercultural Communication: A Reader,* ed. L. A. Samovar and R. E. Porter (Belmont, Calif.: Wadsworth Publishing Co., 1972), p. 6.
3. Ibid.
4. Hudson Hoagland, cited in Gay Gaer Luce, *Body Time* (New York: Pantheon Books, 1971), pp. 15–16.
5. C. T. Tart, "Waking from Sleep at a Preselected Time," *Journal of the American Society of Psychosomatic Dentistry and Medicine* 17, no. 1(1970): pp. 3–16.
6. Edward T. Hall, *Beyond Culture* (Garden City, N.Y.: Doubleday and Co., 1976), pp. 47–48.
7. Leslie Baxter and Jean Ward, cited in "Newsline," *Psychology Today* 8, no. 8(1975): p. 28.
8. Judee K. Burgoon and Thomas Saine, *The Unspoken Dialogue: An Introduc-*

tion to Nonverbal Communication (Boston: Houghton Mifflin Co., 1978): p. 131.

9. Ibid., pp. 131–32.
10. Ibid., p. 131.
11. Ibid., p. 99.
12. Ibid.
13. Ibid.
14. Luce, *Body Time,* pp. 87–88.
15. Ibid., pp. 85–89.
16. Ibid., p. 10.
17. Ibid., p. 86.
18. Ibid., pp. 7–8.
19. Eve Scott, "Staying Well: What to Believe about Biorhythms," *Seventeen,* May 1978, p. 90.
20. Vicki Goldberg, "What Makes the Body Tick?" *Family Weekly,* 3 July 1977, p. 12.
21. John E. Gibson, "The Different Ways We Perceive Time," *Family Weekly,* 2 April 1978, p. 20.
22. Scott, "Staying Well," p. 90.
23. Luce, *Body Time,* p. 282.
24. Ibid., pp. 281–82.
25. Scott, "Staying Well," p. 90.
26. Nadine Brozan, "How Owl-Lark Couples Get Along," *New York Times,* week of 29 August 1982.
27. Patricia Yoxall, "Circadian Rhythm . . . The Clock That Makes You Tick," *Family Safety,* Summer 1981, pp. 8–10.
28. Luce, *Body Time,* pp. 35–38, 43–46.
29. Yoxall, "Circadian Rhythm," p. 9.
30. Ibid., p. 10.
31. Ibid., pp. 10, 19.
32. Luce, *Body Time,* pp. 8, 52–53.
33. Ibid., pp. 46–58.
34. George S. Thommen, *Is This Your Day?* (New York: Crown Publishers, 1973), pp. 1–13.
35. Ibid., pp. 9–15.
36. Ibid., pp. 53–55.
37. Ibid., pp. 55–58.
38. Ibid., pp. 18–19.
39. Ibid., pp. 59–60.
40. Andrew Ahlgren, quoted in Scott, "Staying Well," p. 90.
41. Mary Ellin Barrett, "The Rites and Wrongs of Spring," *Family Weekly,* 4 April 1982, p. 16.
42. Luce, *Body Time,* pp. 257–59, 270–80.
43. Ibid., pp. 259, 278.
44. Barrett, "Rites and Wrongs," p. 16.

Color

COLOR CANNOT BE AVOIDED. It is an integral part of everything around us. Where there is light, there is color. Even when we close our eyes, we experience color; and blind persons will tell you they can sometimes feel color by the amount of heat absorbed or reflected by the varying brilliance of colors. Light colors absorb less but reflect more heat than do dark colors. For this reason, car seats with dark upholstery are warmer to sit on than ones with light colors; and pastel clothing, which reflects the summer sun, feels cooler.

But color is more than a physical separation of visible light into its component parts. It is a powerful stimulus upon human beings, both physically and psychologically. Our use of color is constantly communicating messages to ourselves and others.

Color Symbolism

Even when color isn't physically present, we use it in language, with effect. We describe ourselves as "feeling blue" or "in the pink." When we're happy, we're "tinkled pink" and greet the world "with flying colors." After we "paint the town red" on the weekend, we're apt to wake up feeling "a little green around the gills" and have a "blue Monday." When we're angry, we "see red," and some people even go into a "white rage." Envious people "turn green" when they see others with things they'd like to have, and cowards are "yellow" in the face of danger. Color symbolism is used by all cultures and appears in all languages.

Some symbolism is very old. Purple, for example, has been considered a symbol of royalty and rank since ancient days. Not commonly found in nature, a few precious drops of purple dye were extracted from the shell of the tiny murex snail as early as 1600 B.C. to color the clothes of wealthy Phoenicians. The depletion of the species was nearly total in some Mediterranean areas, and the consequent rarity of the dye made the color even more valuable as a status symbol.[1]

In heraldry, not only does purple symbolize rank and royalty, but red is symbolic of courage and zeal. Yellow or gold represents honor and loyalty; green, youth and hope; blue, truth and sincerity; black, grief and penitence; and white or silver, faith and purity.[2]

In modern times, color symbolism has been written into some laws. When Congress passed the Occupational Safety and Health Act (OSHA) in 1971, a set of color symbols became part of the law. OSHA yellow is to be used to indicate physical hazards and a need for caution; OSHA violet, radiation hazards; OSHA orange, dangerous parts of equipment and machinery; OSHA red, fire protection equipment; OSHA blue, equipment for preventing and reducing hazards; and OSHA green, safety and first-aid equipment.[3]

Most color symbolism is derived from tradition, not law. And tradition means that different cultures and different times associate slightly different meanings to certain hues. The Pueblo Indians, for example, had the colors yellow, white, red, and blue associated with the points of the compass. Medieval physiology associated colors with the four basic humors: Blood was red, of course; choler, yellow bile; phlegm, green; and melancholy, black bile. In China, yellow indicates royalty, white is worn for mourning, and red for festive and joyous occasions. In Egypt, yellow symbolizes happiness and prosperity; blue, virtue and truth; green, fertility and strength; and purple, faith and virtue.

The Personalities of Color

Let us, for a few minutes, engage in a bit of fanciful imagining, pretending that each hue is a separate person. Each of our personified colors, then, would have an identifiable personality and associate with a certain crowd of friends. Compare your imagined characterizations to those offered below and see if we don't agree fairly well.

Red is bold and aggressive, a stimulating creature. To call it an extrovert would be an understatement. In its company are fire, heat, courage, and patriotism but also sometimes anger, blood, sin, and danger.

Blue, on the other hand, is serene, pleasant, and cool. Its retiring and modest nature mark it as an introvert. Blue is associated with devotion, truth, and justice but also sadness and discouragement.

Yellow is a touchy character. Sometimes friendly, cheerful, and warm, it can on occasion be irritating, hostile, and unpleasant. Its associates also vary from sunshine and glamor to sickness and jealousy.

Green is always pleasant. It tends to be peaceful, calm, and leisurely. It never puts on airs but is always natural. Green is associated with freshness, youth, vigor, and prosperity. Sometimes, however, it keeps company with envy and inexperience.

Orange can be two-faced. Sometimes it is lively, exuberant, and bright, a stimulating and glowing creature. At other times, it turns noisy and unpleasant, its strident tones irritating our nerves. Orange doesn't have a lot of associates, but fruitfulness and harvest are always in company.

Purple is rich, stately, and dignified. It is usually aloof but sometimes lonely and nostalgic. We help it associate with victory, authority, royalty, passion, memory, and penitence.

White is an airy sprite, delicate, sparkling, cold, and clean. It is associated with purity, innocence, chastity, joy, and hope.

Finally, there's black, melancholy, solemn black. It is profound and sometimes mysterious but oh so sad. In its company are night and death, wickedness, sorrow, and despair.

How have my imagined personalities compared with yours? Not far off? That's really no surprise since colors affect us all in similar ways physically and psychologically, and perhaps we've been exposed to the same traditions, literature, and history. In other words, we share a common pool of reference. And in using colors, we draw upon that pool of knowledge, feeling, and experience. This is why colors communicate.

Color and Human Personalities

A couple of decades ago Dr. Max Lüscher, a professor of psychology in Switzerland, designed an interesting turn-about of our effort to ascribe personalities to colors. He constructed a test showing that our individual preferences for colors can be used to describe our personalities.

The Lüscher Color Test is currently available in a paperback book of that title, translated and edited by Ian Scott.[4] This do-it-yourself test offers the reader eight color chips to consider. Based on one's selection or rejection of the individual chips, ratings are assigned to be matched with descriptive, psychological information. Although Lüscher's conclusions are not universally recognized as valid, this test is simple, enjoyable, and for most people uncanny in its accuracy. However, the author, editor, and publisher warn, "It is *not* a parlor game and most emphatically it is not a weapon to be used in a general contest of 'one-upmanship.' " Psychiatrists, psychologists, and other professionals can use it as a "deep" psychological test.[5] Some industries have also used the test to screen job applicants.

The scientific basis upon which Dr. Lüscher built his test is one more bit of evidence supporting the claim that the encoding and decoding of color messages are similar enough in all people to make color a significant communication language.

Color Preferences

The Lüscher test shows and is in fact based upon the premise that not all persons like the same colors equally well, and under changing conditions, an individual may alter his or her preference ratings. Studies have shown that certain colors are perennial favorites, however. Blue and red are by far the favorite colors of most adults. Green usually comes in third and purple fourth with yellow and orange vying for last place.

Ratings from another set of tests show that women tend to prefer different colors than do men. The top three preferences of adult women were red, purple, and blue, in that order. For men, the favorites were blue, red, and purple. Fourth, fifth and sixth places were the same for both sexes — green, orange, and yellow.[6]

Age seems to make a difference, however. Babies are attracted to pure hues only. Their mothers may choose pastel pinks, blues, yellows, and greens for the nursery, but they'll reach for bright red almost every time. Young children seem to have difficulty distinguishing orange and purple from red, yellow, and blue. Orange is frequently confused with either red or yellow. Tell preschool children that an object is purple and not blue, and they'll begin identifying blue objects as purple.[7] Between the ages of three and four their overall preference for red gives way to yellow.

By ages thirteen and fourteen, adult preferences begin to form. Girls like red, boys blue. However, students ages eighteen through twenty-one showed a preference for dark colors except for clothing. There is some indication that pink ranks high among adults between the ages of fifty and sixty. Naturally this does not often show itself in their choice of colors for their home exteriors, cars, or even clothes. Tests prove, time and time again, that the colors, designs, and patterns selected as favorites in test situations do not carry over into the subject's product purchases.

Obviously, there are other factors involved. Research done by the Color Research Institute in the 1950s showed that persons with higher incomes and educations tended to prefer delicate colors. Persons whose incomes placed them at poverty level or whose educations left them illiterate preferred brilliant colors. Louis Cheskin, director of the institute, concluded that people who have many emotional outlets available to them or who have the ability to purchase emotional satisfaction select the diluted and neutral colors. People whose lack of education and/or low income provides them limited opportunities for emotional outlets prefer pure hues, especially those from the warm end of the spectrum.[8]

Other studies seem to show that geography also plays a role in color preference. Societies that live near or in the tropics seem to prefer bright colors, white, and dark shades close to black. Those from the temperate climates prefer muted shades or pastels except for bright accents. Scientists have linked this to the human perception of color. In tropical areas, the angle of the sun's rays makes shadows distinct. Therefore, people who live there are not accustomed to seeing hues in other saturations and brilliances and don't select them for art or clothes. Those in northern Europe, Canada, and the northern United States are accustomed to seeing shadows that blur at the edges and are therefore attuned to more muted tones and tints.[9]

This may account in part for some of the ethnic preferences recorded by investigators. A certain orange-red was the runaway favorite of Italians and Mexicans. Another shade of red was preferred by Central Americans, and a third by Slavs. Scandinavians, however, liked bright blues and greens.[10]

Your home environment might also affect your choice. People who live in the mountains seem to like bright cool or neutral cool tones. Grass green is not particularly popular in rural areas, where presumably people see a lot of it. But for those from inner city areas, green ranks high on their list of favorites.[11]

Color and Visibility

Because the fast pace of our lives often makes visibility of a distant sign a matter of life or death, many studies have been done regarding the visibility of color pigments on various backgrounds. The traditional contrast of black on white was found to rate a poor sixth. In first place was black on yellow, the color of most U.S. cautionary road signs. Second was green on white; and third, red on white — combinations infrequently used in this country. Blue on white ranked fourth; and white on blue, fifth. Informative signs using the latter combination have become more common since the introduction of graphic symbols to identify places for international participants at the 1968 Olympic Games in Mexico City. Filling the last four slots on the top ten visibility list are (7) yellow on black, (8) white on red, (9) white on green, now used to route traffic on American interstate highways, and (10) white on black.[12] Combinations of red and blue, red and green, and blue and green pigments are nearly illegible.

Yellow filtered lighting provides the best environment for good visibility. Orange-yellow illumination ranks second; yellow-green, third; and green, fourth. Deep blue and violet lighting were least desirable. Blue light made focusing of the human eye difficult and caused objects to appear blurred or surrounded by halos. Red light was discovered to be useful in extremely dim environments. When the human eye must adapt from darkness to light in order to read dials and gauges in ships, airplanes, and control rooms, red light allows excellent acuity.[13] Unfortunately, conditions for good visibility (in a factory or office, for example) may have psychological side effects that interfere with productivity or human relations. This issue will be considered later in the chapter.

Color Selection and Marketing

For years merchants have realized that the appearance of the product or package in which it is wrapped is one of the four pillars of success in marketing (the other three being product quality, price, and promotion effectiveness).[14] Unless an item looks good, no one who has a choice will buy it.

But to package products by relying on color preference ratings alone is to consider only part of the psychology of consumer sales. The need for visibility must be weighed, as must the image retention value and the association of colors and products packaged within. Yellow, as we have seen, appeals to few people but ranks high in visibility. As one color engineer pointed out, Yellow Cabs are not as common as one may think. They simply stand out among other automobiles. Blue ranks high in preference ratings but is hard to see at a distance and escapes from the mind easily too. Orange-red ranks outstanding in both attention-getting value and retention level; but except in tints of peach, it doesn't appeal to many people. Peach, on the other hand, loses impact and is hard to remember.[15]

A study by the DuPont Corporation showed that 78 percent of supermarket purchases were made as a result of package design and eye appeal. Another study attributed 53 percent of drugstore sales to impulse buying.[16]

When we go shopping, we are thinking about the products within the wrappers, and our minds seek packages that are psychologically associated with the products inside. Pictures of the assembled or prepared product are always effective, but even then coloring can be important. Blue, for example, helps sell hardware. No metal is naturally blue, yet we have been sold on the fact that blue blades are the best steel and that good hardware has a blue tinge to it. Peach and pink, on the other hand, sell cosmetics. For elegance a little gold may be added but not bright yellow.[17] However, don't expect men to select products in pink or pastel wrappers. "A man wants to feel like a man," according to the manufacturer of one product in a deep-toned package.

The Color Research Institute carried out one experiment using three different detergent boxes. One was predominantly yellow, the second blue, and the third blue with splashes of yellow. Subjects were given one of each of the boxes without being told that the contents of all three were identical. They were asked to take them home, try them, and report their evaluations of the detergent inside. The majority of the users adjudged the detergent in the yellow boxes to be "too strong." That in the blue boxes "left the clothes dingy." The contents of the blue and yellow boxes, however, were "fine" and even "wonderful."[18]

An orange-red is easily identified with the kitchen and will help sell food packages, but the same color is too strident to be considered for living room or bedroom items. Deep green has been found effective in jewelry sales but not for food packages.

For consumer appeal, foods need to be wrapped in appetizing colors — warm red, pale yellow, clear green, peach, tan, and golden brown. People consider yellow-green, purple, and gray unsavory. This attitude has caused microwave oven manufacturers to design all sorts of devices for browning meats. Beef and pork cooked in a microwave oven without browning are just as nutritious but don't have the psychological appeal of golden brown portions. Psychologically, pink has been judged the "sweetest" color.

Libby's hit the jackpot when they selected a crusty brown–colored label with a touch of red and yellow for their Deep-Brown Beans. Another rich brown shade with similar accents has sold a lot of coffee. Consumers associate the color with the prepared product. They never truly match, but the ideal sells the package. Brown has also been used effectively by a number of tobacco companies.[19]

One of the long time standards on supermarket shelves is the box containing Betty Crocker cake mix. General Mills adopted the package in 1954 and is not about to abandon its bonanza. A close-up photo of the prepared cake, ideally colored, provides the background for an oval red spoon containing the logo. Ovals are more pleasing to the subconscious mind than shapes with sharp angles. Betty Crocker red is the kitchen shade of red mentioned earlier. When General Mills first introduced the box, sales of all cake mixes doubled in the next two years. The sale of its Betty Crocker mixes, however, quadrupled in the same period of time.[20]

Selective color application will even sell telephone calls. When the phone booths in Grand Central Station were repainted from olive green to bright red, the number of calls originating from those phones increased 600 percent in the next two weeks.

The Clothing Industry's Marketing Psychology

Selling clothes requires a different set of color guidelines. The garment industry knows what it's doing when it promotes a new shade as the color for the season. Many people want to stay in style. Yet the season's promoted color may not be one an individual prefers, or even one that flatters his or her figure and natural coloring.

In his book *The Hidden Persuaders,* Vance Packard records the sales record of three identically styled dresses. One was made up in turquoise, another in fuchsia, and a third chartreuse. Louis Cheskin, whose Color Research Institute made the study, reported that only 20 percent of the women who bought the dress selected it in turquoise, which the majority indicated was their natural preference. Fuchsia was purchased by 40 percent because they had been told it "would do something" for their complexion, and 40 percent bought the season's vogue, chartreuse. One woman actually said the color made her want to vomit, but when she was reminded that it was the latest style in color, she ended up buying it.[21]

There's no question but that certain colors are more flattering to a person than others. Generally the rule is "complementary is complimentary." Colors from the complementary or opposite side of the color wheel from one's natural color are the most flattering. A golden blonde, therefore, looks good in blue. Brunettes find warm colors from the yellow family—beige, light brown, and cocoa—most complimentary. A redhead looks striking in aqua, but his or her hair appears rusty next to red.

A drab complexion may gain sparkle with white near the face, but you need to be a raven-haired blushing bride to look your best in all white. For blondes, too much white seems to drain them of color and only adds to their girth. Black is psychologically the worst color a person can wear, but by contrast, it makes a plain woman more beautiful. To help sell more clothes, some quality stores are now giving their sales personnel training in the analysis of natural coloring so that they can recommend flattering colors. Professional color analysts command high salaries.

But natural color preference cannot be ignored. Cheskin tells of one woman who bought two coats, a blue one because it was the "in" color that fall and another in beige, her favorite color. "In four weeks she had worn the blue coat three times and the beige twenty-one times.[22] Thus it appears that the clothing industry is designing to sell us three times the clothes we need, so that we can be in vogue, compliment our natural coloring, and satisfy our own preferences.

A good friend chooses her daily wardrobe using a fourth guideline, her mood and the weather. On drab, overcast days or when she's feeling down, she wears bright, warm colors to give herself a lift and communicate cheerfulness to others. On a bright sunny day when she's in high spirits, she wears cool, subdued colors.

Color Names and Human Perception

Color consists of visible wavelengths that blend into one another without perceptible breaks. Humans determine the divisions, labeling the hues, tints, and shades in any way they please. Chapter 1 pointed out how a group's need for color distinctions affects its vocabulary and perceptual acuity. Newton's color circle consisted of red, orange, yellow, green, blue, indigo, and violet. He tied these seven colors to the seven then-known planets and the diatonic musical scale. Artists, who deal with object colors, will tell you they mix their palettes from the primaries—red, yellow, and blue—and add black and white for shades and tints. Physicists working with colored lights have the additive primaries of red, blue, and green and the subtractive primaries—magenta, cyan, and yellow. Most Americans today divide the spectrum into six colors—purple, blue, green, yellow, orange, and red.

Some highly localized African societies, who have had little interaction with outsiders, divide the spectrum quite differently. The Bassa of Liberia separate the color world into *hui* and *ziza*. *Hui* is the violet, blue, blue-green portion, while *ziza* refers to yellow-green, yellow, orange, and red.[23]

The Shona of Rhodesia have a three-way split: Orange, red, violet, and blue-violet are all *cipsuka*. Blue and blue-green are *citema,* and yellow-green and yellow are *cicena*. Of course, the Shona speaker is able to perceive variations within the basic divisions just as Americans can; but when he looks at the rainbow, it seems to naturally divide into the portions for which his language has convenient labels.[24]

In the United States, children's color perception is generally controlled by the Binney and Smith Corporation, the Crayola makers.

Defective Color Vision

As stated earlier, defective color vision affects about 8 percent of the world's males and almost 1 percent of the females.[25] Normal observers are trichromats, which means that they can match all colors with mixtures of three colored lights—blue, green, and red.

The most common color vision problem is known as anomalous trichronism. This means that the subject sees all colors but not in a normal way. He can match any color with a mixture of three colored lights but will require different amounts of these lights than the normal person will. If his color vision is green weak (the most common type), he will need more than the normal amount of green in a green-red mixture in order to match a given yellow. Other anomalous trichromats have weaknesses for blue or red.

About 2 percent of white males and 0.03 percent of females are dichromats.[26] A dichromat can match all colors with mixtures of only two primary lights, most commonly yellow and blue. Such persons are red-green color-blind. Dark reds, greens, and grays are confused and a natural gray is seen instead of blue-green and purple. People with this deficiency have difficulty finding bright red strawberries among their green leaves or determining when lean beef in a frying pan has turned brown. A rarer color vision problem is that of the dichromat who does not see yellow and blue.

It is is interesting to note that although color blindness occurs predominantly in males, their daughters are carriers of the gene. While they may not be color blind themselves, these women frequently give birth to sons who have the same deficiencies as their grandfathers had.

The Physical Illusions of Color

We've all seen drawings called optical illusions in which lines seem to curve or straighten, shorten or lengthen as a result of their proximity to other lines and figures. Color sends its own set of illusional messages to the brain.

In a warehouse where briar pipes were stored and shipped, employees frequently complained that the black metal boxes containing the pipes were so heavy as to cause back strain. When the boxes were painted green, employees commented upon the light weight of the new boxes.[27]

A more scientific experiment asked people to move one of two crates to tables across a room. The two crates were the same size and weight; but one was painted blue, the other dark brown. Subjects always selected the blue crate because it gave the impression of being lighter. Subjects also had a choice of moving the crate to a red table or a blue one, both equally distant. They almost invariably went to the red table because it appeared to be at least a step closer.

Because the focus of the human eye is not the same for all hues, different colors appear to be near or far, large or small. The illusions of color can be so strong as to overrule our judgments of depth, perspective, and visual orientation.

Not only are single colors capable of creating an illusion, but against different colored backgrounds, colors can be distorted or induced. That is, the background color can alter our perception of the color of objects or figures set against it.

Those of us who have normal color vision perceive colors in pairs, for example, red and green, yellow and blue. Instead of seeing each color individually, we actually see complementary colors together through one particular part of the optic nerve. As a result, the mind may receive a false message known as a color afterimage.[28]

Try this experiment. From a sheet of bright red paper cut a one-inch disk. Lay it on a table and stare at it for thirty seconds. Then shift your eyes to a sheet of white paper you've placed on the table beside it. Wait a few seconds. Suddenly you'll see a cyan green afterimage. Try the same thing with a bright yellow disk. The afterimage will be blue. With a green disk, you'll see a magenta-red afterimage. The explanation given by most scientists is that staring at a bright color spot for a time fatigues the color receptors so that when you shift your gaze to the white paper, the fatigued receptors can send only a weak signal to the brain, the complement of that color.

Afterimage was discovered to be the cause of a meat market nearly going out of business. In an effort to spruce up his store, the owner of a meat and a sausage shop painted the walls a bright, cheery yellow. To his dismay, his business went straight downhill in the following weeks. Even previously regular customers stopped buying his products. A color expert resolved his problem by suggesting that he redecorate once again, this time applying bright blue-green paint. The results were unbelievable. Within a few weeks business had reached an all-time high.[29]

Here is what had happened. The eyes of customers entering the bright yellow shop were attracted by the decor. Then when they looked down at the meat display, the afterimage, blue, made the meat appear old and spoiled. Bright blue-green walls, which attracted attention because they'd been freshly painted, produced a bright red afterimage.

Color can even affect the sense of taste. A study conducted at Colorado State University showed that the color of what a person eats or drinks plays an important role in determining how it tastes. Yellow was discovered to decrease the subjects' threshold of sensitivity to sweet tastes. Green, on the other hand, increased sensitivity for sweets. In other words, candy tinted yellow does not seem as sweet as does the same candy colored green. Both yellow and green decreased subjects' sour taste threshold, and red diminished their sensitivity to bitter tastes.[30] Thus sour lemon- and lime-colored foods do not seem as sour as the same foods in other colors, and bitter red medicine seems less bitter than the same medicine with another tint.

Samuel G. Hibbing, a lighting engineer, invited a number of guests to a dinner that was a social and gastronomic disaster but a powerful illustration of the effects of color. Hibbing arranged to have the best foods served to a group of interesting and unusual people. He even arranged for fine background music. Nothing was overlooked. Everything was perfect, except the lighting. Hibbing filtered the room illumination to eliminate all colors except red and green. The big, juicy steaks looked gray. The celery was pink. The chocolate dessert, yellow. The guests appeared sad and unhealthy. One by one they lost their appetites. Some became physically ill and had to leave.[31]

The Curative Powers of Color

Properly used, colors can also help to make people well. But judging from the number of years it took for hospitals to become white and sterile, it will probably be the twenty-first century before color is employed in a truly therapeutic role.

Using color to cure is not a new concept. History records it being used by the ancient Egyptians and classical Greeks, but modern medicine took off in another direction.[32]

Joseph Lister spent most of his life trying to convince the medical profession of the need for antiseptic conditions. Clearly the need was great. Hospitals were breeding grounds for bacteria that killed millions through infection. By about 1885, doctors were beginning to listen, and for the next thirty years hospital employees chased bacteria with a vengeance: Ornate walls and woodwork could appear to be clean when they weren't. Bring in the plasterers and painters with white enamel. Patients' and employees' personal clothing is certainly unsanitary. Lock it away till they're ready to leave. To be sterile, cloth must be boiled. Get bleached muslin for uniforms, gowns, and bed linen. Replace those wooden beds with metal ones, enameled white. Metal pans and pails rust. Throw them out together with china dishes, which harbor germs in the cracks. Get porcelain-glazed utensils. No, not gray, white!

By the 1950s our hospitals were so sterile, cold, and white that patients literally suffered from a lack of sensory stimulation. No one is suggesting abandoning antiseptic conditions. But modern materials and cleaning products make sanitation possible without everything being a cold white. Blue has been suggested for the walls of operating theaters and recovery rooms. Its sedative qualities would help calm and assure patients. Warm, bright colors, especially in intensive care units would make patients there feel more cheerful and eager to get well. The mentally depressed also need stimulating hues, but nervous and excitable patients would do best in rooms with cool colors.[33]

Curing and alleviating pain by the application of color-filtered lighting has many supporters, some of them respected physicians; but much more research needs to be done. Evidence already supports the belief that green or turquoise light reduces the pain for burn patients and promotes healing. Since using this light in no way interferes with other, standard burn treatment, further experimentation is probably ongoing in many burn centers.[34] Blue light seems to help patients relax and sleep without drugs. Sufferers of "thumping" headaches and high blood pressure caused by nervous tension also report relief while relaxing under blue illumination.[35]

Red-orange light, it is said, helps people with respiratory ailments, asthma, and emphysema.[36] Red light aids sufferers of skin diseases, eczema, urticaria, rheumatoid arthritis, and sciatica—as long as they don't have elevated body temperature or blood pressure.[37] In fact, some people believe that there is a specific colored light that can help stimulate each of the body's glands when such aid is needed.[38] Research is clearly needed in this field.

In 1980 researchers found that a certain shade of pink in large doses is physically debilitating and calming on people who are emotionally upset or violent. When paint of that color, known as Baker-Miller pink, was tested in jails and other correctional institutions, the results were consistent and impressive. Previously aggressive and violent inmates were calmed within minutes of being placed in cells painted with that color. Alexander G. Schauss, director of the American Institute for Biosocial Research in Tacoma, Washington, tested its effects on himself by using an eighteen-by-twenty-four–inch cardboard sheet of the pink. He found that his heartbeat, his pulse, and his blood pressure all dropped more rapidly upon exposure to that shade after a period of intentional hyperexcitement than when viewing any other color.[39] The implications of this discovery are indeed exciting.

Color Psychology and Interior Decor

Reports of the positive effects of the scientific application of color in shops, restaurants, churches, schools, and factories throughout the world are both plentiful and consistent. A few certainly bear repeating.

A New York–based color engineer, Elizabeth Banning, accepted a West Coast assignment to help redecorate a San Francisco shop where business was bad. Upon arrival, she discovered the shop exterior was painted in eight different colors. The same colors were repeated inside. Banning analyzed the merchandise stocked and the nature of the customers for whom it was designed. Then she proposed repainting both the interior and exterior in Windsor blue. She also recommended the use of soft pink lighting. Her suggestions were carried out and business improved immediately.

Another contract challenged her to find appropriate colors for a chain of fast-food restaurants. Leisurely eating may be better for digestion, but the restaurant owners were interested in fast customer turnover. Banning suggested a South American flavor and color scheme with bright, busy colors.

Think about the colors used by the fast-food chains in your area. There's not a cool color to be seen. In the Midwest, Wendy's, Colonel Sanders, McDonald's, Hardee's, A & W, Burger King—all keep people moving with reds, oranges, and rich browns.

For a more expensive, elegant restaurant Banning recommended soft harmonious tones of purple and magenta accented with lemon yellow. When toned down even more by the use of candlelight, customers were encouraged to linger for the evening.

An East Coast factory gave its cafeteria a face-lift by painting its previously peach-colored walls a light blue. Patrons responded with complaints of being cold and frequently entered wearing sweaters and coats although the thermostat was set at a level generally considered comfortable. When the room was painted peach again, complaints stopped.[40]

Some readers may remember a film named *Hell Fighters* in which John Wayne played an aging oil-well firefighter turned member of the board of a large oil company. In one scene, Wayne was subjected to a session with a color consultant proposing possible colors for the restrooms of company service stations. Wayne couldn't care less, but the actor playing the consultant showed that the script writers did their homework. Painting the restrooms a soft willow green, the consultant said, will make them seem soothing and restful. Royal blue would be preferred by chic women, but flaming heart red would make people hurry.

For restrooms where obnoxious graffiti is a problem, building managers often request that the walls be painted dark shades, assuming, presumably, that wall artists will be discouraged when their work is less noticeable. Experience shows that they don't stop. They simply become more creative in their choice of writing implements. When the walls are painted with clean pastel tints instead, they remain unmarked longer. No one seems to want to be the first to defile an innocent, clean surface.

Another often retold story concerns the redecoration of an old, but well-established church. The interior had been dark. The walls had dark oak paneling, and deep red cushions covered the pews. The minister and congregation leaders decided on a modern airy appearance. Walls were painted white, and blue carpeting and pew cushions were installed. The difference was impressive. The auditorium, the nave, seemed to have nearly doubled in size, and in the white chancel, the minister seemed small and less imposing. Attendance at regular services dropped, to the dismay of all concerned. Members were heard to remark that the services seemed cold and unsatisfying. Yet only the colors had been changed. The minister, the organist, the music, and order of service – all had continued in traditional manner.

A German research team wondered whether the appearance of children's playrooms had any effect on the IQs of the children who played inside. To find out, they assigned one group of children to a suite of brightly colored rooms and another group to rooms painted white, black, and brown. Immediately the IQ scores of children in the "happy rooms" increased by twelve points while those in the "ugly rooms" dropped fourteen points.[41]

The behavior and performance of children in three new schools was measured and carefully observed over a two-year period to see the effect of differing colors in their environment. One school was painted in the traditional way, with buff walls and white ceilings. The second school was left unpainted. The third had been painted using color dynamics. The corridors were yellow with gray doors and baseboards. North-facing classrooms were pale rose; south-facing rooms, blue or green. In all classrooms the front walls were darker shades than the side walls. Chalkboards were a nonglare green. The art room was painted a neutral gray so as not to clash with the children's creative use of color. The children were followed through their kindergarten and first-grade years in these schools. Students attending the colorful school showed the greatest improvement in social skills, health and safety habits, language arts, arithmetic, social studies, science, and music. The least improvement was recorded for children in the unpainted school. Those in the traditionally painted building ranked second.[42]

Since bright warm colors stimulate, it has been suggested that the best place for creative thinking might be a red room. But for visual and mental concentration to carry out creative ideas, a room painted in soft cool colors is much preferred. A pastel blue or green room might best allow attention to be directed inward. Brain-damaged children, however, often need completely gray environments. Otherwise they become too highly stimulated to learn anything.

As might be expected, color psychology has invaded athletic team locker rooms. When Amos Alonzo Stagg was head football coach in Chicago he had his team's dressing room painted a relaxing blue for use during rest periods. For pep talks, he called the men together in a brilliant red anteroom. Knute Rockne tried to stimulate his players by using a red-walled locker room, while the opponents were lulled in restful blue quarters.[43]

Before OSHA color symbolism added bright accents, many factories were dull, gray places. A few, however, have discovered that color on walls and machinery can improve production and employee morale, decrease absenteeism, and reduce accidents and waste.

A London factory, confronted with high absenteeism among its female employees, had its plant examined by a color engineer. Iron gray walls and blue lighting were discovered to make employees look sickly, especially when they looked at themselves in a mirror. Although there was no proof that this caused the women to become physically ill or call in sick, repainting seemed to be worth a try. To offset the blue lighting, the gray walls were painted warm beige. Miraculously, absenteeism was no longer a problem.[44]

In another factory, employees were in the habit of standing around a drinking fountain and visiting. When the soft green walls of the area were repainted vivid orange, workers took a drink and left.[45]

Employees of a radio station, highly trained and skilled individuals, were in a state of constant tension with one another. Internal bickering and failure to cooperate disrupted performances and came to a head when two talented persons threatened to resign. The manager, who had recently heard a lecture on the benefits of natural light, suddenly realized that the pink fluorescent lighting, installed for its aesthetic appearance, might be a problem. He immediately had the pink tubes replaced with natural ones. Within a week tempers ceased to flare, cooperation returned, and the resignations were withdrawn.[46]

Black Friars Bridge in London with its extensive black iron work was well known for its frequent suicides. When the city fathers painted it bright green, they were surprised to discover that suicides declined by more than one third.[47]

Considered individually, such reports attributing changes in human behavior to changes in color can easily be challenged. In most cases, conditions were neither scientifically controlled nor measured. Yet most people are convinced by the plentitude and consistency of these reports.

Using Color Communication Principles

Color consultants have worked apparent miracles in business and industry, but they also charge higher rates than most of us can afford. Nevertheless, the messages communicated by color in our homes and personal lives are loud and deserve analysis. Fortunately, the intelligent selection of colors for clothing and home interiors does not usually require a color expert. An understanding of the principles in this chapter, combined with an assessment of available lighting and the kind of activity that will take place in a given room, should result in a comfortable selection.

When choosing clothing colors, one must decide what is most important: wearing the season's fashionable color, complimenting one's natural coloring, being comfortable with a favorite color, or trying to affect oneself and others with color.

Finally, we must not forget the "personalities" and "associates" identified for each of the basic colors. These psychological and symbolic qualities should help us to select appropriate colors for communicating a particular message and to understand how the colors we see communicate to us.

Activities

1. Examine a copy of *The Lüscher Color Test* by Max Lüscher (Pocket Books, 1969), a relatively inexpensive paperback, which is widely available at book and department stores. Try it on yourself and a group of friends. Report their reactions.

2. Try wearing clothes with colors chosen to complement your moods and/or the weather. (For example, if you are depressed or the weather is gloomy, wear a bright outfit.) Do you notice any difference in yourself? In the reactions of others?

3. Examine the colors associated with various holidays. What symbolism is involved?

4. Research the color symbolism used in most Christian churches. What concepts are symbolized by the various colors used in the vestments?

5. Collect magazine ads to illustrate a booklet in which you summarize the use of color to sell merchandise.

6. Design a package and a series of visual ads to sell a product or your own selection or creation. The design and colors must suit both the product and the intended consumers.

7. Read the book *Color Me Beautiful* by Carole Jackson (Ballantine Books, 1980), available in most public and many school libraries. Using the author's guidelines, determine your own "seasonal palette" by analyzing your hair and eye coloring and skin tone.

8. Examine the colors used in various restaurants, or in schools, or in another category of publicly used buildings. If possible, talk to someone who made the color decisions and find out why certain choices were made.

9. Experiment with colored foods on your family. For example, use food coloring to make mashed potatoes blue or spaghetti green. Report the reaction of each person served.

Or divide a batch of taffy or divinity candy into three bowls. To the first add pink food coloring, to the second green, to the third yellow. When the candy is finished, ask people to sample each for sweetness. Is it true that most people think pink is the sweetest?

10. Read the poem "My Mother Taught Me Purple" by Evelyn Tooley Hunt (see Appendix). Discuss the use of color symbolism in the poem with your class.

11. If you've never seen a test for abnormalities in color vision, ask your ophthalmologist, optometrist, family physician, or school nurse to show you one next time you visit. If they have the facilities for actual testing, you'll find the procedure more than interesting.

Notes

1. Hal Hellman, *The Art and Science of Color* (New York: McGraw-Hill, 1967), p. 92.
2. Faber Birren, *Color, Form and Space* (New York: Reinhold Publishing, 1961), p. 60.
3. Lawrence B. Rosenfeld and Jean M. Civikly, *With Words Unspoken* (New York: Holt, Rinehart and Winston, 1976), p. 170.
4. Max Lüscher, *The Lüscher Color Test,* ed. and trans. Ian Scott (New York: Random House Pocket Book Edition, 1969).
5. Max Lüscher, *Color Test,* back of paperback cover.
6. Herbert Paschel, *The First Book of Color* (New York: Franklin Watts, 1959), p. 38.
7. Louis Cheskin, *How to Predict What People Will Buy* (New York: Liveright Publishing, 1957), p. 232.
8. Cheskin, *How to Predict,* p. 177.
9. Elizabeth Burris-Meyer, *Color and Design in the Decorative Arts* (New York: Prentice-Hall, 1940), p. 37.
10. Cheskin, *How to Predict,* pp. 189, 201.
11. Judee K. Burgoon and Thomas Saine, *The Unspoken Dialogue: An Introduction to Nonverbal Communication* (Boston: Houghton Mifflin Co., 1978), p. 106.
12. Paschel, *First Book,* p. 39.
13. Birren, *Color, Form,* pp. 44–45.
14. Cheskin, *How to Predict,* p. 26.
15. Ibid., pp. 120, 188.
16. Howard Ketcham, *Color Planning for Business and Industry* (New York: Harper and Brothers, 1958), p. 74.
17. Cheskin, *How to Predict,* pp. 175, 223.
18. Vance Packard, *The Hidden Persuaders* (New York: David McKay Co., 1957), p. 16.
19. Cheskin, *How to Predict,* pp. 184–87.
20. Ibid., pp. 73, 162.
21. Packard, *Hidden Persuaders,* pp. 126–27.
22. Cheskin, *How to Predict,* p. 226.
23. H. A. Gleason, Jr., *An Introduction to Descriptive Linguistics* (New York: Holt, Rinehart and Winston, 1961), pp. 4–5.
24. Ibid.
25. Clarence Rainwater, *Light and Color* (New York: Golden, 1971), p. 113.

26. Ibid., p. 115.
27. Linda Clark, *The Ancient Art of Color Therapy* (New York: Pocket Books, 1975), pp. 55–56.
28. Hellman, *Science of Color,* p. 126.
29. Cheskin, *How to Predict,* p. 232.
30. John E. Gibson, "Truth *Is* Stranger Than Fiction," *Family Weekly,* 2 January 1977, p. 8.
31. Cheskin, *How to Predict,* pp. 231–32.
32. Clark, *Color Therapy,* p. 66.
33. Ibid., pp. 56–57.
34. Ibid., pp. 100–101.
35. Ibid., pp. 17, 120–26.
36. Ibid., pp. 111–14.
37. Ibid., pp. 105–10.
38. Ibid., p. 67.
39. John Feltman, "Healing with Light and Sound," *Prevention,* June 1981, pp. 86–91.
40. Cheskin, *How to Predict,* p. 231.
41. I. Silden, "Psychological Effects of Office Planning, *Mainliner,* December 1973, pp. 30–34.
42. Ketcham, *Color Planning,* p. 97.
43. Ibid., p. 88.
44. Clark, *Color Therapy,* p. 55.
45. Ibid., p. 59.
46. Ibid., p. 39.
47. Ibid., p. 56.

11

And the Feat Goes On

READERS WHO THINK the range of nonverbal communication has been covered in the last ten chapters aren't using much imagination. We've examined only a small portion of a huge, multifaceted subject. A single trip to the library can put you in touch with volumes regarding additional, related nonverbal languages. This chapter will suggest a few you might find interesting to learn more about.

Pheromones and the Olfactory Sense

The messages conveyed by the sense of smell are only beginning to be known, as you may remember reading in chapter 2. In recent years, scientists have given special attention to a group of odors they call pheromones. Pheromones are the odoriferous sex attractants excreted by animals, which affect the behavior of other members of the same species. Recent studies have isolated a male scent, called androsterone, in hogs and wild boars. Now available commercially in spray form, androsterone helps pork producers calm nervous sows for breeding or artificial insemination.[1]

Of greater interest is the discovery that androsterone is also produced by men. Most women given a sample were able to recognize an odor to the substance, which they described as pleasant or musky. Only half of the men queried said they could detect any odor at all. In 1978, researchers at the University of Birmingham, England, published a report indicating that humans unknowingly exposed to the chemical seldom notice it but react with significant changes in social behavior. It does not function as an aphrodisiac, but humans become happier and more friendly when it is present.[2] In England today, pure androsterone is being sold as a spray for men called

Attract. In the United States, Jovan is producing Andron for men and a slightly different formula also called Andron, for women.[3] Both, they say, are blends based on pheromone formulas.

Robert Henkin, a biologist at Georgetown University Medical Center, is researching the use of fragrances to reduce anxiety and stress in workers. He believes that scientific use of fragrances might improve efficiency in offices and factories and lower the incidence of violence and aggression in correctional institutions.[4]

Synchrony

Another human phenomenon noted by many current researchers is synchrony, the unconscious way in which human beings synchronize their rhythms and movements as they interact. In the early 1960s, William Condon, a kinesicist, was analyzing, frame by frame, films of people conversing. As humans talk, Condon discovered, their every body movement down to the last eye blink is in sync with the words.[5] Not only do a speaker's movements follow the rhythm, but his attentive listeners follow as well.

The chapter on kinesics in this book noted how people who tend to agree with one another in a group often assume congruent or mirror postures, but Condon's discoveries go far beyond this. Infants will sync with a human voice regardless of the language being spoken, but adults seem to be attuned to the rhythms of their own language and culture and respond to them more adeptly. Autistic children, schizophrenics, and people with Parkinson's disease, epilepsy, or aphasia have been found to be out of sync, not only with others but even with themselves as they speak. When Condon wired a number of interacting subjects to an EEG (an electroencephalograph) and recorded their brain waves as they talked, he was amazed to find that even the configurations of the recordings swung in synchrony, not perfectly so but together nonetheless.[6]

Another researcher accompanied a silent film of children at play with carefully selected rock music. So well synchronized were their movements that some viewers found it hard to believe that the children had not heard the same rhythm when the film was made. Frame by frame examination revealed that one very active little girl was the director and orchestrator of the playground rhythm.[7]

An entirely separate research study shows that women living together in dormitories and sorority houses for long periods of time even tend to synchronize their menstrual periods.[8]

The fact that interactional synchrony varies, sometimes being highly pronounced and sometimes only faintly perceptible, seems to reflect subtle but important variations in human relationships. Psychologists and therapists are, therefore, continuing the research in hopes of using it in their work.

Clothing and Accessories

Much more obvious, and easily studied firsthand, are the messages we convey via the clothes we select to wear. The dozens of available variables in clothing offer interesting possibilities for questionnaires and reaction inventories.

Choice of style, for example, sends a loud message to others. Does a young man most often wear tennis shoes, boots, moccasins, slip-ons, brogues, or wing-tips? Does he like to wear blue jeans, cords, tailored slacks, or suit pants? Does a woman prefer her dresses flowing, figure revealing, or tailored? For casual wear, does she like a full skirt, a straight skirt, pants, or jeans? And with that choice, does she prefer a T-shirt, halter top, smock top, classic shirt, or ruffled blouse?

General interest in clothes might also be surveyed. Is a person interested in the latest styles and colors? How much do cut and fit matter? How important is comfort? Would one prefer a few designer and quality outfits or several economy separates to mix and match?

What colors does a person wear most frequently? Bright warm colors? Cool greens and blues? Muted earth tones? Solid colors only? Tweeds and textures? Plaids and prints? Varied shades of the same color? Dark tones with bright accents?

What fabrics are one's favorites—denims, corduroys, wool flannels, lightweight cotton blends, light cotton knits, gauze sheers, soft acetates and dacrons, polyester knits, heavy wool knits?

To what extent does the subject conform in his or her choice of clothes? How do people who have to wear uniforms feel while in uniform? Do they feel any different while dressed in clothes of their own choice? To what degree does a given person's selection of clothing express individuality?

The results of such surveys might be matched with each subject's self-analysis or personality characteristics, social attitudes, and group memberships to see what patterns evolve.

Another interesting investigation might probe the decoded messages conveyed by clothing. Photographs of faceless models wearing a wide variety of clothes might be shown to people representing various age groups, asking them to describe the type of person who would wear such clothes to school.

On the international level, people of many cultures have not adopted what we call Western dress. An examination of specific costumes and the reasons behind their continuation in different societies will reveal male and female standards, religious laws, cultural mores for variations in marital status and those for mourning, availability and use of materials, and adaptation to climatic variation. As an interesting start, one might investigate the Aymara women's polleras and felt bowler, the stiff stovepipe hats worn in Peru and Bolivia, the Japanese kimono and obi, the Hindu sari, or the kavai worn by women on the island of Karpathos, Greece. The white jellaba and turban seen in the Arab world on Muslim men and the hide-all clothing of the women who follow Islamic law also offer interesting research possibilities.

Manual Sign Languages

Hundreds of nonverbal signs and symbol systems have been designed to meet special human needs. Sign language is used when speech or hearing is impaired or impossible or when a common spoken language does not exist. The manual (deaf) alphabet, like Braille for the blind, is not a separate nonverbal language but simply a set of symbols for the phonemes (individual identifiable sounds) of a spoken language. The same is true of Morse code, whether sent by flashing lights, sound impulses, or flags. Semaphore flags can also convey alphabet equivalents.

Most of America's fifteen million hearing impaired citizens use a system of signing based not on the alphabet but on concepts or ideas. For greater efficiency, hand signals are often accompanied by facial expressions. The message "I am not going to comprehend" becomes just four signs: "I (negative) (future) understand." The negative sign may be conveyed by either a hand motion or a facial expression. *Comprehend* and all other synonyms of *understand* use the same sign. As the needs of the handicapped are recognized, more and more noncredit courses are being offered and books written to teach signing to the public.

The American Plains Indians developed a sign language for an entirely different reason. Each tribe had a well-developed oral language, but they lacked a common medium of communication. At the time the white settlers arrived, some thirty to thirty-five tribes inhabited the region, each with its own language. Some — like the Commanche, Arapaho, Kiowa, and Blackfoot — were nomadic hunters. Others — such as the Pawnee, Hidatsa, Mandan, and Arikara — were agrarian but liked meat with their vegetables and also needed hides, horns, and other animal products. Thus all Plains Indians became hunters at certain times of the year. This meant they often encountered bands, families, or tribes who did not speak their language but with whom they wished to communicate. By necessity, then, they developed a system of several hundred hand signs and gestures with which they could identify themselves, their needs, and desires. Some Indians became very skillful in using sign language and employed it within their own language group while stalking animals or whenever silence was to their advantage.

Anthropologists have declared the American Indian sign language to be the most complex and well-developed gesture language in the primitive world. Today the Boy Scouts have adopted the sign language of the Plains Indians as their official international language and use it at worldwide meetings or jamborees.

Sign languages also developed elsewhere on the North American continent and as far away as central Australia. Most societies that required widows to observe a period of silence in mourning developed hand signal systems, as did monks who took vows of silence in Trappist monasteries.

Whistles, Bird and Animal Calls

American Indians, like efficient hunters the world over, also acquired the ability to imitate various bird and animal sounds in order to lure game within range of their weapons. Sometimes these calls were used in interpersonal communication because they carried across long distances better than did a human voice. At other times, hunting or scouting parties used animal calls to warn others of impending danger or to keep their communication secret. In many parts of the world, counterfeit bird and animal calls still serve these purposes.

In La Paz, Bolivia, groups of boys develop and use bird calls as a means of signaling and recognizing one another. Some trill, some warble, some twitter. My husband chirped. There have never been as many birds in the city as there are birdlike calls for friends. Such whistling will help a boy find his friends in a crowded movie theater or let his family know he's at the patio gate and wants to come in. Above all the traffic and city noises, these whistles can be heard clearly.

On La Gomera, one of the Canary Islands off the coast of Africa, Spanish-speaking natives send messages across gaping canyons by using a whistle language based on Spanish rhythms and pitches. The whistled notes carry and can be understood up to six miles away. A similar whistle language has been discovered in Oaxaca, Mexico, again using tonal phonemes instead of vowels and consonants.

Swiss and Austrian Tyrolean shepherds have developed a yodeling language to serve the same purpose. A yodel is no more than rapid transfer back and forth from a natural singing voice to falsetto, which gives it carrying power across Alpine valleys.

From Alpenhorns to Talking Drums

Elsewhere in the Alps and in the Andes of South America, natives use long horns to send simple messages. Polynesians use conch shells. But by far the most common message-sending instrument is the drum.

Talking drums are still used in Africa, New Guinea, and the Amazon jungles of South America. In most cases these signal drums are huge hollowed-out logs up to twelve feet long and four feet in diameter. They vary in tone depending upon where and how hard they are struck. From two to nine drums of different sizes may be used in combination. Their messages usually carry five miles or more, but important news will be rebroadcast from village to village.

Most African languages emphasize stress and pitch to a much greater degree than does English. Every syllable of every word has a more or less arbitrary tone or musical pitch. Thus, many words are distinguishable solely by their patterns of tone, which drums can imitate. In cases where the absence of vowels and consonants might lead to misinterpretation, stock phrases are attached to clarify ambiguous words.

Naturally there's no secrecy possible when messages are sent by whistle language or talking drums. Anyone who knows the spoken language of the area can quickly learn the tonal equivalents used by whistlers and drummers. But in heavily wooded areas and mountainous terrain where they are used, only aural messages will be received.

Picture Writing and Petroglyphs

Years before humans devised a writing system to record the phonemes of speech, they were drawing pictures and scratching signs on rocks. Rocks with such drawings, called petroglyphs, found in France and northern Spain have been estimated to be up to twenty-five thousand years old. The first use of symbols for separate consonants and not for syllables or entire words is believed to have occurred about three thousand years ago at the eastern end of the Mediterranean Sea.

But in North America, phonetic writing came with the Europeans. Indians north of southern Mexico never devised an alphabet system. Petroglyphs have been found in practically every part of the United States — wherever rock surfaces could be incised. In the western states, Indian petroglyphs were particularly common. Most museums have some local examples on exhibit. If you live near a state or national park or memorial, you may be able to see some in their natural condition.

Trail Markings and Smoke Signals

Most modern Indians can give few clues to the significance of the ancient petroglyphs, but when the first white settlers came, Indians were still using ancient methods of trail marking: blazing trees, piling stones, knotting grasses, or breaking branches in a manner that would indicate direction or warn of danger.

To communicate messages over long distances in open areas, smoke signals were sent. Westward moving wagon trains repeatedly reported seeing them; but unfortunately, the elaborate code used was never recorded.

In the Vatican, the public watches for smoke signals every time the cardinals enter into conclave to elect a new pope. Traditionally, the cardinals have no contact with the outside world until a pope has been chosen. They meet each day in the Sistine Chapel to vote. After each count, the voting papers are burned in a stove in the corner of the chapel. The smoke, passing up an iron pipe through a window, enables the crowd assembled in the piazza of St. Peter's to guess how the voting has gone. A majority of two-thirds plus one is needed. If a majority is not reached, the ballots are burned with wet straw so that the smoke is black. When a pope is elected, the ballots are burned with dry straw so that the smoke is white.

Road and Traffic Signs

As roads and railroads were built, signs marking direction and distances became more common, but not until recently have most regulatory and warning signs been standardized throughout the United States.

More than thirty countries, most of them in Europe, have adopted a set of international road signs proposed by a United Nations committee established in 1949. Most American signs warning and directing traffic do not conform to the international code, however, but rely heavily on written words. Even our informational arrows and pictographic warning signs differ from the international standard in both color and shape. A comparison of the symbol systems can be done after acquiring a booklet containing the United States signs accepted in 1970, from the motor vehicle licensing department of any state. The American Automobile Association and most city libraries have copies of the international signs used in Europe.

An attempt to standardize service and guide signs for international use followed the introduction of a carefully designed series in 1968 at the Olympic Games in Mexico City. These new signs, free from words in any language, employ pictographic symbols to communicate accommodation and service information to people of most cultures.

Hobo Signs

A less visible, but equally effective, system of road warning and accommodation signs was used by hoboes, the "Knights of the Road," during the heyday of the railroad. Real hoboes were neither bums nor thieves but men who wanted to travel and see the country without taking time to earn money or spending what little they might have. They usually traveled alone, hopping freight trains from one place to another, but maintained a loose fraternity with other men who lived the same kind of life.

They often slept in empty boxcars or, in nice weather, camped out in unimproved campgrounds, better known as hobo jungles, not far from the railroad tracks. Hunger or illness took a hobo into town, however. There he often scratched signs on a tree or fence or chalked messages on a sidewalk or telephone pole to notify other hoboes of fierce dogs, thieves, angry townsfolk with guns, and unfriendly police. He also scratched symbols to let those following him know where handouts were easy to get, which doctors would help without charge, and where people would give a man a good meal if he was willing to work for it.

Many hobo signs, it is said, are international and can be translated by gypsies and vagabonds around the world. That claim is relatively hard to prove, but wandering gangs were known to leave symbols along European roads as long ago as the Middle Ages. Later, gypsies and itinerant peddlers identified by signs good places to stop or sell and those that more likely offered danger.

Navigation Signals

Another rich category in the history of nonverbal communication is that used to communicate to and from ships at sea. One of the original seven wonders of the ancient world was the lighthouse in the harbor of Alexandria, Egypt. Called Pharos, after the island upon which it stood, it was built in 240 B.C. during the reign of the Greek king, Ptolemy Philadelphus. Signal fires, most assuredly, predate it by centuries.

Colored international flags, hand-held semaphores, and flashing lights using alphabet codes have transmitted messages for hundreds of years and still augment sophisticated electronic and radio systems on occasion.

Much navigation information cannot be broadcast just once or even from time to time. A sailor needs to receive certain facts whenever he might look for them. Storm warnings are conveyed by standardized weather flags during the day and by red and white lights vertically displayed at night. River and harbor channels are marked and ships guided through them by a variety of colored buoys, some lighted and/or carrying bells. Inside a harbor, these buoys may be no larger than a five-gallon drum. Farther out, they are usually large, high structures, which can be seen at long distances. Ships and even small craft carry colored running lights to help avoid nighttime collisions, and foghorns are no strangers to anyone living near navigated waters. Learning to read a navigation map will provide a challenge in nonverbal communication requiring considerable time and effort.

Scientific and Technological Symbol Systems

Cartographers, as map makers are called, are only one group of persons concerned with the efficient communication of scientific and technological information. Specialized signs and symbols must be learned by persons interested in agriculture, biology, geology, chemistry, astronomy, physics, architecture, engineering and drafting, medicine and pharmacy, and transportation and communications.

As technology enters Americans' lives like never before, we are all being exposed to new symbols on appliances, machinery, and power tools. We must learn new languages not only to program computers but simply to operate our cameras, stereos and recorders, microwave ovens, sewing machines, and automobiles. Clothing care labels frequently bear nonverbal symbols, and television meteorologists bombard us with information in symbolic form.

Numerals and Counting Systems

Many of the scientific and technological symbol systems are relatively new, but at least one, the graphic representation of numbers, is thousands of years old. The base-ten, or decimal, system of counting and writing numbers appears in Egyptian records as early as 3400 B.C. The Egyptians did not, however, use a symbol for zero, which made calculation difficult using their numerals.

Because humans have ten fingers, it is no surprise that the base-ten system evolved in various societies the world over. Knotted cords to record numbers have been found in various parts of Europe, China, Japan, Tibet, and North and South America. Most of these too indicate the use of a decimal system of recording. However, the Mayas in Central America evidently counted on both their fingers and toes. Their written symbols use a base-twenty (vigesimal) system. The Babylonians, sometime between 3000 and 2000 B.C., developed a system with base-sixty (a sexagesimal system). Thus, the base-ten system was not without challengers.

The Greeks, starting much later, based each written numeral on the initial letter of its name, a natural practice for civilizations with alphabet writing systems. To some degree this practice can be seen in the two thousand-year-old Roman numerals where C stands for one hundred (*centum*) and M for one thousand (*mille*). Roman numerals have survived not because of their simplicity in calculation certainly but because of the early strength and power of Rome over all of Europe.

About the same time that the Romans developed their system (ca. 300 B.C.), Hindus in India invented a positional system of calculation and a group of symbols that have come to be known as arabic numerals. At first, they too employed no zero symbol but wrote numbers like 302 by simply leaving a space between the 3 and the 2. Later they marked the space more clearly with a dot or small circle. Being traders, the Hindus carried their system to the Arabs, who in turn took it to Europe. This is why we refer to this system as arabic. Interestingly enough these numerals never were, and are not now, used by the Arabs in a form we would recognize.

Musical Notation

Examination of the evolution of musical notation as used for European and American music today is an equally interesting study but covers a far shorter time span. Scores written as recently as 1600 may be unclear to modern music students.

The first aids to musical performance were copies of the words of Christian liturgical chants. From earliest times, the church demanded that authentic music and manner of performance be preserved, a tradition that evolved from Jewish liturgical recitation. By the eighth century, accent marks, dots, and curved lines frequently appeared above some words. In the next four hundred years, these hand-drawn *neumes* slowly changed in shape and were placed on a five line staff so as to indicate relative duration and pitch relationships. But it was well into the fifteenth century before the notes looked like the whole, half, quarter, eighth, and sixteenth notes we use today.

The treble (or G) clef sign was originally an elaborate capital *G* that curled around the second line of the staff. The resemblance to a *G* is now gone, although the clef sign still curls around the appropriate line. The bass (or F) clef sign was an elegant script *F*. The colonlike pair of dots that follows the modern bass clef sign is all that remains of the crossbar of the *F*.

The symbol for flat notes (♭) looks a little like a lower case *b,* because at one time that's exactly what it was—the letter *b* written on the staff's B line to indicate that that note was to be performed a halftone lower. The symbol now applies to all notes lowered by a halftone.

The greatest period of development occurred between the fourteenth and sixteenth centuries. However, not until after the seventeenth century did the bar lines between measures become standard practice along with time signatures expressed as fractions.

Old musical scores are frequently reproduced in books of music history and volumes tracing the evolution of church liturgy. One need not go farther than the local public library to find them.

Symbolism in Religion and Beliefs

In addition to being indirectly responsible for the development of musical notation, religious practice has given us numerous symbols of its own. A person looking into the subject would be surprised at the number of symbols, even within one religious group. Almost everyone recognizes the star of David and the menorah (seven-branched candelabra) as symbols of Judaism, but few know the significance or origin of these symbols and others used in Jewish homes and synagogues.

The cross, in dozens of forms, has become the symbol of Christianity, but perhaps a hundred other symbols also have special meanings to Christians. Figures of a fish, a lamb, and a descending dove have special significance as does a palm branch, a lily, or a white rose. Even colors take on new meanings in Christian churches. Purple signifies repentance and is used for vestments during Lent and Advent. White (for purity) is used at Easter and Christmas, black on Good Friday. Green, the color of all growing things, is worn during the long season after Pentecost.

Symbolism such as this is used by all religions and is recognized, if not always fully understood, by all members. Islam, Brahmanism, Hinduism, Jainism, and Zoroastrianism — all have their own symbols, as do the Far Eastern religions, Buddhism, Confucianism, Taoism, Shintoism, and Sikhism.

Even ancient beliefs — astrology, alchemy, witchcraft, and superstitions — have their symbols, many of which were said to grant special powers or protection to those who wore them as talismans. The signs of the zodiac have recurring popularity, as do circles, squares, and triangles, which have been given special significance by hundreds of groups throughout history. The tarot cards contain much of the European symbolism prevalent during the Middle Ages.

Emblems of Identity and Ownership

Also dating back to medieval times are the symbols and colors of heraldry, the Crusades, and royalty. With the resurgence of interest in genealogy, information regarding the colors and emblems appearing in coats of arms is readily available.

Universities perpetuate the century old practice of dressing graduates in robes and hoods signifying the highest degree attained and the school from which it was received. Each degree—bachelor's, master's, and doctor's—has a separately styled robe and hood. Each hood is banded in velvet of the color corresponding to the college or department in which the degree was earned. The satin lining of the hood, and sometimes the gown itself, depends upon the identity of the university conferring the degree.

Most of the symbols of craftsmen, shopkeepers, unions, and lodges are also older than the United States. Before the days of lighted signs, carved boards hung outside of buildings. A huge boot indicated the shoemaker's shop. A painted red and white barber pole told people where they might have their hair cut or their blood let. The druggist's shop had a mortar and pestle sign hanging outside its entrance. The societies of merchants and artisans called guilds, which began in medieval times, each had an emblem shield. Modern trade unions, lodges, and fraternities are simply following an age-old tradition.

Animal branding began as long as four thousand years ago in Egypt. Many European cows and horses during the Middle Ages were branded with a modification of the owner's coat of arms. The open ranges of the United States brought animal branding to an all-time high. When similarity of brands became a problem, laws were passed prohibiting duplication and requiring that all brands be registered. Designing and reading brands is a language in and of itself. Letters and numerals may be forked, flying, rocking, tumbling, running, swinging, lazy, or crazy. Frequently recurring symbols are those read as *bar, circle, bench,* and *cross.*

The lumbering industry in the United States early began using symbols that resembled cattle brands for marking logs that were left in the forest for later recovery or set floating downstream to a sawmill. Many of these early symbols have now become registered trademarks of companies dealing in lumber, pulp, and paper products.

Logos and manufacturing trademarks are now used by most large companies. Michelin Tire Company, Prudential Insurance Company, Texas Instruments, John Deere, MacDonald's hamburgers, Columbia Broadcasting System, Nabisco, and Eveready batteries—all have easily remembered symbols associated with their names. The Procter and Gamble trademark, a circle of thirteen stars and a crescent moon, was first registered in 1882 but has recently been accused of having satanic implications.[9] Procter and Gamble officials have had to make repeated explanations because their old trademark is more elaborate than modern company seals. Back in the early days of Procter and Gamble products, using thirteen stars to represent the original thirteen states was not unusual.

Sports teams and schools, too, frequently decide upon a crest, emblem, and mascot format that can be standardized for use on all helmets, shirts, jackets, banners, rings, and printed materials.

Even countries are recognized by symbols, which may or may not appear on their flags. The maple leaf, Union Jack, the rising sun, the hammer and sickle, and the fleur-de-lis say Canada, England, Japan, Union of Soviet Socialist Republics, and France as clearly as do these words.

Art as a Medium of Communication

Many people believe that the visual and expressive arts communicate as clearly as words, and on the international level, more effectively. A painting, sculpture, dance, or musical performance can effectively convey a message to all people—regardless of their language and cultural background. The cognitive denotation of the message may not be as precise as one communicated verbally, but on the affective and emotional levels, communication is achieved. This is the level that is important to the imaginative artist. No one, least of all such an artist, would attempt to organize and convey facts through music or visual art—that is left to the engineer and draftsman through their medium. The imaginative and creative artist will more likely suggest life forms and rhythms but handle them in such a way as to heighten their effect on the viewer or listener.

To be able to decode and internalize the most from a work of art, one must be familiar with the medium of expression used by the artist. In many respects attending one's first ballet, opera, symphony, or art museum is not unlike attending one's first football game. In each case the neophyte may be caught up by the emotional tone of the event but will probably understand little of what's being seen or heard. Few people would advise formal instruction in football or ballet before seeing one's first game or performance. However, to appreciate either fully, a person ultimately has to understand the rules within which the action is performed and the nature of the options undertaken. The first time you attend a ballet, or a football game, you'll get from it what you can. Only after several more exposures will you begin to realize its intricacies and appreciate a quality performance. At this point you may want to seek further information to refine your perceptive skills.

Learning about art, like learning about sports, must never depend upon verbal study, for words cannot adequately create the total experience. One has to live with art, or sports, to enjoy them. Most teenage Americans have grown up with rock music and have come to like it very much. Many persons who have not had this exposure react to rock much as they do to impressionistic modern art. They are jarred and unnerved by its intensity.

A person who appreciates and enjoys football will not automatically enjoy watching a boxing match or bowling tournament. Each sport must be experienced and learned separately. The same is true of the arts. A lover of classical sculpture must experience romantic painting and baroque music separately if any understanding or appreciation is to develop.

This experience will help the decoder recognize the conventions and limitations of each art form. A painter or sculptor may intentionally distort reality in order to heighten the desired message and emotional impact. Mimes and caricature artists also exaggerate and distort reality to their own ends. Photographers try to convey their messages by the handling of light, field of focus, camera angle, and arrangement of elements.

The beauty and grace of ballet grows from its precision of movement and elaborate formal technique. Knowledge of ballet movement and the story behind the music that guides the dancers' movements will greatly enhance the enjoyment of any audience. Program music, which is composed so as to tell a story, describe an event or action, or create a mood or musical picture, lends itself well to ballet interpretation.

Such music makes good concert fare also. Composers manipulate rhythm, tempo, tonality, harmony, and instrumentation to elicit feelings of joy, triumph, restlessness, melancholy, loneliness, and other emotions. Each theme, or leitmotif, in program music is associated with a different situation, mood, or character contributing to the whole. In Prokofiev's *Peter and the Wolf,* for example, different leitmotifs featuring different orchestral instruments are associated with each character—Peter, his grandfather, the cat, the duck, the bird, the wolf, and the hunters. Interaction between the themes and variations on them carry the story along.

Whether such program music takes the form of a symphonic tone poem or provides the fabric against which ballet is performed, the musical experience is more enjoyable to those in the audience who have learned to listen for the themes and recognize them as recurring forces.

The three-hundred-year-old Japanese Kabuki theater uses music and dance, plus elaborate costumes, stylized acting, and pantomime to convey nonverbal messages. Oriental and Polynesian dances regularly incorporate stylized gestures and movements with specific meanings well known to those who regularly attend performances of such dances.

Tradition has also set a pattern for sonatas, concertos, and symphonies. Each has four movements, and each movement is written according to a different form. The first gets the audience's attention. The second sets them dreaming or contemplating. The third offers a chance to relax, and the fourth puts them into a cheerful or exalted frame of mind. Differing tempos and rhythms, repetition, and variations on themes are blended into a unified whole.

Architecture, it has been said, is frozen music. Early twentieth century banks and the buildings along Wall Street in New York City attempt to communicate solid strength and security to those who pass by. Minarets, spires, and steeples direct our attention heavenward. The interior of famous temples and cathedrals awe those who enter and make them feel the insignificance of humans in the presence of God. A knowledge of Greek, Byzantine, Romanesque, and Gothic architecture will make visiting examples of each more meaningful. Travelers often enjoy seeking out specific architectural details wherever they go. Some especially like rose windows. Others will go out of their way to see gargoyles that serve as downspouts for rainwater.

These are only a few examples of works of fine art that can be better appreciated by studying their underlying structure and form. Objects of folk art and artifacts used in daily living throughout history can be equally interesting to study for their communicative qualities. Pitchers, jugs, and vases; jewelry; furniture styles; rug, blanket, and textile designs; quilt patterns; basketry; and tombstone art—all frequently incorporate symbolism and provide decoding pleasure.

One need not be a creative artist—composer, musician, dancer, architect, sculptor, or painter—to communicate through the arts. Anyone who turns on a radio, selects the station, and sets the volume sends a message, be it country and western, rhythm and blues, jazz, rock, classical, or easy listening. The mother humming lullabies to her baby, the ball player adding his voice to the national anthem, people singing hymns in church are all communicating through music in a variety of ways. Young people have been known to make, or forget, new friends on the basis of the tapes they play in their cars and trucks. And music certainly can affect the success of a party or social gathering.

Music and the visual arts are such powerful and universal languages that everyone associated with them in any way becomes either a sender, a receiver, or both. The design and interior decoration of a home and yard, even the pictures or artwork on the walls, communicate not only from the designers to all viewers but also from the owners and residents who selected their works. When a young man selects a piece of fine jewelry for his fiancée, it's the craftsman primarily who communicates to him through his art. But when the buyer delivers it to the woman, both the craftsman and the giver send a message via that piece of jewelry. As the recipient wears the item, she too becomes a communication sender, together with the designer and the buyer.

And the feat goes on.

Graphology

Handwriting analysts have long believed that much can be learned about humans' personalities by examining their handwriting. This study, known as graphology, has fascinated observers for hundreds of years. As early as the second century, peculiarities in the penmanship of Octavius Augustus were recorded. Today books to aid beginners learn the principles underlying graphology can be found in any well-stocked library. The fundamentals are not difficult to learn, but combining the discovered clues into accurate personality profiles requires professional training.

Many of today's professional graphoanalysts have been trained and certified by the International Graphoanalysis Society. The president of this group, V. Peter Ferrara, says that graphoanalysis is as accurate and scientific as is any other test of personality.[10] Many certified handwriting analysts work as consultants in business and industry. Others assist police and law enforcement groups.

Graphoanalysts systematically examine a number of qualities of a subject's handwriting. One of the first things they note is the baseline of the writing. Is it level, going straight across the page, or does it slant upward or downward on an unlined sheet? If a slant is apparent, its angle is recorded. Two other aspects considered are the overall size of the writing and width of the strokes.

Still another characteristic weighed heavily by analysts is writing angle. Do all letters slant backward, stand upright, incline slightly forward, or lean far forward? In the United States, children are taught to write at a slightly forward angle. Persons whose letters recline, or slant backward, are often reserved, rebellious, or otherwise detached from society. Those whose writing inclines forward more than the norm reach out toward others and tend to be highly emotional.

Conclusions must not be drawn too quickly, however, for spacing between lines provides an additional clue to the writer's personality, as does spacing between words and letters. Beginning and end strokes and connected and disconnected letters are also noted.

Capital letters are examined in comparison to the rest of the writing sample. Capitals that are particularly large or small, ornate or plain, graceful, disjointed, or printed are significant.

Finally, the lowercase letters are studied individually. The *i* dots and the *t* bars offer a wealth of information. Other letters, specifically *o, a, d,* and *g,* are examined to see if they are open or closed. Letters with ascending or descending strokes or loops are also studied and their peculiarities noted.

Each of these aspects of handwriting offers professional graphoanalysts information to use in their composite personality profile. The study of handwriting analysis is a legitimate field, but it does require years of specialized training and practice to be done accurately. Learning its principles from a library book will not make you a qualified analyst any more than reading a book on anatomy and human disease qualifies you to practice medicine. Nevertheless, both graphology and anatomy are enlightening studies and will contribute to your background as an educated person.

Subliminal Perception

Subliminal communication refers to messages that reach our brain without our conscious knowledge. In recent years, two machines capable of sending subliminal messages have been developed. The first is a slide projector with a high speed shutter capable of flashing an image as briefly as 1/30,000 of a second in duration. This machine, called a tachistoscope, has been used to project a message over another film in progress. When the machine flashes an image for 1/1000 of a second, a viewer may receive the message without any conscious realization of its being sent. No one can actually "see" an image of such short duration, yet the unconscious mind may pick it up and understand it.

As early as the mid-1950s, marketing researcher James Vicary used the tachistoscope to project the words "Hungry? Eat popcorn," and "Drink Coca-Cola" over the feature film in a Fort Lee, New Jersey, theater. Nobody remembered seeing the words, for they flashed across the screen so quickly that the average individual was unaware of their presence. However, popcorn sales increased 57.7 percent and Coke sales rose 18.1 percent.[11]

Further research failed to support the early claims that subliminal stimulation could initiate action. The fear that people might be stimulated to do something against their will was proven totally unfounded. Today scientists generally agree that subliminal perception is possible. However, the message received by these means has no greater impact on a person than does a message received in normal, recognizable form.

A second machine capable of transmitting messages below the threshold of awareness has recently been developed by Dr. Hal Becker. The little black box, as the device is popularly called, is basically a sound mixer not unlike those used by radio disc jockeys. A message is broadcast at very low volume together with background music, applause, or another sound track. Becker has used the machine in stores where music is played continually. The black box mixes the music with such phrases as "I will not steal" and "Stealing is dishonest" rapidly repeated at very low volume. The music is heard, the message is not. However, many of the fifty department stores in the United States and Canada currently using the device report a noticeable drop in both customer and employee theft.[12]

Other audio attempts at subliminal communication have also been reported. Song lyrics have been manipulated so that they contain hidden meanings apparent only to an in-group. Slow chants are vocalized behind instrumental melodies so as to reach the brain unconsciously while the listener focuses on the melodic theme. Words and phrases are even recorded backward on a tape or phonograph record.

Visually, taboo words and drawings have been embedded into paintings or airbrushed onto photographs. In other cases, models and objects have been arranged so that the viewer's mind receives messages that would be morally unacceptable if presented overtly.

The practice of employing subliminal persuasion may not be as widespread or as intentional as some writers would have us believe. Nevertheless, the techniques described here are capable of leaving a subconscious impression in the right hemisphere of the human brain, which does not care if messages are reversed, inverted, logical, or even complete. At least one man, Wilson Bryan Key, has become so upset by these practices that since 1973 he has written three books on the subject. According to Key, many bills have been introduced in Congress forbidding devices and techniques designed to make an impression on the subconscious mind, but none has become law.[13]

Extrasensory Perception

Persons who think that extrasensory perception (ESP) is not worthy of serious study may be surprised to learn that several prestigious universities, both in the United States and abroad, are engaged in parapsychology research.

Parapsychology may have its roots in nineteenth century spiritualism, but its modern thrust is scientific testing of extrasensory perception. Research has tried to measure subjects' powers of telepathy (sometimes called thought transference or mind reading), precognition (the ability to foresee the future), and clairvoyance (knowledge of events not detectable by the normal senses).

Results of research done before 1970 have been widely published — and widely criticized. Scientists have questioned the objectivity of the researchers and their methods and statistics.

Advocates of extrasensory perception say that ESP abilities are stifled in a laboratory setting. They point out that ESP responses are the product of highly emotional situations or stimuli relevant to the subject's life. Laboratory experiments that require people to guess cards and push buttons do not generate the kind of charged atmosphere that gives rise to ESP.

Currently several European scientists are working on the hypothesis that ESP can be explained by natural laws that have not yet been discovered by mankind. Perhaps study of subatomic physics or the electrical nature of the nervous system will provide an answer.

And the Feat Goes On

If by now, you're beginning to think people communicate in one way or another practically every waking moment of their life, you've got the right idea.

Look around you. What messages do your senses perceive? Tammy's bored; she's doodling. . . . Jeff must be worried about the biology test or he wouldn't be studying his notes so hard. . . . Poor Todd is working too many hours. He can hardly stay awake.

Your mind is constantly interpreting the messages sent by others, be they intentional or unintentional. In school, at home, in the store, on the road, wherever you look, others are transmitting messages about themselves, their feelings, attitudes, and goals.

Even when people can't be seen, you receive their messages and internalize them. For example: They must be making pecan rolls for lunch. It sure smells good. . . . The jazz band really sounds great. By contest time it will be a winner. . . . Cindy's absent; her cold must be worse.

How about the messages you send? Can you see how you too are constantly transmitting messages for others to decode even when you don't say a thing? Take, for instance, the day you hadn't read your American history assignment and didn't want to be called on during class discussion. The bright T-shirt you wore that day, the location of your seat, the mutual eye gaze you unsuccessfully tried to avoid, the way you slouched in your seat, your nervous movements—all communicated to your classmates and teacher. You never had a real chance of being overlooked.

You can't avoid encoding nonverbal messages and your decoding skill develops with practice. As a product of American culture, you have no trouble speaking English or understanding other Americans. Nevertheless, you study in English, speech, and language arts courses to be better able to speak and write (encode) and listen and read (decode) your native verbal language. Hopefully, this book has helped you improve your skills in sending and receiving nonverbal messages as well.

Notes

1. ABC News, "Sex and Scents," on "20/20," 24 June 1982.
2. Lowell Ponte, "Secret Scents That Affect Behavior," *Reader's Digest,* June 1982, pp. 123–24.
3. "Sex and Scents."

4. Ponte, "Secret Scents," p. 125.
5. Flora Davis, *Inside Intuition* (New York: McGraw-Hill, 1973), pp. 98–111.
6. Ibid.
7. Edward T. Hall, *Beyond Culture* (Garden City, N.Y.: Doubleday and Co., 1976), pp. 71–78.
8. Hall, *Beyond Culture,* p. 79; "Sex and Scents."
9. Ann Cooper, "Procter & Gamble Says It Has Licked a Real 'Devil' of a Rumor Problem," *Baltimore Sun,* week of 7 November 1982.
10. Thomas G. Aylesworth, *Graphology: A Guide to Handwriting Analysis* (New York: Franklin Watts, 1976), p. 10.
11. Wilson Bryan Key, *Subliminal Seduction* (Englewood Cliffs, N.J.: Prentice-Hall, 1973), pp. 22–23.
12. "Secret Voices: Messages That Manipulate," *Time,* 10 September 1979, p. 71.
13. Key, *Subliminal Seduction,* pp. 21–22.

Appendix

[Chapter 6, **Silence**]

SILENCE

Edgar Lee Masters

I have known the silence of the stars and of the sea,
And the silence of the city when it pauses,
And the silence of a man and a maid,
And the silence for which music alone finds the word,
And the silence of the woods before the winds of spring begin,
And the silence of the sick
When their eyes roam about the room.
And I ask: For the depths,
Of what use is language?
A beast of the field moans a few times
When death takes its young:
And we are voiceless in the presence of realities—
We cannot speak.

A curious boy asks an old soldier
Sitting in front of the grocery store,
"How did you lose your leg?"
And the old soldier is struck with silence,
Or his mind flies away
Because he cannot concentrate it on Gettysburg.
It comes back jocosely
And he says, "A bear bit it off."
And the boy wonders, while the old soldier
Dumbly, feebly, lives over
The flashes of guns, the thunder of cannon,
The shrieks of the slain,
And himself lying on the ground,
And the hospital surgeons, the knives,
And the long days in bed.
But if he could describe it all
He would be an artist.
But if he were an artist there would be deeper wounds
Which he could not describe.

There is the silence of a great hatred,
And the silence of a great love,
And the silence of a deep peace of mind,
And the silence of an embittered friendship.
There is the silence of a spiritual crisis,
Through which your soul, exquisitely tortured,
Comes with visions not to be uttered
Into a realm of higher life,
And the silence of the gods who understand each other without speech.
There is the silence of defeat.
There is the silence of those unjustly punished;
And the silence of the dying whose hand
Suddenly grips yours.
There is the silence between father and son,
When the father cannot explain his life,
Even though he be misunderstood for it.

There is the silence that comes between husband and wife,
There is the silence of those who have failed;
And the vast silence that covers
Broken nations and vanquished leaders.

There is the silence of Lincoln,
Thinking of the poverty of his youth.
And the silence of Napoleon
After Waterloo.
And the silence of Jeanne d'Arc
Saying amid the flames, "Blessèd Jesus" —
Revealing in two words all sorrow, all hope.

And there is the silence of age,
Too full of wisdom for the tongue to utter it
In words intelligible to those who have not lived
The great range of life.

And there is the silence of the dead.
If we who are in life cannot speak
Of profound experiences,
Why do you marvel that the dead
Do not tell you of death?
Their silence shall be interpreted
As we approach them.

Reprinted with permission from Edgar Lee Masters, *Songs and Satires,* Macmillan Publishing Company, 1916.

Silence

Marianne Moore

My father used to say,
"Superior people never make long visits,
have to be shown Longfellow's grave
or the glass flowers at Harvard.
Self-reliant like the cat —
that takes its prey to privacy,
the mouse's limp tail hanging like a shoelace from its mouth —
they sometimes enjoy solitude,
and can be robbed of speech
by speech which has delighted them.
The deepest feeling always shows itself in silence;
not in silence, but restraint."
Nor was he insincere in saying, "Make my house your inn."
Inns are not residences.

[Chapter 7, **Tacesics and Stroking**]

Cipher in the Snow

Jean E. Mizer

It started with tragedy on a biting cold February morning. I was driving behind the Milford Corners bus as I did most snowy mornings on my way to school. It veered and stopped short at the hotel, which it had no business doing, and I was annoyed as I had to come to an unexpected stop. A boy lurched out of the bus, reeled, stumbled, and collapsed on the snowbank at the curb. The bus driver and I reached him at the same moment. His thin, hollow face was white even against the snow.

"He's dead," the driver whispered.

I didn't register for a minute. I glanced quickly at the scared young faces staring down at us from the school bus. "A doctor! Quick! I'll phone from the hotel. . . ."

"No use. I tell you he's dead." The driver looked down at the boy's still form. "He never even said he felt bad," he muttered, "just tapped me on the shoulder and said, real quiet, 'I'm sorry. I have to get off at the hotel.' That's all. Polite and apologizing like."

At school, the giggling, shuffling morning noise quieted as the news went down the halls. I passed a huddle of girls. "Who was it? Who dropped dead on the way to school?" I heard one of them half-whisper.

"Don't know his name; some kid from Milford Corners," was the reply.

It was like that in the faculty room and the principal's office. "I'd appreciate your going out to tell the parents," the principal told me. "They haven't a phone and, anyway, somebody from school should go there in person. I'll cover your classes."

"Why me?" I asked. "Wouldn't it be better if you did it?"

"I didn't know the boy," the principal admitted levelly. "And in last year's sophomore personalities column I note that you were listed as his favorite teacher."

I drove through the snow and cold down the bad canyon road to the Evans place and thought about the boy, Cliff Evans. His favorite teacher! I thought. He hasn't spoken two words to me in two years! I could see him in my mind's eye all right, sitting back there in the last seat in my afternoon literature class. He came in the room by himself and left by himself. "Cliff Evans," I muttered to myself, "a boy who never talked." I thought a minute. "A boy who never smiled. I never saw him smile once."

The big ranch kitchen was clean and warm. I blurted out my news somehow. Mrs. Evans reached blindly toward a chair. "He never said anything about bein' ailing."

His step-father snorted. "He ain't said nothin' about anything since I moved in here."

Mrs. Evans pushed a pan to the back of the stove and began to untie her apron. "Now hold on," her husband snapped. "I got to have breakfast before I go to town. Nothin' we can do now anyway. If Cliff hadn't been so dumb, he'd have told us he didn't feel good."

After school I sat in the office and stared bleakly at the records spread out before me. I was to close the file and write the obituary for the school paper. The almost bare sheets mocked the effort. Cliff Evans, white, never legally adopted by step-father, five young half-brothers and sisters. These meager strands of information and the list of D grades were all the records had to offer.

Cliff Evans had silently come in the school door in the mornings and gone out the school door in the evenings, and that was all. He had never belonged to a club. He had never played on a team. He had never held an office. As far as I could tell, he had never done one happy, noisy kid thing. He had never been anybody at all.

How do you go about making a boy into a zero? The grade school records showed me. The first and second grade teachers' annotations read "sweet, shy child"; "timid but eager." Then the third grade note had opened the attack. Some teacher had written in a good, firm hard, "Cliff won't talk. Uncooperative. Slow learner." The other academic sheep had followed with "dull"; "slow-witted"; "low I.Q." They became correct. The boy's I.Q. score in the ninth grade was listed at 83. But his I.Q. in the third grade had been 106. The score didn't go under 100 until the seventh grade. Even shy, timid, sweet children have resilience. It takes time to break them.

I stomped to the typewriter and wrote a savage report pointing out what education had done to Cliff Evans. I slapped a copy on the principal's desk and another in the sad, dog-eared file. I banged the typewriter and slammed the file and crashed the door shut, but I didn't feel much better. A little boy kept walking after me, a little boy with a peaked, pale face; a skinny body in faded jeans; and big eyes that had looked and searched for a long time and then had become veiled.

I could guess how many times he'd been chosen last to play sides in a game, how many whispered child conversations had excluded him, how many times he hadn't been asked. I could see and hear the faces and voices that said over and over, "You're dumb. You're dumb. You're a nothing, Cliff Evans."

A child is a believing creature. Cliff undoubtedly believed them. Suddenly it seemed clear to me: When finally there was nothing left at all for Cliff Evans, he collapsed on a snowbank and went away. The doctor might list "heart failure" as the cause of death, but that wouldn't change my mind.

We couldn't find ten students in the school who had known Cliff well enough to attend the funeral as his friends. So the student body officers and a committee from the junior class went as a group to the church, being politely sad. I attended the services with them, and sat through it with a lump of cold lead in my chest and a big resolve growing through me.

I've never forgotten Cliff Evans nor that resolve. He has been my challenge year after year, class after class. I look up and down the rows carefully each September at the unfamiliar faces. I look for veiled eyes or bodies scrouged into a seat in an alien world. "Look, kids," I say silently, "I may not do anything else for you this year, but not one of you is going to come out of here a nobody. I'll work or fight to the bitter end doing battle with society and the school board, but I won't have one of you coming out of here thinking himself into a zero."

Most of the time — not always, but most of the time — I've succeeded.

Two Friends

David Ignatow

I have something to tell you.
I'm listening.
I'm dying.
I'm sorry to hear.
I'm growing old.
It's terrible.
It is, I thought you should know.
Of course and I'm sorry. Keep in touch.
I will and you too.
And let me know what's new.
Certainly, though it can't be much.
And stay well.
And you too.
And go slow.
And you too.

[Chapter 10, **Color**]

TAUGHT ME PURPLE

Evelyn Tooley Hunt

My mother taught me purple
 Although she never wore it.
Wash-grey was her circle,
 The tenement her orbit.

My mother taught me golden
 And held me up to see it,
Above the broken molding,
 Beyond the filthy street.

My mother reached for beauty
 And for its lack she died,
Who knew so much of duty
 She could not teach me pride.

Reprinted from Evelyn Tooley Hunt, "Taught Me Purple," *Negro Digest,* February 1964.

Index

Academic attire, 168
Accessories, clothing, 159–60
Adapters, 48–49
Affect displays, 38–44
Agreement, nonverbal signs of, 44–45
Ahlgren, Andrew, 134–35
American nonverbal dialects
  in behavior
    eye, 59–60
    smile, 42–43
    touch, 86
  in color preferençe, 142
  in feedback, 47–48
  in paralanguage, 70–71
  in personal space, 106
  in punctuality, 126–27
  in time orientation, 122
  in walking, manner of, 14–15, 49
Appearance, physical, 10, 13–14, 18–31
Art, visual, 169–71
Attitude, perceived, 69, 71–73
Audience responses, 36
Auditory sense, 18–19

Banning, Elizabeth, 150–51
Biorhythms, 134–35
Bird and animal calls, 161
Blue Mondays, 132
Body, human
  characteristics, 10, 13–14, 18–31
  modifications, 25–29
  physiques, and temperaments, 22–23,
    29–30
Body language. *See* Kinesics
Bonding, 83–84
Branding, 168
Brown, Helen Gurley, 58
Building design, 114–18

Carter, Jimmy, 42–43
Cartooning, 49, 51
Cerebrotonia, 22, 29–30
Character traits, 70–71
Cheskin, Louis, 141, 144, 145

Chronemics
  concepts, 121–22
  definition, 121
  human orientations, 122
  physiological rhythms, 129–35
  punctuality, 125–29
  timing,123–24
Civil inattention, 54–55
Classroom environment
  color, 152
  seating preferences, 112
Clock-bound cultures, 125–27
Clothing, 159–60
Coats of arms, 167–68
Cognitive cycle, 134
Color
  afterimage, 147–48
  curative powers, 149–50
  in interior decor, 150–53
  in marketing, 143–45
  perception, 15, 146–49
  personalities, 139–40
  preferences, 140–42
  recommendations, 150–51
  symbolism, 138–40
  on taste, effect of, 148–49
  visibility, 142–43
  vision, defective, 20, 146–47
Color Research Institute, 141, 144, 145
Communication, nonverbal. *See also*
    Nonverbal languages
  art as, visual, 169–71
  conveys self-concept, 12–13
  dance as, 170–71
  extent of, 10, 69
  music as, 169–71
Congruent behaviors, 44–45. *See also*
    Synchrony
Contact lenses, 28–29
Contamination, of territory, 100
Content-free speech, 72
Counting systems, 165–66
Cultural variation
  in affect displays, 40–44

183

Cultural variation (*continued*)
  in beauty, concepts of, 24–29
  in body modifications, 25–29
  in color
    perception, 146
    preferences, 142
    symbolism, 138–39
  in eye behavior, 59–60, 62–63
  in gestures, 11, 34–38
  in nonverbal feedback, 47–48
  in office design, 109
  in open spaces, around homes, 97–98
  in paralanguage, 68, 70–71
  in personal space, 105–7
  in punctuality, 126–29
  in receiving criticism, 47
  in silence, use of, 80–81
  in sitting, and standing, 15, 49
  in time, concepts of, 121–22
  in touching, 89–90
  in walking, manner of, 14–15, 49
Cycles, human physiological. *See*
  Physiological rhythms
Cystic fibrosis test, 20

Dance, 170–71
Davitz, Joel and Lois Jean, 72
Daylight savings time, 125
Dialects, American nonverbal. *See*
  American nonverbal dialects
Disagreement, nonverbal signs of, 45
Dischronia, 132
Distance. *See also* Proxemics
  eye gaze and, 55–56
  intimate, 103
  personal, 103
  public, 103
  social, 103
Dormitory, room design, 114–15
Dress, 159–60
Drums, talking, 162

Ectomorph, 22–23, 29–30
Ekman, Paul. *See* Kinesics, classification
Elizabeth II, 42
Emblems, 33–36
Emotion, displayed, 38–44
Emotion, inferred
  from eyes, 57
  from facial expressions, 38–44
  from paralanguage, 71–72
Emotional cycle, 134
Endomorph, 22–23, 29–30
Extrasensory perception, 174–75
Extrovert
  and gaze behavior, 59
  and personal space, 105

Eye behavior
  functions of, 57–58
  gaze, 54–63
  pupil dilation, and constriction, 53–54,
    63
Eye contact, 54–63
Eyeglasses, 28–29
Eye studies, 53–54, 56, 57, 58, 59, 60, 61–
    62, 63

Facial expressions, 38–49, 69
Feedback
  gaze and, 56–62
  kinesics and, 36, 45–48
  paralanguage and, 72–73
Flags, 169
Fliess, Wilhelm, 133–34
Flirting, 58
Forsdale, Louis, 101
Friesen, Wallace V. *See* Kinesics,
  classification

Gestures
  adapters, 48–49
  emblems, 33–36
  illustrators, 37–38
  regulators, 44–48
Gibbs, Ann, 102
Graphology, 172–73
Greetings
  American, 87, 91–92
  Bolivian, 1–2, 35–36, 49
  Greek, 35
  Japanese, 42
  in tactile vs. nontactile cultures, 89

Hall, Edward T.
  classification, of distances, 102–3
  experience, in Japanese hotels, 101–2
  on time, 121, 126
Handwriting analysis, 172–73
Hearing, 18–19
Height, 13–14
Hesitation, 77
Hess, Eckhard, 53–54, 63
Hibbing, Samuel G., 148–49
Hobo signs, 164
Homosexuality, and stereotypes, 21–22
"Hora latina," 127–29

Illustrators, 37
Infradian cycle, 129
Intellectual cycle, 134
Introvert
  and gaze behavior, 59
  and personal space, 105
  and silence, 78

Invasion, of territory, 100

Jet lag, 132
Juncture, 77
Jury foreman, selection of, 109–10

Kennedy, Jacqueline, 41
Kinesics
  classification, 33
    adapters, 48–49
    affect displays, 38–44
    emblems, 33–36
    illustrators, 37–38
    regulators, 44–48
  definition of, 33
  facial expressions, 38–49
  gestures, 33–38
  postures, 13, 15, 49
  walking, manner of, 14–15, 49

La Guardia, Fiorello, 37
Larks, 131
Lead time, 124
Learning, of nonverbal behaviors, 14–17, 34, 37. See also Cultural variation
Leave taking. See Greetings
Leipold, William, 104–5
Life-style, 114–18
Lighting, effects of
  color-filtered, 142–43, 148–49, 150, 153
  experiment on, 148–49
  natural, 153
  on personal space, 105
Logos, 168–69
Lüscher Color Test, The, 140–41, 154
Lying, 12, 59

McEnroe, John, 41–42
Machiavellianism, 59
Marasmus, 84
Marceau, Marcel, 15, 52
Markers, of territoriality, 97–99
Mehrabian, Albert, 69
Mesomorph, 22–23, 29–30
Messages, contradictory, 12
Mohr, Lee, 99
Morris, Desmond
  on territoriality, 95, 97
  on touch, 88
Music, 169–71
Musical notation, 166
My Fair Lady, 38, 40

Navigation signals, 164
Nonpersons, 56, 78, 108
Nonverbal languages
  communicate self, 12–14

compared to verbal, 10–12, 69
female superiority in, 15–16, 74
forces modifying, 11
as learned behaviors, 14–16, 34, 37
relationship, to other disciplines, 95
Nonverbal signs, of agreement and disagreement, 44–45
Numerals, 165–66

Olfactory sense. See Smell, sense of
Owls, 131

Packard, Vance, 145
Paralanguage
  character traits, suggested by, 70–71
  definition, 67
  emotion, communicated by, 71–72
  physical features, communicated by, 69–70
  reaction to, 72–73
  silences, as extensions of, 77
  status, and sensitivity to, 73–74
  study on, 72
  vocalic classifications, 67–68
Pause, 77
Pavlov, Ivan, 90–91
Personal space, 102, 104–8
Petroglyphs, 162
Pheromones, 157–58
Physical appearance, 10, 13–14, 18–31
Physical cycle, 133
Physical features, 69–70
Physiological rhythms
  circadian cycles, 129–33
  circamensual cycles, 129, 133–35
  circannual cycles, 129, 135
Physiques, classification of, 22–23
Pink, Baker-Miller, 150
Posture, 13, 15, 49
PKU test, 19
Prescott, James, 85, 88–89
Privacy, 80–81, 97–98, 108, 115–17
Program music, 170
Proxemics
  classification, of distances, 102–3
  definition, 102
  experiments, 99, 101–2, 104–5
  life-style, and building design, 114–18
  personal space, 102, 104–8
  seating preferences, 110–14
  status and, 108–10
  territoriality, 95–102
Punctuality, 125–29

Queuing up, 106–7

Regulators, 44–48

Religious symbolism, 167
Retirement home living, 115, 123
Ritual stroking, 91–92
Road and traffic signs, 163
Romeo and Juliet, 34
Room arrangement, 114–18

Scent. *See also* Smell, sense of
    body odors, 23–24
    pheromones, 157–58
    as test for PKU, 19
Seating behavior, 109–14
Self-awakening ability, 123
Self-concept, 12–13
Self-description test, 29–30
Sensitivity cycle, 134
Sex differences
    color distinctions, in making, 15
    in color preferences, 141–42
    in color vision, defective, 20, 146–47
    in crowding, reaction to, 105
    in dilation, of pupils, 63
    in emotional displays, 43–44
    in eye gaze, 58–59
    in leg crossing, 49
    modify nonverbal languages, 11
    nonverbal communication, in decoding,
        16
    in paralanguage, 69, 73–74
    in walking behaviors, 49, 90
Sight, 20
Sign languages, 160–61
Signs, of identity, 167–69
Silence
    for concentration, 80
    as emotional response, 79–80
    for mourning, 81
    negative messages of, 78–79
    of shyness, 78
    solitude and, 80
Sincerity, 60–62
Sleep-wake cycles, 132–33
Smell, sense of
    in Arabian culture, 23–24
    pheromones and, 157–58
    as receptor, of nonverbal messages, 18–
        19, 23–24
Smoke signals, 163
Somatotonia, 22, 29–30
Sommer, Robert, 100–101, 104, 110–12,
    114
Southern United States, residents of
    eye behavior of, 59
    punctuality, concept of, 126
    smiling behavior of, 42–43
Spring fever, 135

Staring, reactions to, 56
Status
    eye behavior and, 57–58
    paralanguage and, 71, 73–74
    proxemics and, 108–10
    touch and, 88
Stereotypes, 21–29, 69–70
Stroking. *See also* Tacesics
    definition, 90–91
    positive, and negative, 92
    ritual, 91–92
Subliminal perception, 173–74
Swoboda, Hermann, 133–34
Symbolism
    academic attire, 168
    color, 138–40
    flag, 169
    religious, 167
Symbol systems, technological, 165
Synchrony, 158–59. *See also* Congruent
    behaviors

Tacesics
    bonding, 83–84
    cultural norms, American
        adult, 86–90
        childhood, 84–86
    cultural norms, other, 89–90
    definition, 83
    messages, conveyed by, 88–89
    nontactile strokes, 90–91
    rituals, American, 87–89, 91–92
Tactile sense. *See* Tacesics; Touch
Talbot, Fritz, 84
Taste, 19–20
Teltscher, Alfred, 134
Temperaments, classification of, 22–23, 29–
    30
Territoriality
    in behavior
        animal, 95–96
        human, 96–102
    definition, 95
    markers of, 97–99
    reserves space, 98–100
Territory, intrusion upon, 100–102
Time
    concepts of, 121–22
    dialects of, American, 126
    finding the best, 123–24
    orientations to, 122
    sense of, 122–23
Timing, 123–24
Touch. *See also* Tacesics
    behavior, adult, 86–90
    development of, 19, 83

human development and, 84–86
as receptor, of nonverbal messages, 19
Trademarks, 168–69
Trager, George, 67–68
Trail markings, 163
Turn-taking, 46, 57

Ultradian cycles, 129

Violation, of territory, 100
Viscerotonia, 22, 29–30
Visual sense, 20
Visual stimuli, 63
Vocalics. *See* Paralanguage
Vocalizations

vocal characteristics, 68
vocal qualifiers, 68
vocal segregates, 68
Vocal qualities, 68

West Point, 78–79
Whistles, 161
White noise, 80
Whorf, Benjamin, 15
Winter madness, 135

Yodeling, 161

Zodiac symbols, 167